FINDING BEN

FINDING BEN

A Mother's Journey
Through the Maze of Asperger's

Barbara LaSalle

With Contributions from Benjamin Levinson

McGraw·Hill

New York   Chicago   San Francisco   Lisbon   London   Madrid   Mexico City
Milan   New Delhi   San Juan   Seoul   Singapore   Sydney   Toronto

The *McGraw-Hill* Companies

Library of Congress Cataloging-in-Publication Data

LaSalle, Barbara.
    Finding Ben : a mother's journey through the maze of Asperger's / Barbara
LaSalle.
        p.   cm.
    ISBN 0-07-140225-X (hardcover) — ISBN 0-07-143194-2 (paperback)
    1. Levinson, Benjamin Daniel.   2. Asperger's syndrome—Patients—
Biography.   3. Asperger's syndrome—Patients—Family relationships.
4. Parents of autistic children.   I. Title.

    RJ506.A9 L393   2003
    618.92′8982′0092—dc21   2002034912

1 2 3 4 5 6 7 8 9 0   AGM/AGM   3 2 1 0 9 8 7 6 5 4

ISBN 0-07-140225-X (hardcover)
ISBN 0-07-143194-2 (paperback)

Interior design by Monica Baziuk

McGraw-Hill books are available at special quantity discounts to use as premiums and
sales promotions, or for use in corporate training programs. For more information, please
write to the Director of Special Sales, Professional Publishing, McGraw-Hill, Two Penn
Plaza, New York, NY 10121-2298. Or contact your local bookstore.

This book is printed on acid-free paper.

This book is dedicated to my son,
Benjamin Levinson,
with love and admiration.

These lifelong losses. These necessary losses. These losses we confront when we are confronted by the inescapable fact . . . that we have to accept—in other people and ourselves—the mingling of love with hate, of the good with the bad. . . .

—JUDITH VIORST, from *Necessary Losses*

Are you capable of forgiving and loving the people around you, even if they have hurt you and let you down by not being perfect? Can you forgive them and love them . . . because the penalty for not being able to love imperfect people is condemning oneself to loneliness?

—HAROLD KUSHNER, from *When Bad Things Happen to Good People*

CONTENTS

PREFACE

THE FRIENDS WHO HAVE BEEN in my life throughout this odyssey are astonished that I would want to write a book telling the whole truth. "Have you told Ben?" they ask.

The answer is, of course I have. I went to Ben before I even began, seeking his permission. At first he wasn't sure. Even at thirty-three, Ben still felt shame at having Asperger's Syndrome. Just as I, his mother, had once felt shame too.

I explained that this book is really about me, my journey, my discovery. He still wasn't sure. When I finished writing the proposal, I phoned Ben and read it to him. He was silent for a very long time after I was done. Finally he said, "Mom, this is your story. You need to tell it. Go ahead and write it." And then he added, "Maybe I can help you write it."

Since then, and throughout this process, Ben and I have talked about our shared past in ways we have not before. Ben's memory is photographic, and when I couldn't remember an incident or needed to understand his inner experience, I'd call and ask for his help. I did this again and again. His answers appear throughout the text, as he wrote them. "Tell the truth, Mom," was all Ben asked. "Just tell the truth."

The writing of this book has become an important part of our shared healing experience. It has become an opportunity for both of us to be honest and open with each other. We are friends now and that is the best blessing of all.

IN BEN'S WORDS

WHEN MY MOTHER TOLD ME she wanted to write a book about our life from her point of view and asked whether that was all right with me, I wasn't sure what to say. It's a unique position to find yourself in—having your own life story told from the point of view of your mother. I was concerned that her point of view would differ from mine and that she would write about all those embarrassing, hurtful, and humiliating moments I've tried so hard to forget.

Though I said yes, secretly I hoped this book would never end up in print. Then one day Mom called to tell me she had gotten a contract to write it and asked whether I would help. Since this is my life story, I figured giving my input was a good idea.

I can say that what you read in this book is not pretty. There are so many things in it that I never wanted to remember or discuss with anyone. However, I can acknowledge that what is contained here is the truth. Our collective truths—Mom's and mine.

The process of writing this book has been difficult for both of us. We cried a lot, sometimes alone, sometimes together. But ultimately it does what we wanted it to do: to tell the truth.

Some time early in my childhood, I got the message that telling the truth about myself was something to be avoided at all costs. Revealing my true nature meant showing that side of me that I always regarded as abnormal, the one that others pointed at and made fun of. But the problem with keeping your true self hidden is that one day you wake up and don't know who you are. And even if you did, you could never explain it to anyone.

Helping my mom write this book has forced me to confront aspects of myself I may never otherwise have faced. It has forced me to remember experiences in my life I tried so hard to forget. But somewhere in the process of answering my mother's questions, I realized that talking about these experiences was making me feel better, not worse.

When I realized that this book was really going to be published, I decided that it was going to tell the truth about me, unvarnished. That meant telling the whole, complete story. It meant giving my mom the freedom to share her experiences with me without trying to control the outcome.

What is written here is my mother's story. But it is also mine. Telling each other the truth has brought us closer than I could have ever imagined possible.

FOR MORE ON BEN'S EXPERIENCES as an adult living with Asperger's Syndrome, check out his website at http://aspergerjourney.com. This site includes journal entries from Ben, information on Asperger's Syndrome, links to related websites, and biographical and contact information for both Ben and Barbara.

My Land of Make-Believe

In my land of make-believe
I'm not the boy you see
I'm someone else entirely
And that's the real me

In my land of make-believe
I'm not the boy you know
I'm bigger, better, nicer too
Because I know it's so

The land where all my hopes are born
And all my dreams come true
Is where I like to spend my time
And you can come there too

Come to my land of make-believe
You'll smile at me and say
This boy is king of everything
And everything's okay

—JOHN DANIEL

FINDING BEN

PROLOGUE

"MAKE A LIST, BEN. I'm not taking you grocery shopping without a list."

"I did, Mom," Ben replies.

"Well, where is it?"

"In my head, where everything is."

My son and I are in Costco, the wholesale warehouse store where, for a monster supply of toilet paper, paper towels, chili, tuna, and frozen boneless chicken breasts, you think you're getting a bargain.

Ben is pushing the cart and I'm trailing behind, keeping track of him. We have done this ritual for years now.

"Cheese? You're allowed to eat cheese? Why do you have to eat cheese? Cheese is fattening. It's full of cholesterol. It's not good for your asthma." Thirty years of advising, commenting, suggesting. What *hasn't* been said in that much time? It's enough for both of us. I'm fed up with trying to change my son. I'm tired of how it feels to look at him and see layers of fat, to listen to him and hear a constant low-grade wheeze, to flinch at his flat feet, at the fixed, unchanging expression on his face, at his glazed, vacant eyes. I'm tired of trying to get a straight answer from a crooked person, even though that crooked person is my son.

But, as tired as I am of Ben's being the way he is, I'm just as tired of my being the way I am. I'm tired of trying to change what I'm powerless to change. I'm tired of monitoring his shopping cart, of reminding him to pull up his pants, of asking him if he took his inhaler or if he's made a friend.

"Barbara?"

I turn and see a familiar face.

"Oh, hi," I say.

Instantly I'm plagued by two embarrassments: Ben, and the fact that I can't remember the woman's name. One of my eyes smiles at the nameless woman, while the other keeps track of my son. I'm hoping a familiar hope, an impossible hope, a shameful, guilty, awful hope: I'm hoping Ben has wandered off ahead so I won't have to introduce him. But he hasn't. There he is, as he has been for thirty years, hovering, invisibly hooked to my side, all 465 pounds of him. And before I can make a quick escape, the woman points in Ben's direction and guesses what I don't want her even to dream of guessing.

"Is this your son?"

"Oh." I feign surprise. "Yes. This is Ben . . . my son."

He shakes her hand. "Hello," Ben says. "Nice to meet you."

I watch him as he answers her questions. "Yes. I live here in Culver City." Ordinary words from a most unordinary man. But for the words, there is nothing about Ben that is ordinary. Just as there is nothing ordinary about me, a mother who would wish her son to disappear.

Yet our bond, though twisted and tangled, is inextricable. In each other's eyes we find our worst and best selves.

Ben is as different, as unblended, as *other* as I seek to be normal, an irony that does not elude me. Rather it haunts, punishes, taunts me. But what it does to Ben is worse. Because—despite his Asperger's Syndrome; his obesity; his chronic asthma; his Crohn's disease; his cortisone-damaged organs, bones, and glands; his destroyed and unforgiving metabolism that will not yield an ounce of fat—he knows.

My son is aware that the last time I *wanted* to introduce him was when he was four. When I was still proud of him. When I wanted the entire world to know he was my son because, *Look at him! He can recite the entire preamble of the Constitution by heart; he knows each and every London street although he's only seen London on a map; he can recite a chronological list of every dictator, president, prime minister, governor, and mayor and each of their respective dwellings. You don't even have to ask.*

Benjamin Daniel was born the same year "Sesame Street" made its debut, which is how he claims to have learned to read. At eighteen months of age.

We were on the plane, just the two of us, returning from a visit to my parents in Florida, when I made the discovery. I had brought along Play-Doh and pretzels, puzzles, and "persons," Ben's beloved miniature wooden Fisher-Price figures. And of course the books. Always the books. I wouldn't think of going anywhere without them. Other mothers bribed with TV, toys, candy, and games. Not me; I bribed with books. Ben could sit for hours staring at books, anywhere, any time, eager to turn the page when I finished it.

Soon enough he began saying the final word on each page, and I thought, *Oh, of course—why not? After all, he's heard it so many times, by now he's committed it to memory.* But then on the plane that day, when he was eighteen months old, I discovered that my supposition was wrong. My son was not merely regurgitating words; he was reading.

At first he pointed to the overhead signs—"No Smoking," "Seat Belts," "Exit"—and read each one. I was surprised and pleased, but not startled, because of the pictures: he was probably "reading" the pictures. But then he spotted the American Airlines magazine in the seat pocket. He grabbed it, handed it to me, and demanded, "Mommy read." What was there to read in a trade magazine? I turned the pages, searching for pictures of planes or people doing interesting things, like skiing or sledding or biking. Concrete, little-boy pictures that I could point to and create stories about. But Ben wouldn't be fooled. "No, Mommy," he insisted, pointing to a page of fine print, a page with no pictures. "Read this." And so I began reading the dreary travelogue about a remote place in Switzerland. I was midsentence when Ben broke in, pointing to the next word. "Was," he read, and then, "far," followed by "away."

I remember the moment. The way Ben remembers the color of his first bedroom. "It was yellow, Mom."

"But how can you be so sure? We moved when you were only nineteen months old."

"It's my memory," Ben replies. "It's like a moving picture with all these freeze-frame images adding up to whatever's stored in my brain." And then he pauses, staring somewhere off into his own private world where I cannot find him, where once I tried with so much hope in my heart, until the day—I cannot say when—I knew I never would. "I'm sorry, that's just the way I am."

That's just the way he is.

Thirty years have passed since that yellow bedroom where Ben spent the first nineteen months of his life. But even now I haven't the means or the mind to grasp his astonishing capacity for memorizing single afternoons, single mornings, single minutes from his childhood and spitting them back up whole, detail for boring detail. What I do understand is their shared common denominator: information. The glistening, magical slant of a newfound fact, a precious gem meant only for Ben, for his prodigious brain, for the way he tucks it into a hidden corner of his bosom and dusts it off whenever he needs it. Sometimes he needs it for comfort, when he's lonely because no one wants to play with him. Sometimes he uses it to show off, just the way I once showed him off; but mostly he uses it because it is the way he knows himself.

"Say it, Ben, say it," the kids used to tease. "Say the Declaration of Independence."

He dusts off his beloved data, his sweet sanctuary of cherished knowledge, his truest, most loyal home, and swims in its familiar warm current, away from the kids who don't understand, away from the grownups who egg him on for the sake of entertainment, and especially away from me, his mother with the fake smile.

My son with the astonishing memory, my son with the gigantic brain, the boy I'd expected to know by my heart's own beating, without benefit of a single word. But the boy spoke a thicket of words and I couldn't find the path. I couldn't find the boy.

There is more to a boy's life than information, than bare, cold facts. But not to Ben. Information was his life, his nourishment. He collected it, memorized it, and stored it like a computer, squirreling it away like a manic chipmunk preparing for a winter that would never turn to spring. But I didn't want a computer for a son; all I ever wanted was a real little boy.

I was so ready to be a better version of myself. I was so ready to be a good mother, but something was horribly, terribly wrong. And when I began to let the truth in, it felt like a stab to my heart. My pride, my self-celebration, turned to fear, and I felt a partition slamming down between the life I had expected and the life I had.

Would I have been a better mother to my son if I had known from the beginning that so many of my disappointments and embarrassments weren't Ben's fault? Would Ben have been more accepting of himself if he had known he was born with a baffling neurological condition called Asperger's Syndrome? Would our journey together have been easier?

I don't have the answers to these questions. All I know is what it was like when we didn't know, and what it is like now that we do. This is our story.

1

A CHILD IS BORN

I sometimes wonder what it would have been like to know I had Asperger's Syndrome from the beginning. Would my life have been different?

———

MY SON BENJAMIN was born three weeks late. "If you haven't gone into labor by next Thursday night, come to my office. I'll induce you there. Then you and your husband can drive across the bridge to the hospital. I'll meet up with you later," said Dr. Green, my obstetrician. By this time I was twenty-seven years old, married for six years, and twenty-one days past my due date.

My husband, Steven, and I were living in Fort Lee, New Jersey, where for three years we had been commuting into New York City to our jobs. I was a kindergarten teacher. Steven was an entertainment lawyer. Together, we were about to embark on the adventure of parenthood. Steven was proud and self-confident. I was scared. What if I didn't do everything perfectly?

I didn't go into labor on time, but once I was induced I labored like hell. I labored all the way across the George Washington Bridge, a trip that seemed to last forever, with sweat and tears all the way to the hospital door.

But then, just as suddenly as it came, the pain disappeared. The doctor had to induce me again. Was I going to do this job properly or not?

The gap in my memory begins from the moment my husband sat down on the chair next to my hospital bed. He held my hand while I waited for the pains to resume. Soon after, the doctor pulled up another chair. How many hours did we wait like this?

I remember nothing. Not even the birth of my baby, which did eventually take place.

But *why* don't I have a single memory of that forever moment, that once-in-a-lifetime, singular second, the memory every other mother has? There are no dots connecting the "day you were born" story my own parents recounted to me, and which I never tired of hearing, to the one I would someday recount for my son. That story is missing, blank, gone forever. I have no story to give him, no favorite bedtime tale to pass on, beginning with the words, "It was the happiest day of my life."

I remember the pain and I remember the doctor being frustrated because I was doing the pushing wrong. I remember two nurses, on either side, lying across my stomach, doing it right. And finally I remember another nurse handing me my newborn, swaddled tightly in a yellow blanket. His face was red, but a blotchy sort of red, with spots of yellow.

I thought babies were pink.

The nurse seemed irritated when I asked about the blotches. "Eczema. Infant eczema. He'll grow out of it." Then, she turned on her heels, carrying my baby as if he were hers to carry, and left the delivery room.

"Congratulations," said the doctor, removing his scrubs. "You've given birth to a perfectly healthy son."

Back in my hospital room, drifting off to sleep, I felt relieved that the hours of labor were behind me, glad that it was this time today, not this time yesterday.

The next thing I remember was the nurse carrying my baby into my room and laying him in my arms. She was smiling. She was turning away. She was walking away. She was leaving us alone together.

Wait, I wanted to call out, *come back! What am I supposed to do now?*

What was supposed to happen next? What was I supposed to do with this baby struggling to fit his tiny mouth to my nipple?

Benjamin Daniel did not sleep in my room, but in a giant nursery, with glass on all sides, as was the custom in that era. It adjoined the room for new mothers. We could hear every cry and whimper, and we were permitted to "look" at our babies to our hearts' content; but "under no circumstances" were we to touch.

All was quiet in the nursery, except for the piercing wail of a single infant. Call it a mother's instinct, call it an inkling, call it a premonition, but I knew, without even looking, that the wailing infant was mine.

A force impossible to resist was tugging me, wrenching me, jerking my heart in a direction I'd never taken before. My baby—inside the glass—his tiny body heaving up and down, desperately gasping for breath, imploring, beseeching, begging to be soothed; and me, his mother—outside the glass—being good, following orders, obeying rules.

I put pillows over my ears, phoned a friend, walked the hospital corridors. Still, I heard him. Wherever I went, whatever I did—I heard him. And when I returned to the glass, I could see, lying limp in the crib, next to my son, the ghost of my own reflection.

I was no mother. I was a coward. A fainthearted, pluckless, gritless coward.

How long I stood there staring at this authentic picture of myself, I cannot say. I only know that suddenly, through the cry of my son's true nature, the invoking of his most naked, primal self, I could hear the sound of my own voice.

This is your baby. He needs you!

And there I was—a tigress—charging the nursery, rushing to my son. Suddenly I was—as I picked up my baby, rocked him, comforted him—the woman I'd been preparing all my life to become.

I was Benjamin's mother.

2

THE PAUSE

The room was yellow. My crib was white. The dresser was blue, with white knobs. I remember because when we moved, the knobs fell off.

———

"No. No. No." The words spat out of Mrs. Chantelle's oversized mouth in staccato speed. Mrs. Chantelle, my baby nurse, was rejecting my selection of clothing for Benjamin's trip home. That was the way she said hello, firm and forbidding, establishing the rules in her thick French accent, rules that were to circumscribe us for the next fourteen days and fourteen nights.

I could have said, "No, I'll do it," but Mrs. Chantelle was too tall—basketball-star tall—too husky, too grim, and too intimidating for that. So sure of herself. But wasn't that what had impressed me about her in the first place? Well, yes and no. Yes, because with all those babies listed on her resume, surely I could count on her to do the right thing. And no, because even then I knew that by hiring a baby nurse I was simply seeking more rules to follow.

The first few days home from the hospital are a blur. No, on second thought, I'm the blur. I remember Mrs. Chantelle perfectly: her huge, sure-of-themselves hands, her swift, stern, know-it-all manner, her hurry-up, never-changing daily routine. And I remember the blotchy baby in the crib down the hall. But the room I had prepared so carefully had become Mrs. Chantelle's room. *My* baby was missing, and in his place was an infant stranger, sleeping next to the bed of a giant stranger. Because, just like that—dwarfed by her basketball-star size, struck dumb by the stern staccato of those three soldier-stiff "no's," there I was again, mute, my mother-voice lost, for the second time in my son's first week of life.

I took to my bedroom and returned to my baby books, which I had expected I'd have no time to read once I'd given birth. I'd be too busy, I thought, too engrossed, too in love with my baby to read. But I was wrong. Here I was, with a real live baby—but still, I *wasn't* too busy, I *wasn't* too engrossed, I *wasn't* too in love with my baby to read. In fact, I read all day, poised in my role as wet nurse, waiting from one four-hour interval to the next for Mrs. Chantelle's knock on my bedroom door.

"Time to nurse, dear." And like a zombie, a mother-mummy, I'd close the pages of *Your Baby: The First Three Months* and follow behind Mrs. Chantelle into my son's room, sit in the rocker, and do as I was told.

The rocker was next to the crib, next to the bed where Mrs. Chantelle slept. And she'd place the infant-stranger in my arms, position my nipple to fit his little mouth, and stand over me, making clucking sounds with her tongue, jerking him off one breast and onto the other, her beady eyes watching, watching. "Wake up baby!" she'd demand, tapping her giant finger against his cheek each time he fell asleep too soon to suit her.

Wasn't I going to be the best mother? But how could I be, when it was Mrs. Chantelle, not I, who smelled of my milk?

Every day at exactly twelve o'clock, after I'd fed Ben, Mrs. Chantelle fed me.

"But I'm not hungry."

"Yes you are, dear. Remember, you're eating for two now."

"But I can feed myself."

"Yes, dear, of course you can, but now it's *my* job."

It was during one of these noon lunch hours, waiting for the toast to pop, that Mrs. Chantelle turned to me and smiled. She said, "You know, dear, all my babies are beautiful."

And then she *paused*.

I remember the pause the way Benjamin remembers the color of his first bedroom. It took only seconds, but in its midst I knew that whatever was to follow was not going to be good. It was going to be bad. Very, very bad.

And then she said it—the words I will never forget. Just as Benjamin has never forgotten a single word of his beloved book, *A Child's History of the World*.

"Even this one."

These were her exact words. I heard them, memorized them, and despite the fog, the deadly daze of those first fourteen days when my son was lost to me and I lost to him, I understood their meaning. "Even this one" surely meant, "This one isn't." And when I bit into my melted cheese sandwich, I tasted fear.

Why did Mrs. Chantelle say such a thing? *Why* wasn't this baby beautiful, *like all the others*? Was there something I couldn't see beyond his blotchy skin, something other, something unbeautiful?

Any good mother would have said, "Shut up, get out, how dare you, and in my own kitchen no less, open your big fat mouth and say, 'All my babies are beautiful . . . even this one'!"

I wasn't even good at breastfeeding. Mrs. Chantelle said I wasn't. That's why Ben cried so much, she told me. "The poor child is starving." So I switched to formula, which may have been good for the short run but, because formula can produce phlegm, turned out to be very bad for the long run. But how could I know then that my son's infant eczema was a harbinger of the asthma waiting in the wings? Just one more chronic, unrelenting condition we could only manage but, in his case, never cure. Just another burden Ben would have to carry for the rest of his life. For the rest of mine.

Mrs. Chantelle's fourteen days were up on Valentine's Day, the sweetest gift of all. She packed up her carpetbag, took her paycheck, and disappeared out into the night to her next assignment. And then, just as suddenly, I sprang back to *my* life, rejoined *my* assignment: my baby.

IN THE INSTANT of my return, Ben became mine. Maybe Mrs. Chantelle was right after all about the crying, about his being starved—because, just like in the hospital when I'd made a run for my son through the glass-gated nursery, Ben's crying abruptly ceased. But it wasn't milk he was desperate for; it was me.

Some things you *know*, because they *are* you—the who, why, and what of you—so it had to be, didn't it, that my child *knew* he couldn't possibly have belonged to a mother who looked to a clock to decide when it was time to dispense comfort, when it was time to burp, when it was time to sing, when it was time to love her baby?

Ben and I held onto one another for dear life, for the fear of separation, for the fear of loss, for the fear of my betrayal and his abandonment. And never, it seems as I look back now, ever loosened our grip.

Running into each room, opening the curtains, I was blessed by the sun glancing off the snow. It was as if the sun had chosen but a single home to shine its entire light on, because that one home had suffered too long from hopelessness.

Holding my son in my arms was delicious, and so was his sweet baby smell, and his brown eyes locking onto mine as if they were his only home. We clung to one another day and night, and suddenly I could be anyone, do anything—even sing. I took out my repertoire of kindergarten songs—"The Wheels of the Bus," "The Itsy-Bitsy Spider," "Open, Shut Them"—and Ben squealed and stared and sighed and loved them as much, I thought, as he loved me. They were me, these songs. And so were the dances we danced each morning in the living room: the tango, the merengue, the cha-cha. We were each other's cast and crew, one another's fan club, all either of us would ever need.

The New Jersey winter kept us locked inside, but I was glad for the excuse to nest in our second-floor apartment. Once a week we went grocery shopping, and every three weeks we drove down the Jersey Turnpike to the pediatrician's office. We sang our songs in tunnels, over bridges, when the light turned green, and when it turned red.

Before the birth of Ben, I was a songless, serious person, collecting days like baseball cards, stacking them, rubber-banding them, storing them away. As if each day were something I could claim credit for, as if the more days I collected the better I was. But now, first thing every morning, as I stumbled into Ben's room, still groggy, I'd find my son fascinated, gurgling at the mobile hanging over his crib. And I became a singing, laughing person. With Ben, I was a better person. I still collected days, still cherished them, but only because they were days with Ben.

AND THEN, JUST AS SUDDENLY, I changed from a better person into a worse one. As usual, I sang my song—*The wheels of the bus go round and round*—as we drove down the Jersey Turnpike to the doctor's office for Ben's six-month checkup. And, as usual, Ben giggled back. But only a few minutes later, the singing stopped.

In the office, Ben's pediatrician looked at me in a brand-new way. "I'm glad you're here today. There's something I've been considering," said Dr. Pierce, in a lowered, almost reverential tone, the kind of voice you might expect to hear in church.

"What is it? Is it bad?" Of course it's bad—why else would he be touching my shoulder and telling me to please sit down? He's not smiling, he's not cracking jokes, he's not the jolly baby doctor he used to be.

"I've been noticing some anomalies in Ben—"

"What kind of anomalies?"

"Well, his eyes cross, his forehead tilts back, his feet are flat, his chin recedes, his—"

"What does this mean? Is he sick? Is he retarded?"

That's when the good doctor switched back from his church voice to his professional voice. "I can't answer your questions, which is why I suggest you take photos of your son and send them to Boston Children's Hospital. I did a rotation there."

Then he paused.

"They specialize in this kind of thing."

I remember the pause the way Ben remembers the contents of each wing of the Los Angeles Public Library.

"What kind of thing?"

But Dr. Pierce was finished talking.

"Photos of Ben, front and back, face and limbs." "Boston Children's Hospital." These were the words going round and round in my head like the wheels of the bus. The day before it had been laughter and kindergarten songs. Now it was a nightmare chorus, and the beginning of a whole new repertoire.

All at once I was accumulating days again, stacking them up, storing them. My album of most hated memories, a mother's collection of bad days I will always remember.

Each one of the bad days is held together by a bad sentence, a string of words shattering my expectations. And tagged onto each bad sentence, each painful string of words, is the haunting refrain even more painful—that *pause*. For it is the pause I remember most of all. The still and silent seconds marking the place I was standing before the beginning of the bad day, and where I lay when I was knocked down.

3

THE OTHER MOTHERS

I still see better with my ears.

———

"THE DOCTOR IS CRAZY," said Steven. "There's nothing wrong with Ben."

"Well, he seems to know about these things."

"What things?"

"You know . . . bad things . . . bad things about babies."

"*Everyone but you says he's perfect.* A miniature adult! Would you want a kid like Bradley, for God's sake? A hell-raiser, a hooligan? All we have to do is talk to Ben . . . read to him and he's happy. *What more could you want from a six-month-old?*"

"Nothing, Steven. But the doctor—"

"To hell with the damn doctor," yelled Steven, storming out of the kitchen. The kitchen was the warmest room in the apartment, so I had told him there.

I didn't want to tell him, or my parents, or his. I didn't want to tell anyone, not even myself, especially not myself, even though it was I who heard it, I who had driven home hearing it, I who couldn't stop hearing it. It was like refusing to comb the back of my hair—I couldn't see it, so why should I bother? If I hadn't seen the doctor's face when he told me about Ben, if I hadn't heard his words, I'd be singing again. But different songs, with more advanced tunes, World War I songs, like the ones my father used to sing to me—my father, who had been songless until I came along. By this point, I'd be singing "Over There," "The Caissons Go Rolling Along," and "It's a Long Way to Tipperary." And when I looked at my little boy now, I'd see him the way I had before, the way my mother once saw me, the way mothers are supposed to see.

On the warmest day in July, we did what the doctor had told us to do. Holding the camera in one hand and the soft blue blanket in the other, I walked down the stairs of our apartment and out and around, into the backyard. Steven followed, carrying Ben. It was a slow, sad walk, the kind where no one speaks, no one laughs, no one smiles. It was like a walk to the dentist's or principal's office, or to your parents when you got a bad report card.

My son was counting on me to be on his side, to banish any human—hospital nurse, baby nurse, or doctor—who dared even to *suggest* that he might be less than perfect. Mothers do that; it's their second most important job. Their first is to gaze at their child with stars in their eyes, and their second is to bark at trespassers. *Get away! Stand back!*

It had taken me fourteen days to do the gazing part. I had promised myself afterward—no matter who or what tried to come between us—never, ever to abandon my son again. But wasn't I, as I bent to smooth out the blue blanket, on the verge of breaking that promise?

I should have growled at the doctor the moment he switched into his church voice. I should have argued that Ben's chin, his eyes, his forehead, his feet, were *not* anomalies. *How dare you say such a thing! Don't you have eyes? Can't you see that my son is perfect just the way he is?* That's what I should have said.

We sent the photos and waited. Boston Children's Hospital wrote back two months later. As if my lungs weren't bursting from not breathing in all that time, as if torturing mothers was in their job description. "Your son falls into the range of normal."

"I told you the doctor's crazy," said Steven.

"Change doctors," said my mother, and Steven's mother, and the downstairs neighbor. So I did.

I didn't tell Dr. Olson what Dr. Pierce had said. Dr. Olson was an old man. He'd been seeing babies forever, so I shouldn't have to tell him. Why should I?

In the summer of 1969, when Ben was not yet seven months old, we began venturing out of the house, in search of other mothers. I met loads of them in the park, sitting on benches, swapping funny stories about their babies, glad for the few hours of adult company. It became our midmorning ritual, these park outings. But in the fall, when Ben was approaching nine months, the mothers' conversations changed from funny to serious. The mothers appeared to be on some kind of mission. They were collecting names. Some even came with little pads for writing down the names. Mostly the names were about babysitters—their ages, experience, references, and phone numbers. But more and more the mothers talked about how-to books on making better babies. The mothers were especially interested in seeing to it that their kids would be early readers and early talkers.

The mothers complained a lot. Their kids wouldn't sit still. The ones who were sitting up were starting to crawl, and the ones who were crawling were starting to stand, and the ones who were standing were starting to walk. If only they would sit still, they could look at the picture books; and if they would look at the pictures, they could say the words; and if they would say the words, they could learn to read.

I had nothing to say.

I had nothing to say because I didn't understand what they were talking about. I understood their words, but not their problems. *Why* wouldn't their kids sit still? Isn't that what babies do? *My* baby sat perfectly still. *My* baby looked at picture books. *My* baby sat and looked and listened for hours. I didn't have to chase him around, or baby-proof the house, or make sure he didn't suffocate from turning over in his crib and getting stuck between the bars.

My baby never turned over. He just lay or sat where I put him. Totally alert. I saw his alertness with my own eyes: even though he wasn't turning over, or crawling, or standing, and didn't seem to have any interest in locomotion, he did lean. I saw him leaning with my own eyes. He leaned into words. People speaking words, people reading words, words coming out of the TV, words coming out of the radio.

And he didn't like being out of listening distance when I was on the phone. He would sit for hours in his high chair when a friend came to call, leaning in the direction of the words, his brown eyes moving back and forth as if they were tracking a tennis match—words from this side of the court, words from that side.

The park mothers noticed how quietly Ben sat in his stroller, how still he lay in his carriage. Sometimes I'd bring a picture book to the park and set Ben on my lap, turning the pages. "He seems so interested," they'd say, or, "What did you do to get him to sit still like that?"

"Nothing," I'd reply. "It's just what he does."

Was Ben better than their kids? The mothers seemed to be on some kind of search to make their kids more like mine already was. Everything that came naturally to Ben was a big deal to the mothers. Maybe Ben *was* better, but maybe not; maybe he was worse. After all, could all these babies who were so busy exercising their bodies, driving their mothers to exhaustion, be slow?

Better or worse?

Before I met the mothers, I didn't wonder or worry about Ben's lack of locomotion, his preternatural interest in the spoken and written word. It was just who he was, and it was wonderful. But now, I wondered and worried all the time. Now, whenever I was in the supermarket and saw a youngster in a shopping cart grabbing for this, pointing to that, his body contorted in a sitting dance of kicking feet and bobbing head, I'd ask the exasperated mother, "How old is your son?"

I was trying to answer the question of better or worse, but I had no frame of reference because I didn't know what I was looking for. I didn't know what normal was.

"YOU GET THE TAMBOURINE," Ben told the first guest who entered our home for the bon voyage party we were throwing for ourselves. Steven had gotten a terrific job offer in Los Angeles, and in two weeks we'd be off to our new life.

"And you get the triangle," he said to the next one.

"Now the bongos. You each get one of these."

The instruments were on the tray of his walker, which, when he wasn't sitting, peering into a book, or watching "Sesame Street," was his chief means of transportation. He was, at eighteen months, too big to carry.

"OK, now make a parade. When I say *go*, everyone play. I'll be the conductor. Everyone watch me."

The guests were bewitched. They followed Ben's lead, walking in single file, marching from room to room, bemused, off-key, and embarrassed.

I was embarrassed, too, because as much as I had envisioned scintillating dinner conversation, Ben's performance, his imagination, and his vocabulary were all my guests could talk about.

"Maybe he's a genius," a couple of the lawyer men said. "Like Einstein or van Gogh."

"But he's not walking yet," I replied. As if my remark were on the same page, not from a parallel universe, as if these men with crawling, standing, walking children understood I was pleading my case, a case I was begging them to refute.

"COME ON, BEN, walk to Mommy. You can hold on to this stick. Keep your eyes on Mommy. Come on, big boy, you can do it."

"No walking, Mommy. I'm afraid." Ben said that day, just as he had for days and weeks before.

"Try it with the stick. Hold on to the stick. Try it like that, Ben."

Then it happened. Maybe he was tired of my nagging or maybe he had noticed other kids—smaller, younger kids—doing the walking thing, or maybe, late though it was, he had at last caught up developmentally and was finally *ready*. But at last, the day came when he did take a few wobbly steps, first holding on to the sides of tables, the corners of sofas, my skirt, anything to steady himself. And then, miracle of miracles, he reached for the stick I had been holding out for weeks, grabbed an end in each hand, as if it were a horizontal balancing bar, and walked all the way from his end of the room to mine as I ran to the opposite end to cheer him.

"Good job, Ben!"

"No more walking, Mommy."

I remember that day less for the steps than for the terror I saw in his eyes. It was the first time I had seen that look, that deer-in-the-headlights look. But it wouldn't be the last.

"It's his eyes—they're not working together," said Dr. Grey, the ophthalmologist we were referred to by Ben's pediatrician.

"How can you say that? He just read the entire eye chart top to bottom. You didn't even have to ask," I said, holding my eighteen-month-old in my lap.

"It has nothing to do with reading. He reads like a savant. It's just that his eyes don't team. They don't work in unison."

"Oh . . . is that bad?"

"If he wants to be a fighter pilot it is," Dr. Grey laughed.

I laughed too—who cared about that?

"Maybe when he's three or four he can do eye exercises, you know, wear a patch on one eye—"

"But he's OK? His eyes are OK?"

"Lots of people do fine without depth perception."

"Lots of people do fine without depth perception," I told Steven that night. "That's what Dr. Grey told me."

"What else did he say?"

"That Ben will never be a stuntman or a downhill skier."

Steven chuckled.

"That's not funny," I said.

"Why? You want him to be a stuntman?"

"No, of course not. But I'm still worried. I mean, if his eyes don't work together—"

"There's nothing wrong with Ben," Steven insisted. "Lots of people do fine without depth perception. That's what he told you."

"But his eyes—"

"Barbara, what more do you want? Listen to the doctor. The doctor's right. There's nothing wrong with Ben."

4

JUST LIKE A REAL DAY

In the real world, I never knew what was coming. Anything could happen and it was often disappointing. But not when I made it up. Then it came out just right.

"HI, MY NAME IS BEN. What is your name, I used to live in New Jersey, then we took an airplane, did you ever take an airplane, now I live in Los Angeles, where do you live, I also like San Francisco, but I never saw San Francisco, except in my book, *This Is San Francisco*, do you like San Francisco, would you like to see my book, *This Is San Francisco*, I'll get my book *This Is San Francisco*, and I'll get my book *This Is London*, do you like London, I never saw London, except in my book. . . ."

This was two-year-old Ben's greeting to his new "friend," two-year-old Heather. I met her and her mother, Gayle, along with Carol and her son, Griffin, and Nancy and her son, Matthew, when I placed an ad in a local Los Angeles newspaper seeking a playgroup for Ben.

The mothers spoke on the phone and planned to meet in my home with their kids. Gayle arrived first, and Heather, who had the exact same birthday as Ben, trailed behind. Little Heather didn't want to meet me, and she certainly wasn't interested in meeting Ben. But she had no choice, because Ben, who just a few months before had taken his first shaky steps, assaulted both of them. Not with his fists or his feet, but with his mouth.

Ben stood inches from little Heather's face, announcing himself. He could have been saluting, but he wasn't. He was shouting in soldierly fashion, his words delivered in stiff, military precision—forceful, loud, and monotonous.

Ben's speech, this onslaught of words, violating the rules of personal space and introduction, was met with stunned silence. Gayle and Heather stood, mouths gaping, their bodies only half in the door. If there had been a breeze that day, the flurry, plus the avalanche of words pouring nonstop out of Ben's mouth, would have been enough to tip them over.

I couldn't know it then, but the silence on the other side of Ben's hello was more than a pause. It was an ominous preface to Ben's future.

So much to say, so few people who'd listen, who'd want to listen, who'd be equipped to see past Ben's transgression of social code.

Social code—its manners, its hundreds of unwritten rules about what to say, when to say it, how long to say it for. Other ones about how close to stand and where to look when you're standing. Even rules about tilting your voice up and down when you're doing the standing and the saying. And other rules, too, about taking turns, about sharing, and even rules about making faces—happy faces, sad ones.

An afternoon of very young playmates engaged in parallel play. That's what I'd imagined. Ben on the sofa, Heather on the floor beside Matthew, and Griffin off somewhere nearby. Each involved in his or her own interests but aware of each others' presence and somehow learning how to be social from the experience.

It was a failure. At least for Ben it was. Not that he was aware of it; not that he cared. He was perfectly fine doing what he always did, company or no company—sitting far apart from the others and reading his book, while Heather, Matthew, and Griffin played in close proximity to one another, every so often exchanging a word or even a toy.

We set our second playgroup date for the park. We met there the following month, four mothers, four children, and because the initial awkward meeting part was behind us, it felt easier, more relaxed. Even for Ben, things seemed to be going better. All of the kids—Heather, Griffin, Matthew, and Ben—headed off to the sandbox. The mothers brought blankets that we spread over the grass, strewn with bags of colorful toys, pails, little plastic shovels, each kid's favorite napping blanket, cans of juice, bags of pretzels, several alphabet picture books, and, of course, the two books that followed Ben wherever he went: *A Child's History of the World* and *A Child's Geography of the World*.

Carol, Nancy, Gayle, and I sat on the wooden bench closest to the sandbox. The women had just begun to thank me for having placed the playgroup ad in the paper when I looked up to check the sandbox. Ben wasn't there. "Where's Ben?" I called to the children. They pointed to the blanket, and sure enough, there was my two-year-old, sitting on the blanket reading *A Child's History of the World*.

"Is that the same book he was reading the last time we came to your house?" asked Nancy.

"Probably," I said.

"You mean he really *reads*? I thought he was just turning the pages," exclaimed Gayle.

"Oh, he reads all right. He started at eighteen months."

"*Eighteen months!*" the mothers gasped in unison.

"I've never heard of such a thing!" said Nancy.

"Maybe he's one of those geniuses you sometimes read about," said Carol.

"What is it like to have a kid like that?" said Gayle.

"I don't know," I said. "What is it like to have a regular kid?"

"LET'S GO SEE THE TRAINS, MOMMY. Let's go to the Museum of Science and Industry."

"Ben, I'm tired of that museum. How about the Museum of Natural History instead?"

"That one's boring. I like the diorama of the trains and the one about the airplanes and the display about the phone system. Isn't it interesting how signals travel across wires and that's how telephones work?"

"Yes, very," I lied.

So off we went, once again, for the fifteenth time in seven months, the same number of months we had lived in Los Angeles. By now Ben was two and a half years old, probably the youngest kid in Los Angeles who could talk about phone systems, let alone understand how they work.

"OK, Mommy, now don't forget how to get there—last time you got mixed up. Remember?"

"I did, didn't I? It's a good thing you have such a good sense of direction or we'd always get lost."

"Now get on the Hollywood Freeway. Take it to the Downtown four-level interchange and then change to the Harbor Freeway."

"Hold it, Ben. I can't remember all that. Tell me one freeway at a time."

"OK, but don't forget to go south, not north, on the Harbor Freeway, otherwise we'll be going in the wrong direction and we won't go through the tunnel, which is my favorite part."

Which was worse? A two-and-a-half-year-old giving his mother directions, or a thirty-one-year-old mother who needed to get them? Ben sat in his car seat singing "The Wheels of the Bus," plus a brand-new song I'd composed myself, "We're Going Through the Tunnel." It was about a little boy with uneven brown bangs who loved tunnels, trains, and cities as much as he loved books about tunnels, trains, and cities. It was about a boy who was going to the Museum of Science and Industry to see his beloved model train diorama. It was about Ben and his mommy going on an adventure, all the way to Exposition Park, where the Coliseum and the Sports Arena were. It was about love.

When we got to the museum, Ben had an agenda to follow. "Hurry up, Mommy! Don't forget we have to walk up all those steps to the second floor. I want to go there first. I like to imagine that I am one of the people riding the train."

The model train diorama filled the circumference of the entire second floor. The detailed model trains, replete with stations for passenger and cargo loading and unloading, were protected behind glass cases. Ben would stand in front of the glass, gazing for long stretches of time, transfixed, moving ever so slowly, ever so lovingly from one scene to the next.

"I love the farm scene, Mommy, don't you? I love the barn and the grain elevator. It's not real, I know it isn't, but it looks real, doesn't it?"

"It does." I wasn't bored with Ben's fascination; I'd never get bored with that. My son's enchantment was what brought me back again and again to the museum with its unchanging model train exhibit.

"See, Mommy, the train always stops here to get loaded up with grain and flour. If you look closely, *Mommy, you're not looking closely*, you can see the grain being put into the hopper cars."

"I see, Ben. Now can we go?"

"No! We haven't seen the harbor scene yet. Don't you want to see the ships being unloaded? Don't you want to see the cargo transferred onto the train?"

"We saw it last time, Ben. I'm tired of standing in one place for so long."

"We can't go home until we see the cranes putting the cargo into the trains."

My two-year-old had the vocabulary of a ten-year-old and—when he was interested in something—the attention span of a grad student, but he was as inflexible as any two-year-old I'd ever met.

"OK, Ben. *Then* can we go home?"

"No, Mommy. We have to finish *all of it*. Just like last time. Just like always. What about the factory scene? Don't you want to see the steel being delivered by train? Remember they go in as steel on one side and then there's the part where they come out as cars on the other side. Don't you want to see that? That's how cars get delivered, by train, they don't just drive on the freeway one by one, don't you want to see that?"

"We already saw that. You know it by heart."

"That's why I love it, Mommy."

What did that mean? Did Ben love what he knew by heart because he could count on it being just the way he remembered, never changing, never varying, never surprising with a torque or a twist or an alteration in routine? Did he love routine and sameness for its own sake, or because there was something about change that unsettled him?

"The best thing about this whole diorama is how everything connects with everything else. Just like a real city with streetcars and buses and stations and people. One day I'm going to build a real city of my very own."

OUR FIRST WINTER in Southern California was a very wet one. In February it rained every single day, and although Ben was content to sit for hours reading his books and the giant world atlas my father had sent as his birthday gift, I was going stir-crazy. "Let's go outside and play in the puddles," I would say the minute the rain stopped.

"What if it thunders again?"

"Oh, the sun's out. I think the thunder's over for today."

"But I'm scared of thunder. It's too loud."

By that time I had noticed that Ben was extremely sensitive to noise of any kind. He would panic at the sound of every ambulance, fire alarm, or high-pitched beep. It was something about the actual noise level that seemed to throw him, as if it were too much, too loud, too piercing for him to viscerally bear.

"Come on, Ben. It'll be fun. We'll bring your earmuffs, just in case."

So off we'd go, each of us dressed up in our yellow slickers and galoshes. "I'll make a splash first, Ben, and then you make one. How 'bout that?"

"Maybe."

So I found the biggest puddle and jumped in it with both feet. I didn't know exactly what I was doing, or exactly why, but I was aiming for a moment of startle, a surprise, maybe even a flash of shock. I wanted to shake things up.

"Let's go back inside, Mommy."

"No, Ben. We're staying outside. Look at the rainbow forming over the sidewalk, isn't it pretty? It's fun to splash and get all wet. Pretend you're a duck."

"OK." Ben placed one side of his galoshes into the tiniest puddle of water. "Quack, quack, I'm a duck."

"Isn't it fun, Ben?"

"It's OK, but I'd rather be at the Museum of Science and Industry."

"But this is *different*, Ben. We're outside and we're *doing* something."

"Remember the San Francisco Bay diorama, Mommy? Everything—the bridges and ferries and ships, and even the cars—moved around, just like it was real. The water too. Even the sun moved across the sky like a real day."

"But, Ben, we're in a real day now. This *is* a real day."

5

MOMMY, WHAT'S WRONG WITH ME?

I don't remember a time in my life when I didn't think something was wrong with me.

———

"Mommy, am I what that book says?" asks three-year-old Ben.

"Which book?" I ask back, as if I do not know. As if I'm not, this very moment, placing my body directly in front of its red hard cover, blocking the big black terrible words of the title, hating myself for having left it on the bookshelf in clear view of my little boy. My blameless son, in love with the printed word. Even if the words break his innocent heart.

"That one, Mommy," he says, pointing to the new book I bought and placed on the very top shelf of the bookcase: *MBD: The Family Book About Minimal Brain Dysfunction*. It was 1973, when everything wrong with the brain that could not be explained, certified, or diagnosed was labeled MBD.

"Of course not."

"Then what is wrong with me, Mommy? What is wrong with me?"

This first part is for parents. It describes the physical and psychological aspects of the disorder, which parents should find useful in helping their child. The second part is designed to be read by children, along with a parent.

But what was designed to happen did not happen. Ben did not read the second part of the book the way it was designed to be read, "along with a parent." He read it all by himself.

"Part Two: For Boys and Girls" has pictures, and it comes right after the part for parents, explaining that the label of MBD should not necessarily be seen as "condemning a child to irreparable and lifelong psychological" damage. This kind of thinking, the author warns, may lead to an unnecessary burden for both parent and child.

The picture on the first page of the section called "Introduction for Boys and Girls" shows a man facing a little boy. Sitting behind the boy are a lady and a man. They are the boy's mother and father. The man facing the boy is wearing glasses and holding a piece of paper. He is the child psychiatrist. His mouth is moving. He is the one who is talking. The little boy is sitting in a little boy's chair. His arms are crossed in front of him. His mouth is not moving. He is listening. The mother and father are sitting behind the little boy in big-person chairs. They are leaning forward. The mother's and father's mouths are also not moving. They are listening.

Everyone in the picture is smiling.

But Ben isn't smiling. Ben read every section of the part for children. He read the parts about what the brain does; all the ways people are different; what brain dysfunction is; the kind of trouble children with brain dysfunction have; how children with brain dysfunction can be helped and what they can do to help themselves; worries that children with brain dysfunction often have; and how some children with brain dysfunction worry about being retarded. He also read the parts about what you can do if other children are cruel to you; about how there's something wrong with someone who makes fun of the child with brain dysfunction; about how the things other children say about you may sometimes be untrue. And finally, he read about how bad names cannot hurt you and somewhere there are friends for everyone.

Ben read all of it, but still he wasn't smiling. He was crying. Just like I had cried when I read the book.

No doctor had told me to buy the book, read it, and place it on my bookshelf. I had done that all by myself. I had done that despite the protests of my husband, my mother, his mother, and the downstairs neighbor. I had done that even though Ben's doctors—except Dr. Pierce, who "specialized in that kind of thing"—were concerned only about Ben's asthma.

I had gone to the bookstore all by myself and asked the man behind the counter to show me the section on books about children. Then, when he wasn't looking, when the aisle was clear of customers, when I was sure no one was watching, I searched for the section I wanted. The section titled, "Books About Children with Problems."

"Why are you always looking for problems?" my husband yelled when I showed him the book. It was the fourth argument we had had that week on this same subject. The fourth time Steven had blamed me for looking for problems that weren't there, and the fourth time I had blamed him for refusing to see problems that *were* there.

"He's just super-smart. What's wrong with that?" yelled Steven.

"Nothing, except what about the other things?"

"*What* other things?"

"*That's just what I'm talking about.* Don't you get it? He's three years old and still walks up and down stairs one step at a time, he never runs, he won't go near the jungle gym or get on his tricycle, he can't hop or skip. Something's wrong. Why else would Dr. Pierce have sent us to Dr. Turner?"

"EVERYONE! HERE HE COMES. Here comes Ben!" exclaimed Judy, the youngest of Dr. Turner's staff of seven assistant eye-exercisers. "Say the names of the states, Ben. Tell Beth and Jerry and Don and Nancy. They've never heard you recite the states."

"OK, but as you know, there is no direct route from New York to Los Angeles, so I'll start with New York and go all the way to San Francisco, because that way you can take Interstate 80. OK, here goes: New York, New Jersey, Pennsylvania, West Virginia, Ohio, Kentucky, Missouri, Kansas, Colorado, Utah, Nevada, and California."

"See! Didn't I tell you?" Judy beamed, as if Ben's brilliance was her personal property. "Did you ever see anything like it?"

I was used to this. My son, the performing genius, my son the precocious reader of the printed word, who nevertheless needed to travel forty miles twice a week to learn how to team his eyes.

"Good job with the states, Ben. Now can you do just as well with tracking the ball? Let's start with your left eye. Which color patch would you like today, black or green?"

"No eye patch today, thank you. I'll just read my book."

"Come on, Ben, it's not so hard. Any boy who can recite all those states can track a ball."

"It's hard. It's boring. It's stupid. I'd rather read."

These were the same words Ben said to me each night when it was time to do his eye-exercise homework. "Why do I have to wear that stupid eye patch? I read fine."

"Yes, sweetie, you're a fine reader. But don't you also want to be able to hop and jump and throw a ball?"

"No. I don't like that. I'd rather read."

"But Ben, you can't *only* read. You have to do other things too. You can't read all the time."

"Only if we take turns. One exercise for one chapter of my *Child's History of the World* and one exercise for one chapter of my *Child's Geography of the World*."

"OK."

Judy, Dr. Turner's assistant, had told me the nightly eye exercises should take no more than fifteen minutes. She was wrong. They took ninety.

Ben was eating lunch in his high chair when I heard the first wheeze.

"It sounds like a whistle," I said on my end of the telephone call to Ben's new pediatrician.

"Is he wheezing?" asked the doctor.

"I don't know. What does a wheeze sound like?"

"You'd better bring him in. Stay on the phone while I connect you with my receptionist. Tell her I'm expecting you."

"Yup, he's wheezing all right," said Dr. Larson when we got there. "Give him a shot of prednisone," he said to Maria, his nurse.

"What's that?"

"It's a steroid. And here's a prescription for prednisone to be taken by mouth. Mash it up in applesauce, but give it to him exactly as prescribed—one tablet four times a day, today and tomorrow, followed by three for the next three days, then two for two days, and one for one day."

"But he doesn't eat applesauce."

"I don't care what you put it in. Just make sure he takes it."

On the way out of the doctor's office, Maria grabbed Ben. "OK everyone! Here he comes. Here's the boy I told you about!" she exclaimed in her squeaky, cheerful, very loud voice. Doctors, nurses, mothers, and kids of all ages poured out of examination rooms to see what the commotion was all about.

"OK, Ben. Now read this article in the newspaper. The one about outer space. I told them you can read, but no one believes me. Show 'em, Ben, show 'em!" And then, in what seemed like an afterthought, she looked in my direction as if to get my permission.

"It's up to Ben," I said. "Ben, do you feel well enough to read for all the people?"

"I don't have to read it. I did that already this morning in my own newspaper. I'll just tell them what it says."

6

PERSONS AND PEOPLE

I didn't understand the games of other children. But I understood my persons and they understood me.

———

"Mommy, come look at my city," Ben said. He said this most days, because when he wasn't reading books he was building cities and talking endlessly about them.

"Oh, my!" I'd exclaim each time I opened the door to his room. My "oh mys" were not the standard, obligatory mother-child kind, empty praise dedicated to raising a child's self-esteem. My "oh mys" were authentic, because Ben's cities were authentic.

Gas stations, fire stations, police stations, crosswalks, elementary schools, high schools, parks, baseball fields, basketball courts, banks, supermarkets, two libraries, a bike path, and a multitransit system. The structures came from the toy manufacturer Fisher-Price, but the design was Ben's.

"See, Mommy, the school goes here because it needs to be next to the bike path, and the fire station and police station go there because they need to be near the freeway, but not too close because policemen and firemen need to get in and out quickly. The supermarket is down here in the same direction as the elementary school, so the mothers can pick up groceries when they pick up their kids. I wasn't too sure about the gas station, because there needs to be a lot of them, but I only have one, so I didn't know where to put it."

"Oh." It was all I could say, really, because Ben's cities floored me. Just as Ben himself floored me.

Like other kids his age, Ben would beg for the newest Fisher-Price creation. But unlike his peers, he would sit in his room hour after hour, talking to himself, working and reworking his ideas until he had satisfied every element of his vision.

"Now watch, Mommy," Ben would continue as he pushed his yellow school bus up the path to the elementary school and then down to the supermarket, making a stop at the bank. Following this, Ben would retrieve a bag from his top drawer, reach in, and grab a handful of miniature wooden Fisher-Price figures—Ben's beloved "persons."

"My persons always take the school bus, even the grownups. That's how they get around. That's because Fisher-Price forgot to make a regular bus."

"They did, didn't they?"

What could I say? Ben was three and just yesterday he was crying, worried that something was wrong with his brain. I had cried for the same reason. But look—today his brain had produced this astonishing work of urban planning. Yesterday he read that "some children with brain dysfunction worry about being retarded." Today he was a genius.

Preschool would bring the answer; *I* surely didn't have it. True, I had taught kindergarten and had studied early childhood development; still, I was too close to the question that haunted me day and night: Was Ben better, or was he worse?

"I have to bring my persons, Mommy. I can't leave them home alone. You know I need them with me," Ben said as I was getting him ready for his first day of preschool.

"OK, Ben, you can take your persons, but not your school bus. I'm sure your classroom will have one. You can use theirs."

"Oh no! I can't do that! I need mine. *I have to have mine.*"

Maybe he did. *Other kids brought blankets to school*, I thought, *or teddy bears, so why couldn't my kid bring a school bus?*

But that's ridiculous, the other part of my brain replied. *What kid ever brought a school bus and a bag full of persons on the first day of school? He'll look idiotic, the teacher will think he's a weirdo, the kids will tease him. He won't fit in.*

If my son didn't fit in, how would I? This was my worst nightmare. I'd just have to threaten Ben and make it his too.

"You know, Ben, you may be the only boy who brings a school bus."

"I don't care," he said, stuffing his school bus into his backpack, squashing the three slices of American cheese he'd insisted would be his snack.

"But don't you want a *real* snack, like the other kids? How about a container of Jell-O or a bag of Fritos? American cheese is not a real snack. It's lunch food. How will you feel if you're the only kid who brings American cheese?"

"I don't care."

I had tried suggestion, and resorted to intimidation, but I wasn't going to get my way. For some reason I could not fathom, fear of not fitting in was not a motivator for my little boy. Something else was. I couldn't identify it, this something else motivating Ben, but I felt its presence every day in different rooms of the house. Especially in the kitchen.

"No, Mommy, I already told you. *Only* orange juice, *only* American cheese, *only* Cheerios."

"Why don't you try something new, like an omelet or pancakes?"

"I hate new. I want what I ate yesterday, just like always."

Didn't all three-year-olds have rigid ideas about what they would and wouldn't eat? *Yes, of course,* the other side of my brain replied, *but not like my three-year-old.* Mine had rigid ideas, habits, and routines about *everything.* And the dimension of Ben's routines seemed frighteningly inflexible. They didn't, like other kids, have the flavor of rebellion for the sake of individuating and separating. Ben's ideas, habits, and routines seemed to be about something else.

It was the look of panic on his face when we couldn't find his beloved *A Child's History of the World.*

"No, Mommy, not *that* book! *I need my book!*" Ben sobbed one night before I put him to bed.

"But Ben, we've already read that book. You know it by heart. Why don't we read a new book?"

"But this is the book we read *every* night. This is the book I'm used to. This is the book I love. *I need it, Mommy,* you know I do."

And he did. Ben *needed* his *Child's History of the World,* he *needed* his persons, he *needed* his school bus, and he *needed* his three slices of American cheese.

PLEASE, GOD, I prayed, *let Ben's teacher be kind.*

In the car on our way to school, Ben reached into his backpack and brought out his school bus, once again squashing his three slices of American cheese. He wanted to make the wheels of his school bus go round and round in time to our song. Meanwhile, the wheels of my mind went round and round with questions.

Would Ben adapt to a new routine? Would he overwhelm his classmates with pedantic, boring monologues about streets and cities he had seen only in books? Would he talk endlessly about the beginning of civilization? Would he stand in the center of the classroom and insist that everyone listen as he performed perfect imitations of his favorite radio commercials?

"*No, no, no, no!* You can't go home, Mommy. You can't leave me here all by myself!" Ben screamed, pulling on my skirt, as once again I attempted to say goodbye.

"But Ben, it's already the third week of school. You won't be all by yourself. You'll be with Miss Nicki and Mrs. Marcia and all your friends."

"No! You *have* to stay. I need you!"

So I stayed three more weeks. Miss Nicki and Mrs. Marcia said that my six-week stint was a record.

Ben did eventually adapt to his preschool routine, but he did it his way: with a book.

During recess, when it was time to go outside and the other kids would be riding back and forth playing cowboys and Indians on their tricycles, Ben would go outside, too. But he didn't play cowboys and Indians, and he didn't ride a tricycle. He read a book. If he could persuade one of his classmates—the girls proved most accommodating—he would read aloud to them. Otherwise, he would sit there, reading to himself, on the bench reserved for timeouts and teachers, zipped into his winter jacket, absentminded drool dripping onto the scarf tied around his neck.

He didn't need me to be right next to him. I could be anywhere, as long as he could see me. I could even talk to the other kids or the teachers. I just couldn't leave.

Six weeks was plenty of time to get the answers to most of my questions. Would Ben stand in the center of the room insisting that everyone listen to him do his Tide commercial? To that one, the answer was yes. Would Ben overwhelm the other kids with pedantic, long-winded monologues about places they had never heard of, places he had seen only in books? To that one, the answer was also yes.

But the jury was still out on my most important question—the question of better or worse. Although I had six weeks of informal mother-teacher conversations, plus one official parent-teacher conference, I still didn't have the answer.

"He's the smartest three-year-old I've met in all my years of teaching," said Mrs. Marcia at the parent-teacher conference.

"Yes, but he never gets invited to playdates," I said.

"We've noticed that," said Miss Nicki sympathetically. "But do you think he minds? What I mean is . . . he's usually by himself anyway . . . I mean, here in school. He enjoys playing alone; he seems content. Like he's in his own little world."

I just looked at her, because I knew she was right and I hated that she was right. Ben *did* seem content playing alone. But why? Why was he content in his own little world?

My silence must have made Miss Nicki uncomfortable, because the next thing she said was, "Why don't you plan a playdate at your home?"

"That's a good idea. We'll do that," Steven piped in.

Steven wasn't home to see the results of this good idea.

"Hi, Martha," I said, greeting Greg's mother at the front door. Greg was the best choice because, although he had never asked Ben to play with him, he did once ask if he could borrow Ben's persons to play army.

"Have a good time, Greg," Martha said as she kissed her son good-bye. By this time Ben was standing inches from Greg's face, asking, "Which book—my *Child's History of the World*, my *Child's Geography of the World*, or *This Is Brazil*—do you want to read?" Greg was backing away from Ben, and Martha, who had been on her way out, stopped.

"Maybe Greg wants to do something else," I said, grabbing Greg's hand and guiding him to the backyard. "It's a nice day. Why don't you boys play outside?" I asked, as if these were everyday words and I was an everyday mother.

"That's a good idea, isn't it, Greggy? You like playing outside," his mother coaxed. I could see she was torn: she understood the importance of this event for *my* son, but would she be sacrificing *hers*?

"OK," Greg said tentatively, kissing his mother goodbye.

"I'll pick him up in an hour," Martha said, handing me a slip of paper with her phone number written on it.

"See you soon," I called out gaily, holding each of the boys' hands, walking them quickly to the backyard. "While you boys are playing, I'll be in the kitchen making us some chocolate chip cookies." And I hurried inside, because making cookies is what a mother does when her son is on a playdate.

"Where's Ben?" I asked Greg ten minutes later. He was outside, riding Ben's tricycle. The cookie dough was not even thawed.

"In his room," Greg replied. "Reading."

"Oh."

MAYBE I DIDN'T have the answer to better or worse because I never asked the question. And maybe I never asked the question because it was a bad question, a question I shouldn't have asked in the first place, a question I was ashamed of having asked. Or maybe I never asked the question because it wasn't the *real* question. Maybe better or worse was a stand-in for the question I was afraid to ask, a question I dared ask only in the privacy of my own heart, in the middle of the night, when it woke me shouting its terrible words: *Is something wrong with Ben?*

7

PLAYER PIANO

I have always felt a disconnection between my body and my brain. Sometimes it's as if I don't have a body. My body has failed me. I fall down when I try to run. I have problems seeing. I can't focus. I can't make my hands move the way I want them to.

———

"Stop fighting," Ben pleaded with me and Steven when he was one.

"We're not fighting, sweetie, we're having a discussion," I said.

"No we're not! We're fighting." Steven replied. "Go back to your room, Ben. I'll be right there to tuck you in."

"Too loud. I have to hold my ears. I don't like loud," Ben cried.

"I'm sorry, sweetie," I said.

"I'm sorry, too," Steven said.

The best thing between Steven and me was Ben. But it wasn't enough. We were children when we met and still children when we married, not in years but in maturity. Steven was a conscientious husband and father, and he tried hard to meet my expectations. But how could he? I had married him because he was smart; now I wanted him to be athletic. I had married him because he was the strong, silent type; now I wanted him to talk. I worried about Ben and wanted Steven to worry too. But he didn't, or he wouldn't, so I had to worry alone.

All Ben wanted was a home he could count on. He wanted his persons and his books and his American cheese. He wanted "The Wheels of the Bus" from his mommy and "Frisco Bay" from his daddy.

"Stop fighting," Ben said when he was two.

"We're not fighting, sweetie, we're just talking," I said.

"No we're not. We're fighting. Go back to your room, Ben. I'll be right in," said Steven.

"But it's too loud!"

"I'm sorry, sweetie," I said.

"I'm sorry, too," Steven said.

But sorry didn't do it for Ben.

"You know," Miss Nicki, Ben's preschool teacher, said on the phone one day when Ben was three, "Ben's spending even more time alone than usual. Is anything going on at home I should know about?"

"It's his father and me. We're fighting a lot. I can't say the situation's hopeful," I replied apologetically.

"Oh dear."

"I'm sorry," I said, because Ben *was* dear, and look what Steven and I were doing to him.

"That's the last thing that sweet little boy needs. He relies on structure, you know. He gets agitated when there's a change in routine."

"I know, but what can I do? I mean . . . is there something I can do other than . . . you know . . . not fight so much with his father?"

"Maybe if he was more comfortable in his body, maybe that would give him more confidence—"

"But how? What should I do?"

"Maybe this would be a good time to start motor therapy . . . and, you know, talking therapy wouldn't hurt either."

"Anything. But whom should I call? Where should I start?"

"Start with Miss Reed, the motor therapist. It's a long drive from here, but she's the best."

MISS REED WELCOMED US into her house and greeted us like old friends. "We'll go outside and have some fun in a moment," she said. "But first, I want to show Ben something very special." She led us into her living room. "Do you know what that is, Ben?" she asked, pointing at the contraption in the corner.

"No."

"It's a player piano, Ben. It's a piano that plays all by itself!"

Ben's face, which was usually deadpan, changed to a look of horror.

Miss Reed smiled at me and said, "He's just a little shy. Kids love my piano player. Now let's go outside and I'll show you around."

She gave us the grand tour of her facility, which was actually her backyard, converted to accommodate her growing motor therapy business.

In one corner of her backyard stood an aboveground swimming pool with a ladder leaning against it. In another corner, hanging from a eucalyptus tree, was a huge basket with a seat inside. Along the perimeter of the backyard was a series of balance beams interrupted at different points by what looked like obstacles of various shapes and sizes. And then there were the smaller objects—like the shoe-tying board, a board formed in the shape of a shoe with holes for threading and untied shoelaces hanging loose at the sides.

"OK, Ben. Now this one's fun," said Miss Reed after she had given us the grand tour. "Do you know what this is?" Miss Reed asked, pointing to a giant trampoline, which stood square in the center of the backyard.

"It's a trampoline."

"Have you ever jumped on a trampoline?"

"No," Ben said. "I don't like trampolines and I don't like jumping."

"Why not Ben? *It's so much fun!*"

"Not for me."

"Come on, watch me! I'll go first." Miss Reed used the kitchen stool leaning against the side to pull herself over the rim of the trampoline. She stood up and began to jump, catching my eye as I sat watching. She winked and laughed too loudly. Then she jumped higher—up and down, down and up—and as she jumped her laugh grew louder and she said over and over again, *"It's so much fun! It's so much fun!"*

Ben, who had been standing close to her when she was still on the ground, made an immediate about-face. He walked over to where I was standing a few feet away and clutched my hand.

"Let's go home, Mommy. I don't like it here."

"But it looks like fun, Ben. Why don't you try it?"

"No, I'm afraid," he said, deadpan.

"Would *you* like to try it, Mommy?" Miss Reed called to me, winking and laughing too loudly.

I was steaming. *Don't call me Mommy*, I thought. *I'm not* your *mommy. No, I would not like to try it.* But of course I did. Anything to make the forty-five-minute trip worth it.

"The trampoline works magic for these kids," Miss Reed had told me on the telephone when I called to set up Ben's first appointment. "It helps with coordination and depth perception. It works the large motor muscles. It's just what these kids need to build confidence."

"Sure, I'll try it. It looks like fun," I lied.

"No, Mommy. I want to go home!"

I took off my shoes and climbed up the kitchen stool. I held my skirt and took a tiny jump to the accompaniment of Miss Reed's squeals. *"Isn't it fun? Isn't it fun?"*

I hadn't driven forty-five minutes in traffic, all the way from my home in the San Fernando Valley to Temple City, just to have fun. I had come because Miss Nicki had said Ben needed to get more comfortable in his body. I had come because she had said, "Oh dear," when I told her about Steven and me. I had come because Ben's daddy and I were fighting all the time and it was too loud and my little boy was disappearing deeper and deeper into his own little world. That's why I'd come.

It took Ben five more forty-five-minute trips to take his first step on the kitchen stool, and five more trips after that to begin jumping on the trampoline. But he never laughed and he never said, "It's so much fun, it's so much fun."

"Everything about Miss Reed's house scares me, Mommy. Everything!" Ben told me again and again.

"I know, sweetie. It's hard, but you're doing it. You're doing it!"

"But it's scary! I hate it!"

"But Ben, aren't you proud? You're learning to tie your own shoes. You're even balancing on the balance beams. You can do the backstroke and the crawl. You're jumping on the trampoline! *Aren't you proud?*"

"Most of all I hate the player piano. It's too loud! I hate loud."

"The player piano? You mean the player piano itself?"

"*Yeeks.* That's the worst of all. It doesn't make sense. There's nobody playing it. There's no fingers. The keys move all by themselves. Thank goodness Miss Reed doesn't make me sit in her living room and listen to it. I'd die of fright if she ever did that."

"But Ben. . . ." If a piano that played by itself scared Ben to death, what good were words?

Ben hated swimming day. On swimming day, he had to climb up a huge ladder to get into the aboveground pool. It was the climbing part Ben dreaded more than the swimming part.

Ben hated spinning day, the day he had to spin in space. Miss Reed would put Ben in the basket hanging from the tree, then twist the basket, making it go round and round. This was supposed to help Ben feel more comfortable in space. It didn't.

Ben was afraid of swimming, climbing, jumping, and balancing. He dreaded all of it. But worst of all was the day Miss Reed made him sit in her living room, listening to her player piano. Ben had said if she ever did that he would "die of fright."

But I had reassured him that Miss Reed would never do that, because, after all, that's not why he was there. He was there for outside things, not inside ones.

"It's a piano that plays *all by itself*, Mommy. *How can it do that?* Maybe it won't ever stop. Maybe it will play that way forever and forever. It's the scariest thing I ever saw, and I'm never ever going in there. *Never, no matter what.*"

But Ben did go in there. Into Miss Reed's living room, with the player piano, the place he said he'd never go, *no matter what!* "There's nothing to be afraid of, Ben," she'd told him. "It's just a piano that plays by itself. Just sit here and listen for a while. You'll get used to it."

But Miss Reed was wrong about that. Ben didn't get used to it.

He screamed bloody murder.

I wasn't there when it happened. By that time Ben had agreed to let me spend his therapy hour at the library down the block from Miss Reed's house.

When I returned from the library exactly on time, I was greeted by the sight of an ambulance and two fire trucks parked outside Miss Reed's house. Miss Reed was out there too, with Ben at her side. She was motioning wildly and laughing again, but this time not quite as loudly.

"No, he's fine," she said to the ambulance driver. "Aren't you, dear? Aren't you, Ben?"

"No, I'm not fine. There's a piano in there that plays by itself, and Miss Reed said I had to sit in the same room with it and listen to it play," Ben told the ambulance driver.

When Ben saw me, he started to cry, and then he turned back to the ambulance driver and added, "It's a piano and it plays by *itself.*"

"*What on earth happened?*" I screamed, jerking open my car door and making a beeline for Ben.

"Oh, no big deal," Miss Reed said. "My neighbor heard Ben's screams and thought there had been an accident. So she called 911."

"But he was petrified! Couldn't you see that? Why the hell didn't you help him?"

"Of course he's afraid," said Miss Reed, indignant that I'd challenged her. "That's why you brought him here, isn't it? I'm trying to teach him *not* to be afraid of everything. Exposure is the answer, *not* avoidance."

"Yes, but—"

"Look, either he gets it now, or he never gets it. Do you want him to be afraid the rest of his—"

I didn't wait for Miss Reed to finish her dumb question. Do I want Ben to be afraid the rest of his life? Do I want him to need his school bus and persons and American cheese and his two favorite books the rest of his life? Do I want him to stay upstairs in his room reading when a friend comes to play? No, I didn't need to wait around for the end of Miss Reed's question. Of course, I didn't want Ben to be afraid the rest of his life. But just because you don't want something doesn't mean you won't get it.

Motor therapy was a failure. Just as eye therapy was turning out to be a failure. And talking therapy with Dr. Morris had been a failure, too. Therapies didn't work. It was time to recognize that.

But I wasn't ready to give up. There had to be some therapy that would work. There had to be something I could do.

8

HIS OWN LITTLE WORLD

I wasn't interested in playing with other kids. I much preferred spending time with myself, either playing with my persons or reading. I felt uncomfortable around other people. Even going someplace new, like someone's house or a different restaurant, scared me.

———

AFTER TWO YEARS IN PRESCHOOL, which delivered not a single friend or party invitation, and which left—I would learn later—a permanent mark on the psyches of Miss Nicki and Mrs. Marcia, I set out looking for a kindergarten for Ben.

It's not what I had wanted to do; I had wanted to keep Ben in preschool for another year.

"Are you crazy?" screamed Steven when I proposed holding Ben back. "Didn't you hear what the teacher said? He's the smartest kid she's ever met, and you want to hold him back? *What are you thinking?*"

"I know, Steven. But he doesn't have a single friend."

"Did Einstein have friends?" Steven was furious. "Did he *need* them?"

"Maybe he did. Maybe he was sad without them."

"Are you saying Ben is sad?"

"He could be . . . I can't tell. . . ."

"Well, I can. He's perfectly content in his own little world. Perfectly!"

There it was again—that deadly expression—"his own little world." But this time it came out of the mouth of Ben's father, the man who, like my own father, had been too serious to sing. But Ben changed all that. After Ben, melodies flew, like tiny miracles, from Steven's mouth.

In Frisco Bay
There lives a whale
And she eats pork chops by the pail
By the suitcase
By the bathtub
And also by the wheelbarrow

Steven and Ben bonded in folk songs and in Shakespeare. Father recited *Hamlet*: "To die, to sleep; To sleep perchance to dream," and son followed with "Ay, there's the rub," as line for loving line they exchanged their special vow of devotion. Ben stored his love for Steven in memory, where everything precious was kept—for safekeeping, for never forgetting, for reciting back.

"Steven, I know how much you love Ben. You must be worried too."

"I'm *not worried*," Steven protested. Too loudly.

"But he's still a little boy," I pleaded.

"And it's a big world out there, isn't it?" Steven said.

"Yes, but—" Steven was right. I knew he was, but I couldn't stop.

"You can't protect him forever."

"I can't help it. He's just so innocent."

"He can handle it. He's a smart kid."

And of course Steven was a smart man. I considered him a lot smarter than I was, which is why I'd married him. I'd loved listening to him talk about world events with that tone of authority . . . the kind of authority Ben now showed when he talked about subways and maps.

"HOW DO YOU DO, Mickey Mouse," Ben said as he reached to shake the hand of the famous Disney figure. "My name is Benjamin. Pleased to make your acquaintance. How is Minnie?" Formal words, from the mouth of a proper person. But the person was only five years old.

Ben stood center stage in a circle of Disneyland visitors. He was smiling one of his rare smiles and looking a little like Dopey, with his long, uneven brown bangs, his gaping front teeth, his big ears and crossed eyes. But it wasn't any of Disney's carefully costumed characters—not Dopey or Sleepy or even Snow White—drawing the crowd. It was my drooling five-year-old who was attracting them.

"Nibble, nibble, I hear a mouse. Who's that nibbling at my house?" Ben intoned, loud enough to be heard by all who passed by.

"The wind, the wind; it's very mild, blowing like the Heavenly Child." And the passerby, hearing this, would stop. Dead in his tracks.

Today I'll brew, tomorrow I'll bake.
Soon I'll have the queen's namesake.
Oh, how hard it is to play my game,
For Rumplestiltskin is my name!

Ben continued, without segue, without pause. And the people came. They came and came until all you could find of him were the words.

The words. That's all I could find of Ben—the *words*.

I had brought Ben to Disneyland to enjoy the rides: the Haunted House, the Pirates of the Caribbean, the Matterhorn. But as we stood in line waiting our turn, the squeals and screams coming from the kids inside terrified him and he'd put his hands over his ears as if the sound was too much to bear.

"It's a Small World, Mommy. Let's go."

"But Ben," I tried, "we've been on that ride twice. Come on . . . let's go on something else."

"No! Only that one!"

"But why, Ben? Look at all the other kids." It was a sentence I used more and more, a sentence I hated myself for using, because what did all the other kids have to do with mine? I knew that, but still. . . . "Look at the kids coming out of the Tea Cups," I pleaded. "They look so *happy*!" So *normal*, I thought.

But Ben shook his head. "I don't care."

So again and again we rode through the gentle waters of It's a Small World, until, by the ninth straight trip, it was *my* ears that were covered up.

In between, as we stood in the long line waiting for our little boat, Ben would entertain: "Come one. Come all. See the Incredible Talking Boy." Of course he didn't actually make this announcement in Disneyland, and neither did I. There was no need, because Ben drew the crowds naturally, just by being himself—by reciting big words out of his little-boy mouth—and the people came in droves.

STEVEN AND I WERE AT LOGGERHEADS. "You have to trust me on this one. *I'm* the early childhood specialist, not you," I said. By now, we might as well have pressed "play" on a cassette player. There were no variations anymore in what we had to say to each other.

"That's just it," Steven interrupted. "You're not seeing *Ben*. You're seeing a *textbook*."

"I only pray you're right," I said.

"Then it's settled? Ben will go to kindergarten."

"OK." It was a losing battle, anyway. "But only if I can find the right private school. Public school would kill him."

To this Steven agreed, and I set out looking for the proper school for Ben. But what exactly was I looking for? What questions should I ask? I wanted to sound professional, or at the very least informed; but if I said what I was really feeling, I wouldn't sound professional at all. I'd sound like a whining, defective mother.

"Please . . . is this a kind place?" I longed to ask. "Will you help my son make a friend? Will you teach him to climb the jungle gym and play cowboys and Indians? Will you help him not be afraid of stairs and high places? Will you make sure the other kids invite him to their birthday parties? Will you show him how to look at the person he's talking to and make his voice go up and down while he's talking? Will you help him tie his shoes, hold scissors, color between the lines? Will he learn to enjoy adventure books, not just encyclopedias? Will you help him talk less and play more? Can you make him . . . regular?"

Every day I received at least three school brochures; they all seemed to say the same thing. They were bragging, showing off their success rates in reading, writing, and arithmetic. I searched for the words *play*, *eye-hand coordination*, *large muscle activity*, and *sharing*, and when I didn't find them, I'd cross that school off my list of possible schools for Ben and throw the brochure in the trash.

It was getting closer and closer to the beginning of the next school semester and Ben was becoming more and more isolated, disappearing deeper and deeper into his own little world. Except when I dragged him out of his room for a trip to the market, he spent his entire day speaking to no one but his miniature persons, himself, and me.

Then I met Lisa. She lived two houses down, and I guessed she was about twelve. She was a little odd, in a way I couldn't quite describe, overweight, and not at all shy. One day I asked her about all the notebooks with the beautiful pastel drawings she carried back and forth to school.

"Oh. They're my lessons."

"But don't you have books?"

"No. My school doesn't believe in books. We make our own."

"*You make your own books?*"

And then Lisa explained about the Rudolf Steiner school she had been going to since kindergarten. How the kids and the teacher traveled together from grade to grade. How lessons were taught in subject blocks, and how each of the notebooks was for a different subject, taught in a hands-on format.

I was fascinated. Not so much by the notebooks, although they were lovely to look at, but by the idea of a single teacher moving from grade to grade with the same group of kids. Like a big happy family. The wonderful thing about big happy families is their love for one another, their loyalty. The big ones stick up for the little ones and the little ones study the big ones. That's what Ben needed—a big happy family, where he would be protected, where he could learn to be a regular little boy.

Lisa showed me the knitting project she had done in the first grade. It was a long scarf with a patch of green followed by a patch of yellow followed by a patch of orange.

"You made that?" I exclaimed.

"We all do."

"Even the boys?"

"Everyone."

My mind was racing ahead, imagining Ben next year, in first grade, coming home each night and sitting next to me on the couch, knitting needles clicking away, his school bus and persons abandoned for the comfort of seven rows of purl, seven rows of knit.

The next day I made the twenty-five-minute trip to Northridge. The main school sat high atop a hill in a semicircle of one-story wooden structures. *Those must be the classrooms*, I thought as I drove up looking for the principal's office. But there was no principal's office. *They must not have that either*, I thought as I made my way back down the hill to the kindergarten level.

Mrs. White and Mrs. Cash let me observe their morning Circle Time.

The sun with loving light
Shines bright on me each day.
The soul with Spirit power
Gives strength unto my limbs.

Two teachers, two kindergartens, same ritual. In each room, at precisely the same time, twenty-five kids sat on twenty-five blankets, spread in the shape of a big circle, declaring these memorized words. It was almost hypnotic. The kids settled down and so did I. *This is a gentle place*, I thought as my breathing relaxed. I like it here.

So off Ben went that September to his new school, the only Rudolph Steiner school in the San Fernando area. He took with him his school bus, his persons, and his three slices of American cheese, but this time I didn't worry about that. It was going to be all right, I thought. They made their own books.

Ben was in Mrs. Cash's class, and the mothers got to stay as long as they were needed. It was only five weeks for me this time around. Still, Mrs. Cash, who didn't say much, admitted it *was* a record.

"Ben, you be the daddy," the girls in the dress-up corner prodded.

"No. I will not," said Ben.

"But you're the *only* boy here. We're playing house. We need a daddy."

"I'll be the *radio*," Ben said, holding a toy radio up in front of his mouth and beginning his word-for-perfect-word imitation of car, soap, and shaving cream commercials. The girls ignored him. But that didn't stop Ben from pushing forward. He still had the weather report to do. Followed by the traffic report. And, of course, the test of the emergency broadcast system.

This is a test of the emergency broadcast system. This is only a test.

Beeeeeeeeep!

This has been a test of the emergency broadcast system.

The broadcasters in your area, in cooperation with federal, state, and local authorities, have developed this system to keep you informed in the event of an emergency.

Had this been an actual emergency, the attention signal you just heard would be used to inform you of news and official information.

This station serves the Los Angeles area.

This concludes this test of the emergency broadcast system.

Mrs. Cash's kindergarten classroom had clay, finger paints, blocks of all sizes, a fish tank, two gerbils, one caged snake, beeswax for candle making, a dress-up corner, and an area for water play. It also had a reading corner with a cozy chair, but the books were all children's books, like *Good Night Moon* and *Green Eggs and Ham*, books with plots, not places. So Benjamin insisted on bringing his own, and besides, he said, "I hate nap time. I'll only lie down if I can bring my *Child's Geography of the World*."

Which was about the time Mrs. Cash called me on the phone. "I need to see you," she said. "It's about Benjamin."

Steven took the morning off from work, and we drove the twenty-five minutes in silence. The only words I would have said anyway were, "See? I was right." But until we came face to face with Mrs. Cash, I wouldn't know precisely *what* I was right about.

Mrs. Cash wasn't alone. She was flanked by a teacher on either side. On her left was Mrs. White, and on her right was Mr. Kraft, a teacher in training.

It was recess and the kids were playing on the giant green lawn, running, climbing, riding tricycles, and climbing ropes. Ben, of course, was off by himself, sitting in a corner of the playground, reading his book.

Mrs. Cash got right to the point: "Why did you teach Ben to read?"

"What?" Maybe I'd heard wrong.

"Why on earth would you teach him to read before he can even run?"

"I didn't," I said, confused.

Mrs. White wasn't smiling, nor was Mr. Kraft. "You know, it's very bad for them," said Mr. Kraft.

"What is?" I asked, even more confused.

"Reading before they're ready."

"I know that," I said, but I was angry now. Clearly I was on trial here. Clearly I stood accused.

"Just look at him—alone out there day after day—his nose buried in a book," said Mrs. White.

"That's just how he is," Steven said.

"Well, *someone* had to teach him," said Mrs. Cash.

"It was 'Sesame Street,' " I protested.

" 'Sesame Street?' " The three of them chorused.

"He watches it three times a day." Why should I have to make excuses? Why should I have to defend myself? I didn't do anything wrong.

"Three times a day! *Why do you let him*?" Mrs. Cash was indignant.

Maybe that was it, I thought, *maybe that's what I'd done wrong*. But I didn't really believe it. "But that's all he ever wants to do," I said. "That and reading. That and playing with his persons. That and doing radio commercials. And talking, too . . . reading and talking."

"And tests of the emergency broadcast system," added Mrs. Cash.

Driving to the conference I'd wanted to be right, to show Steven I was right. But now that I was, I'd give anything to be wrong.

9

BATTER UP!

There was no way I could be the best at baseball, but I could do the best Vin Scully imitation you ever heard.

———

"LET'S TELL HIM TOGETHER," I said to Steven the day he found the apartment he would be moving into the next morning.

"Good idea," Steven agreed. "I'll take him to see my apartment this coming Saturday, but I'll still drive him to school in the mornings and I'll still go to his school events, and I'll still—"

"I know you will, Steven. And you can see him every weekend, and anytime during the week—"

"I hate having to tell him. What do you think he'll do?"

"I don't know. I wish it were different."

"Well, it's not. Let's get it over with."

Ben was in his bed reading his newest book, *This Is Switzerland*, when, instead of just Steven going into his room to tuck him in, I came too.

Steven began, "Ben, Mommy and I have something to tell you."

"I know," said Ben.

"You do?" I asked.

"Yeah, you're sorry you're fighting and you won't do it anymore."

Steven and I looked at each other.

"No, Ben. It's different this time, but it *is* on the same subject."

"I'm just on the page about how Switzerland doesn't have a fighting army. I'm busy. Tell me later."

"No, Ben," Steven said. "This is important."

"OK." Ben reached for his library card bookmark and closed his book. "What?"

"Tomorrow, I'm moving into a different place."

"You mean you're going out of town *again*? Why do you always have to go out of town?"

"No, Ben, not out of town, like when I go on work trips. This moving is different. Mommy and I are going to live in separate houses."

"*Why?*"

"Because of all the fighting. It's not good for you and it's not good for us."

"It's OK, I don't mind. You can fight all you want. I'll just hold my ears."

"No, sweetie, it's not like that," I said. "Mommy and Daddy are getting separated and we can't live together anymore."

"But why?"

"It isn't your fault, Ben. Mommy and Daddy each love you the same as always. *We'll never be separated from you.*"

Ben turned his head toward the wall. He was crying. Steven and I covered his body with ours. We were crying too.

Then we began, both of us—Steven and I—talking at the same time, over one another, our frantic attempts to comfort Ben bumping into each other.

Words of reassurance, words of regret and guilt and shame for what we were doing, what we had done, how we were breaking our little boy's heart.

I'm so sorry sweetie, it won't be so bad, you'll see. Dad has an apartment, with a special room for you. I'm so sorry, Ben, you'll see me all the time, I'll drive you to school, Dad will drive you to school every day. I'll call you on the phone, Dad will call you on the phone every day. I'm sorry, Ben, I'm sorry, Ben. I love you so much, I love you so much, you'll always be our little boy.

Ben sat up and retrieved his book. "I'm going to read my book now."

EACH MORNING AFTER THAT, Steven stopped by to take Ben to school. They made the same detour they always did, around the block, and down into the underground parking lot with the giant hill. "Ready! Set! Go!" Steven would shout, and Ben would protest, "No, no, no!" on the way down, and "Yes, yes, yes!" on the way back up.

"It's my favorite part of school days," Ben would tell me each night. "And the funny feeling in my stomach going, down, down, down a million miles a minute."

"That fast?"

"Well, not exactly that fast. But anyway, my persons can't go that fast, because they travel on public transportation, and anyway, it's illegal."

"You have fun with your daddy."

"Besides me, he's the smartest person I know."

"That's what I think too," I said.

"And he knows all the states, and he reads maps just like me, and he speaks Shakespeare, and sings folk songs, and he's a lawyer and he went to law school, and he doesn't play baseball, but he knows all the players and he listens to the games on the radio, and. . . ."

Good afternoon ladies and gentlemen. This is Benjamin Levinson speaking to you from Dodger Stadium in Los Angeles, California, and it's time for Dodger baseball!

Except for the din of the crowd, the smell of Dodger dogs, beer, and nachos, and the calls of "Peanuts! Peanuts!" and "Program, program, get your program here!" it might as well be Dodger Stadium. But it wasn't Dodger Stadium. It was Ben, doing his famous word-for-perfect-word radio imitation of Vin Scully announcing a baseball game.

I was standing just outside his bedroom door, and I could see six-year-old Ben sitting at his desk, a toothbrush-microphone in his hand, a pad of paper in his lap. I had heard it before—countless times—but still I waited for the song to begin, because aside from the commercial at the end of the routine, the song was my favorite part.

> *Let's go, batter up, we're taking the afternoon off!*
> *It's a beautiful day for a ballgame, for a ballgame today.*
> *The fans are out to get a ticket or two,*
> *From Walla Walla, Washington, to Kalamazoo,*
> *It's a beautiful day for a home run, but even a triple's OK,*
> *We're gonna cheer, and boo, and raise a hullabaloo,*
> *At the ballgame today!*

Ben was six, in the first grade, and still without a friend. Jumping on a trampoline and counting backward from ten had done nothing to change that. Neither did wearing an eye patch and tracking the ball every night since preschool, in exchange for one chapter of *A Child's History of the World*.

He still drooled; he still stared off into space instead of looking people in the eye; he still talked too long, too loud, and without interest in what anyone else had to say. And he still coughed, hacked, wheezed, and took puffs from his inhaler.

"Ben, are you wheezing?" became my refrain.

I could have been upstairs in my bedroom, and Ben downstairs in his. Or I could have been downstairs in the garage and Ben upstairs in the den, but wherever I was, whatever I was doing, one ear was always cocked toward Ben. I was just as allergic to the sound of Ben's sniffing, blowing, laughing, or coughing as Ben was allergic to cats. For Ben, a cough meant a wheeze and a wheeze meant "Hurry up and take your inhaler or you'll end up in the hospital."

A YEAR AFTER STEVEN AND I SPLIT UP, I met John. He was in music, as was Steven, but in the creative end, not the business end. There were many reasons I shouldn't have fallen for him—he was too old (thirteen years my senior), too poor, and too much the free spirit. But that's why I liked him. That's why he fascinated me. And there was a softness in his smile that seemed to say yes. Yes to today, yes to tomorrow, and yes, yes, yes to me. And he was beautiful to look at.

On our first date we went to his recording studio, where we listened to demos of a singer he was producing. He sat at the piano and sang songs he had sung fifteen years earlier, when he was an up-and-coming heartthrob performer. I looked at the framed album covers hanging on the walls of his studio and fell head over heels.

Soon we were spending weekends together. Ben stayed with Steven on Saturdays and Sundays, and while I wasn't eager for John to meet Ben, John was.

Most people didn't know what to make of my son. He was smart, all right, that part was clear, but there was something about him, something they couldn't quite figure out. I saw it in the funny, awkward way they looked at him. I heard it in their hesitation as they commented about him when he wasn't around: "Your son . . . he's, uh . . . extremely intelligent. He knows a lot . . . I mean . . . how does he know so much?" It wasn't so much what they did say, but what they *didn't* say. If I was going to prepare John, if I wanted it to go well, how should I do it? What should I say?

Should I say, "Oh, by the way, don't be shocked when you meet my six-year-old. He's smart, but a bit odd. No, I can't exactly say what I mean, because I don't exactly know. Why don't I know? I don't know why I don't know. Maybe because he isn't odd. Maybe because no one's ever said he is. I mean, in words . . . do you know what I mean?" Which, of course, he wouldn't . . . know what I meant . . . how could he?

So I didn't say anything.

"Ben, this is my new friend, John. Say hello." Ben wasn't shy, far from it, so saying anything, even to a stranger, wasn't a problem. It was where he stood when he said it that was the problem.

"How do you do? My name is Benjamin." Ben was hoping for a hand-shake, the kind he saw between grown men, but he was standing so close to John, leaving barely an inch of space between them. So the six-foot man kneeled down, making himself the same height as the little boy, placed one of his big hands on each of Ben's little shoulders, and gently moved him back.

It was so tender, this moment between them, completely wordless and wonderful.

"HE'S NOT VERY COORDINATED, is he?" John commented one day. "He doesn't alternate feet when he's walking up and down stairs."

"I know."

"Isn't that the purpose of his eye exercises and that Miss Reed lady in Temple City?"

"Uh-huh. And by the way, you're such a sport for sharing the driving with me. I used to have to do it all by myself twice a week—"

"You're welcome, but it's not doing much good. When I take him to the park, he still refuses to climb the jungle gym."

"I know. Maybe he'll never do it. . . ."

"*Oh, yes he will.* I taught him how close to stand when he's talking to someone, and I taught him to let go of the banister when he walks down stairs. By God, I'll teach him to climb the jungle gym," said John.

"Lots of luck," I replied, because if anything was going to be a losing battle, I knew it would be Ben and the jungle gym.

"Laaadies and gentlemen!" John said to Ben as they stood together looking up at the jungle gym on their next park outing.

"Announcing the one and only Benjamin Daniel Levinson! He is performing this Saturday morning in the year 1975, right here in sunny California. Come one, come all! See him with your own eyes as he climbs up the first rung of the jungle gym!" Clearly, John understood what Miss Reed failed to appreciate about my little boy. He knew that if he was to help Ben overcome his fears, there was only one way to do it— he must join him in his private world of fantasy.

"No, John. I don't want to!" Ben replied, reaching up to grab the first rung.

"Now boys and girls of all ages, watch him closely. He is about to place his left foot ever so carefully, ever so proudly, on the first rung," John continued. "What a feat of daring, ladies and gentlemen! What courage! See him step on the rung, grabbing it . . . right now . . . in both hands!"

"No, John. I'm not going to," Ben replied, grabbing the bar with both hands.

"Here he goes, boys and girls! See him as he reaches up and does it yet one more time!"

"No, John. I'm scared," Ben said on cue, climbing up to the second rung.

And when he reached the top, when John, my soon-to-be-husband, Ben's soon-to-be-stepfather and ringmaster par excellence, had expertly coaxed Ben's achievement of climbing up the rungs—left hand, right foot, right hand, left foot—up, up, up, and then, just as patiently, down, down, down—they greeted me at home. Triumphant.

"Mommy, Mommy! I did it! I did it! I climbed all the way up to the top! Didn't I, John? Didn't I?"

"You surely did!" John said, beaming. Then he picked Ben up and paraded him on his shoulders, back and forth throughout every room of the house.

JOHN AND I MARRIED when Ben was six years old. It was a cold, damp February day. While we were preparing the house for the ceremony and reception, I heard Ben laughing.

"Ben! Stop laughing!" I yelled from the kitchen. "Stop it right now. I can't take you to the hospital today. The wedding's in four hours."

Ben was allergic to dust, pollen, ragweed, cats, dogs, horses, cattle, dander, mold, mites, trees, grasses, weeds, feathers, nuts, lamb, egg whites, halibut, pork, wheat, and tomatoes. He was at risk in certain weather conditions: cold, rain, drizzle, and wind. Early mornings and early evenings could be hazardous to his health, while chortling, chuckling, giggling, and full-blown laughter were outright dangerous.

"I can't help it, Mommy," Ben gasped between bouts of hysterical laughter. I had plopped him in front of the TV so I could get the house ready for the wedding. He was watching his favorite weekend news show. The commentator must have made some kind of quip, because his panel of fifty-five-year-olds and my six-year-old were hooting with laughter.

"Please, Ben, not today!"

There was a slight mist of drizzle as we set up chairs in the backyard for our small wedding party, and Ben was happy and excited. He would be wearing his first jacket and tie, and soon there would be an admiring crowd of adults who would make a gracious audience.

"How do you do?" Ben greeted each guest as they entered our home.

"How do *you* do, Benjamin?" Each guest greeted him back.

"Ben, I'm going to San Francisco next weekend. Could you tell me the best route to take?" asked my friend Glen.

"I presume you are going by car, because if you are going by rail or plane I'd have to know that of course."

"Of course, Ben. I'll be going by car."

"Will you be taking the scenic route or the freeway, which of course will get you there faster?"

"The freeway route, please."

"Well in that case, take Route 5 to the 5-80, to the 80 going north. As you know, the 80 is the Bay Bridge, which, after you pay the toll, will take you into the center of the city."

"I didn't know you visited San Francisco, Ben."

"I didn't. Now, once you arrive in San Francisco, be aware that many of the streets are one way, so—"

"Thank you, Ben. That was very helpful."

"You are very welcome," Ben said, pleased with himself. He was clearly in his element.

His mommy was marrying John, and that was OK because John liked his persons and they liked him. But it wasn't the marrying part that was the best part of this day. The best part was that all the grownups were there to listen to him talk. Not like the kids in school, who turned around and walked away when he talked. They didn't care about learning about traffic patterns or phone systems or why Switzerland didn't have a fighting army. They just liked to run around in the playground and play games. He couldn't wait to be a grownup.

It was a magical day for me, despite the drizzle. I was marrying the man I loved, and, even more thrilling, in six months John and I were going to have a baby of our own. At forty-seven, it would be John's first child, and our little miracle.

Whenever I looked for Ben that day, I saw him in his glory—talking away—people encouraging him at every turn. I heard the sound of laughter—mine, John's, and Ben's. I didn't hear the sound of wheezing.

"John," Ben said, tugging on the pants leg of his brand-new stepfather. The guests had started to leave and the handheld chuppa had been taken down and placed back in the trunk of the rabbi's car.

"Ben? What's the matter?" John replied, bending down to meet his gaze.

"I'm sorry, John . . . but I'm wheezing."

"You are? Oh . . . OK . . . I'll take you to the emergency room."

"I'm sorry, Daddy."

John remembers both parts of this story in equal measure—the wheezing part and the "Daddy" part. It was a milestone day for him: at the age of forty-seven, he had become a husband and a stepfather. As if that weren't enough to celebrate, his new bride was pregnant with the only child he would ever conceive.

And so, at five o'clock on the day of our wedding, John and Ben made their fourth trip together to the ER. Ben didn't like hospitals or doctors' offices, or breathing treatments or shots or puffers or pills. He hated having asthma because it made him wheeze, and his mother would get all crazy and make him take his puffer, even if he was in the middle of reading a book. So he wouldn't tell anyone he was wheezing, because maybe it would go away. But it didn't go away. It only got worse, and there he'd be again, right back in the ER.

In the emergency room, Ben received a breathing treatment, like always. And he received shots of prednisone, albuterol, ephedrine, and theophylline. When John brought him home five hours later, it was ten o'clock at night. It had been an emotional, exhausting day; all John and I wanted to do was fall into bed.

But Ben, shot full of stimulants, was wide awake. In our bedroom the last sound I heard as I dozed off to sleep was the familiar play-by-play of my very own Dodgers baseball announcer.

For your enjoyment, Dodger baseball is on the air! Dodger baseball is brought to you by Farmer John and by Union 76 Gasoline. Dodger baseball is presented for the noncommercial use of our listening audience, and all broadcast rights are reserved by the Dodgers, who also employ the announcers. Any rebroadcast or use of descriptions or accounts of the game without express permission of the Los Angeles Dodgers is prohibited.

"Beeeen!" I called out. "Not now!"

A pleasant evening to you, wherever you may be. I am Benjamin Levinson speaking to you from Dodger Stadium for tonight's game between the Dodgers and the San Francisco Giants. The Dodgers come into tonight's game on a small winning streak, having won four of their last five games, but they will be going up against a Giants team that is equally hot, having won six out of their last eight games. It should be an extremely competitive game, with the Dodgers starting Fernando Valenzuela on the mound and the Giants countering with former Dodger Tommy John. Both pitchers are neck and neck as far as wins, strikeouts, and innings pitched are concerned, so both teams have to perform to a very high standard to be effective against them. We'll be right back with the starting lineups after this message from our sponsor, Farmer John.

"Ben, please! That's enough for tonight. Do the commercial tomorrow," I called out from my bedroom.

"No, I have to finish. It's almost over, Mommy. Just a little bit more."

Friends, Farmer John is the official hot dog of Dodger Stadium, and for good reason, because only Farmer John uses one hundred percent domestic beef in its hot dogs. Plus, Farmer John smokes its hot dogs the old-time western way, with just the right combination of herbs and spices to give you that most distinctive taste. Easternmost in quality, westernmost in flavor. If you can't make it out to the ballpark, bring the ballpark to you, with the one and only taste of Farmer John hot dogs. Available in your grocer's deli case and at Dodger Stadium.

10

THE ADVENTURES OF THE SNEEZER
AND THE KERCHIEF

No matter how hard I tried, I couldn't be like other people. So I retreated into my own world of imagination. It was safe there.

———

DAVID WAS BORN on a hot August day in 1975 when Ben was six years old. My parents had come to stay with Ben while I was in the hospital, and they greeted us—baby David, John, and me—on the steps of our house. A crayoned homemade "Welcome Home" banner was draped across the living room, and Ben, so excited to meet his new brother, handed me a construction paper greeting card with two stick figures, one large and one small, their mouths meeting in a kiss.

"Mommy, this is me and my baby brother, David."

"Thank you, sweetie, this is lovely. You're the big brother now."

"I know. When David gets bigger we're going to be like the Partridge Family and have a band, and make music, and I'll be the DJ because I'm very good at that."

"But what if David doesn't want to be in a band, sweetie?" I said as I made my way to the nursery. "What if he isn't interested in radio shows like you are?"

"The Partridge Family travels on a bus and when David and I grow up we'll travel on a bus too."

"But Ben—" In the hospital I had had a reprieve from these one-sided dialogues, but now, back home for only twenty minutes, I could feel that familiar frustration welling up. Ben was pushing my buttons and I was buying into it. Why was he so good at that? Why did I let him get away with it? I'll let it go this time, I decided. After all, Ben probably was jealous of the new baby. OK, Ben, I thought. Have it your way.

But John had a different idea. "Ben, did you not hear Mommy's question? What if David isn't interested in music and bands and traveling on a bus?"

"My daddy brought home three more Partridge Family albums, even though they're in reruns, still he's a music lawyer and can get all the albums he wants."

"Ben!" John said sharply.

"John, don't!" I said sharply back.

My parents didn't say a word; they didn't have to. I knew what they were thinking. Ben was their pride and joy, their brilliant, extraordinary eldest grandchild, and John, the interloper, was treating him harshly, not appreciating him, already favoring his biological son, his *own* baby boy.

"So, Ben, what did you do in school on Thursday and Friday while I was in the hospital?" I said, changing the subject. I was good at that.

"Knitting," said Ben, heading toward his room.

"Oh, he must be going to get his yarn and needles," said my mother. She was smiling broadly. "It's quite extraordinary how they teach them so young—"

"Go in through the front, run around the back, peek in through the window, off jumps Jack!" Ben chanted as he returned with his knitting bag.

Oh, how thrilling! I thought, remembering Lisa and her scarf, remembering my fantasy of clicking needles and cozy nights of seven rows of purl and seven rows of knit.

"Show me how you do it, Ben. Will you teach me? I never learned to knit."

"Oh. My *real* knitting's in school, but I can do the knitting rhyme. I like to say the knitting rhyme."

"In school? What about *this* yarn and *these* needles? Can't you show me with these?"

"Not now. Now it's time for my radio show. Now I'm going on the air," Ben answered, turning away.

"*Hold it, Ben!* I don't see any knitting in your knitting bag. Only yarn and needles. *Where's your knitting?*"

John was not happy.

"In school . . . like I told you. Now I have to get my microphone and go on the air," Ben said, heading for the bathroom to get his toothbrush-microphone.

My mother was smiling. "He's so much fun to be around, so interested in everything, so talented—"

"And smart, my God, I've never seen anything like it. And what a memory! I always thought *my* kids were smart—you and Ed—but not like Ben. Nothing like Ben," said my father.

I looked for John's eyes, trying to catch them, needing to land on what was real. What *was* real? But John was changing the baby.

"Steven bought Ben a record player and a tape recorder, and ever since, all he's been doing is playing DJ," said my mother.

"You're listening to 93 KHJ in Hollywood, California, and here's ELO." There was Ben's voice coming through the open door of his room, but on top of Ben's voice, or within it, was the disembodied voice of a radio personality, Mr. 93 KHJ. Once again, Ben had left the real world behind. Now he was where he was happiest: lost in imagination, Mr. DJ on everyone's radio.

"He listened to the DJ show one time in the car, only a single time, and he's memorized it in its entirety. But not only the words—" said my father.

"No, not just the words. The intonation, the deep voice, the commercials, everything!" said my mother.

Suddenly I was hit with a huge wave of exhaustion. "If it's OK with you, I'm going to lie down for a while."

I undressed to the sounds of Ben's record player, and as I lay down between the sheets I waited for his DJ voice to return with the volume turned up so Ben's voice could be heard "going to commercial" or delivering a traffic report.

"The 405 through the Sepulveda Pass is very crowded. Backed up past the Ventura Freeway. It looks like there's lots of folks on their way to Westwood on this sunny Saturday afternoon. Now let's get back to the music. Here's 'No Good' by Linda Ronstadt."

But then, only a few seconds after her voice came on, the song skipped. "Uh-oh," said Ben in his regular six-year-old voice. "What should I do now?"

You should quit now, I wanted to call out from my bed. *You should give it a rest, and give* me *a rest, too.* But he hadn't seen me for three days, and here I was back with a new baby, so how could I say that?

"I know," Ben was saying to himself. "I'll pretend that the skipping is part of the show. I'll pretend that someone just came into the studio and knocked the record player off its groove."

"You're listening to 93 KHJ, and my boss, Mr. Miller, has just walked into the studio. Mr. Miller, you knocked the record player off its groove, and the record skipped," Ben said in his DJ voice.

"I'm sorry, Ben, I didn't see it was playing. Why don't you start the record over again from the beginning, and I'll just get out of your way?" Ben replied in his deeper, Mr. Miller voice.

"Why, that's a good idea. Thank you, Mr. Miller. I'll just start the record over again right now," Ben replied in his DJ voice, turning up the volume.

Here we go again, I thought. I'm home. I'm not in the hospital anymore. I'm home with my new baby, my husband, my parents, and my son, the radio.

I fell dead asleep.

OUR FAMILY SETTLED INTO an easy routine, with John driving Ben to second grade in the mornings while I stayed home with David.

"Joshua lives close by. If it's OK with his mother, would you pick him up too?" I asked John. Another seven-year-old in the car. Another chance for Ben to have a friend.

John agreed, and so began the ongoing radio series *The Adventures of the Sneezer and the Kerchief*, created, produced, and directed by John. It was the saga of two good guys on their morning hunt for bad guys. In real life, in the absence of a sneeze, they were simply two second-graders, Ben and Josh, on the way to school. But then Ben would sneeze, and instantly, magically, he turned into the deadly "Sneezer." Ben's sneezes were his secret weapon, because how could the bad guys know that a sneeze, with its wet and flying fluids, could immobilize, could paralyze, with a single giant airborne blast? Joshua, with his trademark plaid kerchief, was the Sneezer's sidekick, his partner in good, who would, morning after morning, whip off his kerchief and tie the bad guys up.

On some days there was not a single sneeze from Ben. There was not much to do on such mornings, except listen to 93 KHJ on the car radio, or to Ben's own radio show. But on most mornings the sneezes came in a soaring series, and on these mornings the bad guys were quickly zapped by the Sneezer and tied up and hauled off behind bars by the Kerchief.

By the end of second grade, the jails were full.

Once again Ben's trips to school became the best part of his day. Each night he would tell me about the latest episode in the ongoing series of the Sneezer and the Kerchief, and when he did, his otherwise dull, monotonous voice would rise out of his body, as if it and he were soaring up, up, up, joyously freed from a world that did not engage him, could not absorb him.

These times, these flights of fancy, created in his own imagination or in the imagination of his stepfather, were when the true Ben emerged. The delightful and delighted creature of fancy and fairy tale, the boy he was meant to be.

SCHOOL WAS GETTING HARDER and harder, more and more out of his reach. Ben loved the subject blocks—Norse mythology, Greek mythology, languages, music, even art and science—taught by his teacher, Mrs. Kilmore. But loving something—soaking the learning into his pores and being able to know it, remember it, spout it back out—was different, worlds apart, from being able to do what was required.

"Take out your green notebooks, the one for the Pacific Coast," Mrs. Kilmore would begin during the week they were studying that subject block.

And there on the board was the outline of Ben's beloved Pacific Coastline. He knew it like the back of his hand. Hadn't he told one of the guests at Mommy and John's wedding how to get from Los Angeles to San Francisco? Didn't he know every city, every town in every city, up and down the Pacific Coast? Of course he did.

Mrs. Kilmore would fill in the map, city by city, as the class talked about each of them. Ben wanted to be the one standing at the front of the class, explaining how the coastline changed as it moved westward, how the weather was wetter and colder the farther north you went, how the real estate section of the *Los Angeles Times* had, just last week, declared Marin County the seventh wealthiest community in the country.

But Mrs. Kilmore, not Ben, was the teacher, and now she was asking the class to open to a clean page and copy the map on the board.

Ben couldn't do that. His hands didn't work fast enough. His fingers didn't coordinate well enough. What his quick, curious mind heard, saw, and devoured, his hands and fingers could not reproduce. He imagined a perfect, even enhanced reproduction of his beloved Pacific Coastline, but he couldn't draw it; he couldn't make it come to life on paper.

There was no one who loved maps more than Ben. So why did each of his attempts to draw one end up looking like a big lumpy circle, with wiggly lines sticking out from all sides? Drawing maps was the big equalizer. It mattered not how much Ben knew, how many times he had visited a city in his imagination. He simply was not able—no matter how long Mrs. Kilmore made him stay indoors during recess—to "just do it, Ben. You know the coastline by heart. Just copy what's on the board."

Ben's failure had nothing to do with time taken. It was the translation from head to hand that was absent, a lapsed synapse hobbling Ben's spirit where it was meant to soar.

If drawing maps with a pencil was hard, calligraphy with pens and inkwells was pure torture. In that school they taught penmanship the old-fashioned way, which meant drawing even, beautiful, repetitive loops and lines. Dipping a pen point into an inkwell and filling a page with graceful patterns.

All the kids had trouble with calligraphy at first, and in that regard Ben was no different. But slowly, one by one, each of them caught on. The walls of the classroom became an art gallery, boasting of elegant works of beautiful penmanship. All but Ben's work was on display. He was left in the dust.

Ben couldn't draw a straight line, even with the cardboard liner clipped to the back of the page as a guide. He couldn't draw a curve. He was left handed and he drooled, so the spit from his mouth would blend like paint with the black ink from the inkwell, while the quill pen, which was meant to produce lovely, precise lines of calligraphy, would smear, and Ben would be mortified, humiliated, horrified by this treason, this treacherous betrayal of *his brain, which knew but could not do.*

11

THE MIDDLE OF IMAGINATION

My real life was never as good as what I could make up. Even as a little kid, I knew the life I wanted to live and the person I wanted to be would never happen. So I began telling stories out loud. Sort of like playing pretend, except only I knew it was a game.

———

"Guess what, Mommy? Guess what?" Ben couldn't wait to tell me his good news. He was eight at the time, and in the third grade. But he had to search the house first—the kitchen, the bedroom, the nursery—to find me.

"What is it, sweetie? But tell me softly, OK? David is taking his nap."

Ben didn't speak softly. He had one tone of voice, one volume, and it was loud. There seemed to be no variation in rhythm or pitch. I'd ask him to lower his voice and he'd say OK, but his very next sentence would sound exactly as loud as the one before. It wasn't just the pitch of his voice, it was the sameness, as if he were reading a technical journal. Ben could be telling me the most fascinating story, but I wouldn't know it, because before long I'd have a headache from the monotony of his stentorian voice.

I recognized "Guess what?" as a question, not because of the upraised tone at the end, but by the words that asked me to guess at something I could not know. "What, Ben? What is it?"

"You'll never guess, Mommy. I'm on the football team!"

"The football team!"

"Didn't I say you'd never guess?"

"But Ben, your school doesn't even *have* a football team." I was beginning to feel uprooted, as if the ground under my feet were trembling. When I felt that way I wanted to shake Ben, because only he could make it better. Only he could take back the words and make them reasonable, make *me* reasonable.

"Oh yes, Mommy. My school does have a football team and I'm on it."

Three impossibilities packed into one short sentence. His school did *not* have a football team, which is one of the reasons I chose it in the first place. And even if it did, it wouldn't be in third grade. But even if I was wrong on both counts—his school *did* have a football team and it *was* operating in the third grade—Ben wouldn't be on it. To play football you have to run, you have to tackle, you have to fall down and pick yourself back up, you have to catch and throw and kick. Ben couldn't do any of these. He couldn't even ride a bike, which is why he was still seeing Miss Reed in Temple City, and why he was still going twice a week for his eye exercises.

"OK, Ben. *Why are you lying?*"

"I'm not lying. My position is running back," Ben said, his head in the refrigerator. "Where's the American cheese? I can't find the American cheese."

"You're not getting one slice until you tell me the truth. *Tell me the truth, Ben!*"

"I told you! And not only that, I have a jersey and my number is 29."

"This minute, Ben. *Stop lying this very minute!*"

"I'm going in my room now. But I won the game today and my team held me up on their shoulders and carried me around the football field."

Ben's psychologist, Dr. Morris, didn't view Ben's stories as lies. She saw them as extensions of his fantastic imagination. "He so loves his fantasy world. Maybe his stories—"

"You mean lies. Why don't you call them what they are? They're lies!"

By now I was fed up with Dr. Morris and her genteel, misguided good intentions. Ben had been seeing her since he was five. It was three years already. What was she doing with him every Wednesday at four o'clock in the afternoon? She was serving him chicken soup in paper containers. She was letting him choose which one—noodles alone, or noodles with vegetables—and letting him heat his favorite on the portable burner. She was calling his lies stories, because she liked him too much to call them lies. He was so sensitive, so dear, so sweet and endearing; how could she call them lies?

"No, Mrs. LaSalle. I can't say I know exactly what Ben is doing, or why he feels compelled to say these things that are not true, *which I will not call lies*. But I have the sense it has something to do with his rich imagination."

"Well he *has* increased his radio program repertoire to include play-by-plays of football games. . . ." I was picturing Ben, alone in his room, his toothbrush-microphone in hand, doing his latest routine.

"Yes. That's what I mean. How would *you* like to be so bright and still not be able to perform, still not be able to turn in a legible paper or draw a simple picture or copy words from the board?"

"I wouldn't. It would be frustrating as hell."

"That's how it is for Ben. He hasn't actually told me so, but it has to be."

"So what should I do? How can I get him to feel less frustrated?"

"What about that motor therapy in Temple City . . . with the trampoline and the swimming pool and the. . . ."

"Not helping. He's still scared out of his mind whenever he's made to do anything physical."

"COME ON, BEN. I'll teach you how to ride your bike." John had tried this before, when Ben was six, and then again when he was seven. Ben's fear was greater than John's resolve, but when Ben was eight and the boys in the neighborhood were already doing wheelies, making their bikes come to a fast skid and then bringing them to a stop on a dime, John decided to try again.

"No, Daddy. I'm scared. I'm afraid to get on. What if I can't stop the bike when I want to?"

"I'll show you how, Ben. Just try it for a few minutes. If you don't like it we can stop."

"Do you promise, Daddy? Do you promise we can stop?"

"Cross my heart and hope to die."

I watched from the window as John brought Ben's bike to the curb, so the pedals and Ben's feet were on the same level. John held the handlebars with one hand and the seat with his other hand, steadying the bike. But Ben was already protesting and turning back to the house. By now a crowd of neighborhood boys were standing around watching.

"Come on, Ben, it's easy," said Lenny.

"Yeah, Ben," chimed in Doug. Even from the distance, I could see the boys grinning at each other.

"Yeah, it's no big deal. Come on Ben, come on!" taunted Sean.

Lenny, Doug, and Sean were the same age as Ben, but they were not his friends. They didn't come asking, "Can Ben come out and play?" They didn't like Ben. They thought he was a jerk.

I heard them in the street one day as I was parking my car. They were passing by on their skateboards, and they were shouting, pointing to Ben's room upstairs, "What a jerk, what a spazz, what a weirdo." When they saw me they stopped, turning instantly into perfectly polite specimens. "Hi, Mrs. LaSalle. How are you?"

I ignored them, because I was not a perfectly polite specimen. Nor did I have any desire to pretend to be. I was a furious, protective, heart-broken mother.

Lenny, Doug, and Sean were not encouraging Ben, they were daring him, they were teasing him, provoking him. Did Ben know that? No, he didn't. I could see from the window that he didn't. Because he was smiling at them, he was talking to them, in that way he talked with kids his age, which was not exactly talking to, but talking at. He was lifting one shoulder, twisting it, and at the same time cocking his head in the direction of his raised shoulder, his gaze somewhere in the vicinity of the boys. But he wasn't looking *at* them, he was looking *past* them.

John said something softly, something I couldn't hear from behind the glass of my window hiding place. But the next thing I saw was the boys riding off. A few minutes passed, with Ben protesting (I could hear that), and finally—miracle of miracles—lifting one leg up and over the bike seat. I wanted to run outside and applaud, I wanted to shout from the window, "Great job, Ben!" But I didn't. I just stood there, holding my breath to see what would happen next.

Nothing happened next. "That's all," Ben had said after a few seconds of seat-sitting, and John, true to his word, wheeled the bike back to the garage.

It took three more Saturdays of seat-sitting, followed by four more Saturdays of pedaling with John holding the handlebars in one hand and the bike seat in the other. Then on the eighth Saturday, John removed his hand from the handlebars and just held the bike seat. "Careful, Daddy, don't let go! Please don't let go!" But by then Ben was pedaling on his own steam, and John kept repeating, "You're doing it, Ben, you're doing it!" until finally, John simply let go of the bike seat and Ben realized that he truly *was* riding the bike by himself. He was thrilled!

Still, he never rushed home after school to get on his bike.

Ben finally learned to ride, just as he'd finally learned to walk, just as he'd finally learned to climb the jungle gym and jump on the trampoline. But he never liked doing any of it.

He didn't want to ride around the block on his bike like Lenny, Doug, and Sean. He far preferred to ride round and round in his world of fantasy, traveling round and round in his imagination, on his imaginary football field, on the proud shoulders of his imaginary teammates. He wasn't afraid of that.

12

THE STREETS OF SAN FRANCISCO

I carried a map of the city in my head. How could I be lost?

———

"Ben?" We were on Bay Street in San Francisco when I called out looking for him.

John, Ben, and I had taken a weekend trip to Ben's favorite Northern California town. It was to be a special treat for our eight-and-a-half-year-old, who knew every cable car, every BART line, every bus, street, pier, wharf, and block of the city by heart. Just the three of us: Mommy, Daddy, and Ben. No baby brother to bother with.

But now Ben was lost. We had been walking only a little while. Just long enough to notice that Ben was more wrapped up in his book about the city than in the actual city.

"What are you doing, Ben?" John demanded.

"Reading my book, *The Streets of San Francisco*," Ben said, his nose in the book.

"But we're *in* the city. Why do you need your book? We're *in the city right now*," I said. "And anyway, how can you see where you're going? You'll fall if you don't look where you're going."

"And why did we bother to come, if you're not even interested?" John said.

"I am interested." But Ben's nose was still in the book.

"Why don't you look at the wharf? You wanted to see it in real life, didn't you?" John demanded.

"Uh-huh," Ben replied absentmindedly.

Maybe that's how it happened. The getting lost story. "Remember the time Ben got lost in San Francisco when he was eight?" By now, the story is part of our family lore. It's funny in the telling. But it wasn't funny then.

Maybe all that happened that day in San Francisco when he got lost was Ben—his nose buried in a book—meandered off behind us. John and I were just steps ahead and Ben was trailing behind—oblivious—reading his book, *The Streets of San Francisco*, the same book he read every single day and every single night since he spotted it in the bookstore.

In any case, he was lost. For real. "Come on, Ben, cut it out!" John yelled. "It's not funny. *Stop hiding right now!*"

"*Ben, please! Where are you?*" I was crying by then, frantic.

"It's impossible," John said, "he can't *really* be lost. He was just here."

"But where is he? What should we do?"

For forty minutes we walked up and down the streets surrounding the wharf—Bay Street, Jefferson, Northpoint, Beach Street—calling out Ben's name. "Ben? Ben? Where are you, Ben? Where are you?"

He was nowhere. I was hysterical. "Barbara, calm down. He *has* to be somewhere. He was just here. He can't have gone far."

"But we have to *do* something. We have to do something right now!"

Just then a cop car passed by, and John hailed it. While I cried, John explained to the officer that we had just—in the span of a split second—lost track of our eight-year-old.

"Do you live here?" the officer wanted to know. "Does the boy know the area?"

"Well yes and no," John answered.

"What?" asked the baffled officer. "What do you mean, yes and no?"

When neither of us replied, the officer said, "Why don't the two of you get in the car. You, ma'am, sit in the back, and you, sir, sit in the front with me."

"Lost boy, eight years old. Brown hair and bangs. Wharf. Doesn't know the area. Staying in the Granger Hotel on Stanyan," the officer spoke into his two-way radio.

"Officer, is there a loudspeaker in the car? Can we call him on the loudspeaker?" John pleaded.

"Yeah, there's a loudspeaker," said the officer.

"Would you mind if I do it? I mean, there's a special way. . . ."

"A special way of calling his name?" The officer was even more mystified. Nevertheless, he gave John the microphone.

John began his loudspeaker game: "Police to Benjamin Levinson. Black and white to Benjamin Levinson. Come in. Come in."

Usually I was amused when John and Ben played their imaginary games—Master of Ceremonies and Honored Guest, Ringmaster and Circus Performer, DJ and Traffic Reporter, Sneezer and Kerchief—but this time was serious. This time I was in no mood to laugh.

In the midst of my panic I had images of other times Ben was "lost." Times in department stores, when he was three and four and five. These times Ben would manage to be "lost" just so he could be found by the sympathetic store manager, who, of course, was more than eager to have "his mother paged on the loudspeaker."

"Don't worry, little boy. What's your name? I'm sure your Mommy is looking for you right now. She'll be here right away." But if his mother came right away, then the game of calling her on the loudspeaker—"Attention shoppers: I have a little boy here by the name of Benjamin. He is lost. (What's your mommy's name, Benjamin? Barbara? Barbara LaSalle?) Will Barbara LaSalle please come to the front of the store and pick him up?"—would be aborted too early, and there would be no chance for Ben to get his hands on the loudspeaker and make the announcement himself.

If Ben had been in the vicinity of the police car that day in San Francisco, he most certainly would have "come in" when he was called. But as many times as we circled each block, as many times as "Officer" John called out his name, Ben didn't "come in." That's how we knew he wasn't in the vicinity.

"Ma'am, where did you say you were staying? In what hotel?" The police officer had taken back the loudspeaker. The game had gone on long enough. This was real. There was a boy missing, lost on the streets of San Francisco. There would be no more fooling around.

"The Granger," John answered. "The Granger on Stanyan and Oak."

"But that's miles from here. . . ."

"We took two streetcars to get here," I said. "That's what Ben wanted to do."

"Well, at least we know he's not back in the hotel. Did he even know the name? Did he know the address . . . the street, at least?" the officer asked.

"No, how could he? There's no way he could be back at the hotel. It's on the other side of town. We were there only a few minutes. The streetcar was just outside the door when Ben heard the clanging. He wanted to get right on, so we didn't even check into our room. We just left our bags at the desk—"

"Wait a minute," I interrupted. "Maybe he *is* back in the hotel. Maybe he *does* know the street. *Maybe he does know how to get there.*"

If I had been thinking like me as I was then—an adult—or even thinking like me as an eight-year-old, I would never have said that. I would have agreed with the police officer and my husband. I would have agreed that of course Ben was not back at the hotel. How could he be? After all, he was only eight and a half years old; he knew San Francisco only by his books and maps; we had spent only minutes at the hotel. Of course he couldn't have found his way back there.

But I wasn't thinking like me. I was thinking like Benjamin.

"Call the hotel. Call the Granger right now. *Please call the hotel!*"

The officer turned to look at me. Up front, John was nodding his head, as if to say, "Humor her. Do what the lady says."

"Put me through to the Granger, on Stanyan," the officer announced into his car radio.

"Hello, this is the police calling. Is this the Granger Hotel?" This question was followed by a brief pause in which the officer did not speak. He was listening. Then he spoke these words, "*He is?* How the hell did he get there?"

"*He's there? He's there!*" John and I were shouting and hugging each other. Now John was crying, and I was laughing.

It was simple, Ben told us when we pulled up to the hotel minutes later. Nothing to it. "A nice sailor saw me walking along the pier and asked me where was my mommy. I told him you and Daddy were lost, but that I wasn't scared because I knew what to do, and did he know how to get to the Granger Hotel? But he never heard of it, so I had to tell him the address, 2352 Stanyan. Then I told the taxi man to go down Bay Street to Van Ness. Then I told him to take Van Ness to Geary and then, when he got to Geary, I told him to make a right turn. After that I told him to make a left turn to Oak Street, and then when we got to 2352 I told him to stop. So I've been sitting right here in the lobby, reading my book, *The Streets of San Francisco*, while I waited for you. Now can we get on a cable car and go to Telegraph Hill?"

13

THE BIG CITY AND THE GIANT
SPACESHIP

I needed a book on Victoria Station, London. The local library said it would take a month to get it from the central branch downtown. I couldn't wait a month. So I went and got it myself.

———

"GUESS WHAT, MOMMY? Josh and I went to the movies yesterday after school. That's why I got home so late." Ben told me that story when he was ten.

"You did?" I was flabbergasted. But it was possible. I had to admit, it was possible. After all, Susan, Josh's mother, did sometimes take the kids places when it was her turn for carpool. I wasn't home anyway on those days, because I would work late seeing patients.

Somehow, in the midst of the growing storm of *What's wrong with Ben? Is something wrong with Ben?*, I'd gone back to school and become a family therapist. So now, instead of five-year-olds and the wheels of the bus, I spent my days with disgruntled parents of five-year-olds, sullen teenagers, and battle-weary couples.

Once, not so long ago, Dr. Morris, Ben's therapist, had refused to call Ben's fictions, lies. She called them "stories," and now I was doing the same with my patients. I understood that they were only doing what they had to do. They were only protecting themselves from the pain, the shame, and the sorrow. I'd never dream of accusing them of lying.

"That's great, Ben. I'm so happy you got to do that. What movie did you see?"

"Tales of the Giant Spaceship."

"Oh . . . did you like it? What was it about?" It wasn't the kind of movie Ben ever asked me to take him to see. But this was different. This was Josh and *his* mother, not Ben and me.

"Two aliens from Mars landed their spaceship on earth and kidnapped Lars and Laura in their bedroom."

"Lars and Laura?" I just mouthed the words, because all I could think was *My son saw a movie with a friend. A friend, a friend, my son has a friend!*

"Yeah. Lars and Laura. They're a brother and sister and the two aliens kidnapped them, like I said, and brought them back to their spaceship, and—"

"Was it exciting? Did you like it? Is it a good movie, would I like it?"

"Not really. It had good sound effects. The visuals were innovative, but the characters were undeveloped. The plot was weak. The action was slow."

Wait a minute, I thought. Didn't I read a review that said those exact words in the newspaper the other day? Yes, I did. Had Ben read the same review? Obviously. Had he really seen the movie? Obviously not.

"Hold it right there, Ben!" I was shouting, the familiar wave of exasperation overtaking me. "Where exactly did you see this movie? In which movie theater? And how long was it? And precisely how did you get there, and who took you home, and *why are you lying again?*"

Ben was silent.

"Is it because you were disappointed you *didn't* see it?" I asked, begging for an answer I could understand.

"I don't know," Ben said, limp by now, spent by the effort of storing, recalling, and retelling, word-for-regurgitated-word, the memorized review.

"Is it because you thought *I'd* be disappointed if you didn't see it?"

"I don't know."

Almost any answer would do. Any answer that made sense to me. But what made sense to me didn't, couldn't, or wouldn't make sense to Ben. Again and again, I searched for a reason that could satisfy my frustration: *Why was Ben lying?*

So again and again, I asked Ben the questions that my own mind, in its own linear, logical way, could understand. I showed him the way to the water, the well that would satiate my terrible thirst to understand his mind. So why didn't he just drink? Why didn't he take a gulp and satisfy me?

Once, long ago, I had loved Ben's stories. But now I hated them. I hated them because they no longer were stories. They were outright lies, despite what Dr. Morris called them. Lies, lies, and more lies. I hated Ben's lies. I hated Ben. And I hated myself for hating him.

A lot of Ben's lies were about the friends he had, or said he had. His football team. His movie date. Did Ben tell me lies because he wished he had friends? Or did he lie to please me, because he knew I wanted him to have friends?

Ben had traveled from grade to grade with the same group of kids since he was five. Maybe he wanted friends and maybe he didn't. But it didn't matter anyway because he never had any. He couldn't figure out the politics of friendship.

What were the rules you were supposed to follow in making a friend? What were you supposed to say, and what were you not supposed to say? What was a joke, and what was not? When were you supposed to talk, and when were you supposed to listen? When did you look at a person, and when did you not? Should you tell what you knew, and say what you were interested in, or should you keep it to yourself?

No, Ben never had friends.

But he knew what friends did. When friends were five and six and seven, they rode home together in another mother's car and had a playdate. Ben had had a few of those. The first was when he was in preschool, when I invited Greg over to our house, even though Ben had said *no*. But I said *yes*. He had to have friends, and to have friends he had to have a playdate.

The playdate with Greg was a flop. But I kept trying. I tried for years, as Ben got older and older, hoping that social skills would suddenly take hold. I invited Gary over. Then Ronnie. Then Josh, the boy with whom Ben did not see *Tales of the Giant Spaceship*. But these playdates all turned out the same way his playdate with Greg had turned out. After a few minutes, the visiting boy would disappear. He would leave Ben inside, in his room, where he wanted to be, not outside, where the visiting boy wanted to be. And the visiting boy would play outside on Ben's shiny new bike or his unused scooter.

Ben didn't care. He was upstairs in his room, where he always was, reading a book.

Lies, and no friends, and failures at school. These were the sad, bad parts of Ben's first ten years of life. But the good parts were as real and as wonderful as the bad parts were terrible. Take the library, for instance.

I started going to the downtown Central Library when I was eight or nine and kept going every Saturday till the sixth grade. I'd take the number 93 bus on Vineland. It was an express bus and it went straight downtown without stopping.

I'd get off at Main and Fifth Street and walk down Fifth to Flower, where the library was. That took me to Pershing Square and the Biltmore

Hotel, where I always made it a point to go in and use the bathroom because I could count on it being clean.

The library was a big hulk of an old building. It smelled like old books and deodorant. I liked the smell of it because, to me, that's what libraries are supposed to smell like.

The library was constructed in the shape of inner rooms. Each room was surrounded by stacks of books. Sort of like a square within a square. The book stacks were hidden behind the walls, and if you wanted to find a book that wasn't on the shelf you'd have to ask the librarian.

I loved the history and geography rooms best because I loved history and geography. I always went there first. I once looked up the San Francisco Chronicle *from 1906 because I wanted to read more about the earthquake. It was on microfilm. It was very exciting. I used to go to the patent room, too, but that room was always hard for me to figure out.

After I spent time at the library, I would walk over to First and Broadway. That was where city hall was located. It was a bad neighborhood and I was a little kid, but no one ever hassled me, not even the bums. I always used the Main Street entrance going into city hall because it had fewer stairs. Then I would go all the way up to the top of city hall to the observation tower. It had a three-sided view of the city! It was enclosed in netting so people wouldn't jump. I used to imagine I was on top of the Empire State Building or the Transamerica Building in San Francisco.

When I was done with my tour of city hall, I would go across the street to the underground mall and have lunch. I would choose between Carl's Jr. or Bob's Big Boy. There was always a large crowd to watch, which I also liked.

Then around three o'clock I would go to the Los Angeles Times Building, which was catty-corner to city hall, and take the three o'clock tour. I did it so many times—at least twenty—that the tour guides knew my name. I liked that tour a lot because I had decided that one day I was going to be a newspaper writer.

By the end of the tour, it was five o'clock, and I would walk back to Spring Street and catch the bus back home.

Ben didn't need to go to the movies to see *Tales of the Giant Space-ship*. He had a fantastic city to visit every Saturday, a journey as marvelous as any spaceship ride.

Yes, it was true: Ben had no friends. But did he really need them? He had books and buses and libraries and city hall and the *Los Angeles Times*. He didn't have people, but he had things. Ben was fine the way he was. It was I who wasn't.

14

LOSING IT

I knew there was something wrong with me, and I was letting my mom down.

———

"OK, THEN. You take him."

I said these five words on an early summer day in the year 1980. I said them in an attorney's office on the twelfth floor of a high-rise building in downtown Los Angles. The office was decorated in light mauves, pinks, and purples. On the walls hung two de Koonings and one Diebenkorn. The desk was cherry mahogany. Two white sofas faced one another.

I was there with my attorney: we sat on one of the sofas. On the other sofa sat Steven and his three attorneys. Four briefcases rested on the coffee table between us, full of battle plans.

The day was sunny, the office was elegant, and the people in it were at war.

The year was 1980. By then the war was in its fifth year. Ben, the territory in question, was eleven years old. Steven and I had been divorced and divided for almost half our son's life.

I had come to this office to ask Steven for more money. Again. He had brought his team of three soldiers in suits, and I had brought my team of one.

A lot can happen in seven years. A marriage meant to last till death do us part dies an early death, while the child conceived from hope and longing still struggles to survive. Accusations of who did what to whom contaminate the air. People try their best, but make a mess of everything.

But it wasn't till I uttered those fateful words in the lawyer's office, sitting on my side of the battlefield, surrounded by pinks and purples, and not until Steven, flanked on his side by his three suited soldiers, fired his words back, "OK, then. I'll take him. I'll take Ben," that the mess got away from my control—too big to clean up, ever again.

All I really wanted was a rest. A rest from the questions: *who* is this child, *why* is he so peculiar, *what* am I doing wrong, *how* can I help him? All I wanted was a rest from the worry, the guilt, the blame, and the shame. But I didn't say that. I said, "You take him," and Steven said yes, he would.

The meeting had begun as a skirmish. "Steven, all Ben's therapies cost money. Too much money."

"How many times have we been through this?" Steven was plagued by battle fatigue. He was giving it one last shot.

"Too many." I was close to collapse. It was my last shot.

"I already give you money. Two hundred dollars a month, plus all Ben's private school tuition, plus all his medical insurance. *What more do you want?*"

"Money for his eye therapy."

"He's still getting eye therapy? He *still* needs it?"

"Yes, Steven. He does. His eyes still don't team. He only uses his right eye. That's why he's so scared when he walks down stairs or steps on an escalator. To Ben, it feels like falling off a cliff."

"Oh, please!"

"No, Steven, it's true," I pleaded. "His optometrist specializes in eye problems like Ben's. He's given him an eye patch for his good eye. It's supposed to force the bad eye to work. He does eye-tracking exercises. We practice every night." I didn't want to practice every night. I was exhausted from the effort of cajoling Ben, from making the homework into a game. I wanted a rest. I wanted to read a mindless magazine. I wanted Steven to applaud me.

"So what do you want from me?"

"More money. For that and his other therapies."

"Other therapies? What other therapies, for God's sake?"

"Talking therapy, and maybe later sensory-integration therapy and also socialization therapy, and—"

"All that therapy? What's wrong with you? What the hell are you doing to him?"

"Trying to help him. I'm only trying to help him."

"Why can't you just leave him be?"

Believe me, you're not the only one asking that question, I thought. *Believe me, I ask it of myself every day. It's how I torture myself: seeing things that aren't there. Mountains out of molehills. Neurotic mother. Hysteric. Selfish.* I'm *the expert at blaming myself for every one of Ben's problems. Not you.*

But I didn't voice my insecurity to Steven. I remained in control, and I answered, "Because his problems are real. They need treatment. Treatment costs money."

"Well, you're not getting any more. Not a cent." Steven's side replied.

And that's when I lost it.

I lost it for that year in kindergarten, five years before, when I was accused of teaching Ben to read and ruining his chances of being a regular kid.

I lost it for that year in first grade, when, despite my dream of clicking needles and cozy nights of seven rows of purl and seven rows of knit, Ben couldn't coordinate his hands well enough to produce a single stitch.

I lost it for the second grade, when Ben was seven and told his first lie: "Guess what, Mommy? I'm on the football team." I knew he said it because he wanted to please me, and his teacher, and all the grownups he loved, whose love he craved and deserved. I knew he said it because not being able to run and catch made him seem strange and suspect, when he was neither strange nor suspect. He was just a little boy who loved books better than baseball, and everybody, especially his mother, had a problem with that.

I lost it for third grade, when I couldn't get the drooling or the toilet training under control. There were spit stains on every one of Ben's shirts and feces stains on every pair of his underpants. He smelled bad from the top and from the bottom. His room smelled bad, his bathroom smelled bad, his lunchbox smelled bad.

"Yuk! What's that bad smell?" Josh would say every morning as soon as I opened the door to let him into the carpool.

"I don't know," said Ben.

"Neither do I," said Ben's mother.

I lost it for the fourth grade, when Ben, whose only vegetable was peas in the pod, dropped them, spilled them, and squashed them under his shoes before the teacher could spot them and say in her loud and shaming voice, "Ben, you're nine years old! *Why are you such a mess?*"

And I lost it that year, the year leading up to this private war in the attorney's office. Ben had finished fifth grade, as he had fourth, third, second, and first grades, carrying nary a single lovely pastel-colored workbook back and forth from school. His books remained stuffed in his school desk, hidden, out of the sight of those who would make fun of him, criticize him, or blame him for what was not his fault. They lay there, limp and worn out from the frustration of trying so hard and failing so long, their weak, wobbly lines of print dropping, dropping, falling off the page. Just as Ben himself was falling into a hole so deep that my arms, my fingers, even my heart couldn't reach in and drag him out.

I lost it that final day of fifth grade, when everyone but Ben was invited to the out-of-town weekend sleepover. Just as I had lost it every

Saturday morning for all those years when Ben, carrying a half-pound of peas in the pod, three slices of American cheese, and enough money to choose between a lunch at Carl's Jr. or Big Boy, waved goodbye to my broken heart, took the number 93 bus, and set off all alone to the Los Angeles Central Library.

What could I do about Ben's lack of friends, his mess, his smell, and his failure to learn to write or knit? What could I do about his increasingly outrageous lies, the pile of books he read obsessively, his loneliness, his three slices of American cheese? What could I do about his spilled, squashed peas in the pod?

I was his mother, wasn't I? *There had to be something I could do.*

So I lost it.

I gave my son away. I blamed it on Steven. It was easier than blaming myself.

I gave my son away. It was easier than being powerless.

I gave my son away. It was better than forcing sleep each night with a sedative and a glass of wine.

I gave my son away. It was easier than hating him.

15

ALL I HAD TO DO

Don't ever ask me again what happened to me at that school.

———

ALL I HAD TO DO was follow the smell. The stink of feces—by now as much a part of Ben as his lies, his wheeze, his puffy cheeks, his fat, his stash of books, his three slices of American cheese, his squashed peas in the pod, his drool, and his black crayoned notebooks. As much a part of him as I was—his angry, frustrated, at-her-wit's-end mother.

All I had to do was open the closet in his room at Healy School for Boys and step over the clothes lying on the floor. All I had to do was pick up the pile of rumpled pants, shirts, jackets, ties, and pajamas spread over every inch of closet space and toss the entire contents of his wardrobe, item by item, onto the bed, until I uncovered the culprit.

The culprit was a single white, rolled-up pair of Hanes underpants full of Ben's newest problem.

All I had to do was pick it up, carry it past Ben's downcast eyes, and take it to the bathroom. All I had to do was dunk the culprit in the toilet and rub the cotton sides together till the largest brown specks fell into the tank. All I had to do was flush. All I had to do was wait for the hot water to get hot enough and the suds to foam enough. All I had to do was scrub harder than I had ever scrubbed before, until my knuckles were as raw as my nostrils.

Steven did take Ben. But not to his house, as I'd expected, where he lived with his new wife only fifteen minutes away, but to the airport. Ben's destination was Arizona. His father had sent him to boarding school. It was I who had put these wheels into motion, I who'd said, "OK, then. You take him." And now there was nothing I could do about it. Now my hands were tied. Now he was in Steven's custody and I was forbidden even to visit Ben.

Ben didn't say anything, not then, the first time I disobeyed court orders and drove with John and David across the state line to visit him in Arizona.

Just as he hadn't said anything on the phone, when I placed my nightly call from home.

"Hi, sweetie!" I would say, all cheery and light and won't-you-please-be-happy-back.

"Hello, Mom," Ben would reply, but his voice was hollow and farther away from where I could reach him than an entire day's drive or a two-hour plane ride, or the hundred unsaid things between us.

"How's school?" I said as if he had just walked through the door one sunny afternoon, right past me, to the refrigerator, searching for his beloved American cheese.

"Fine."

"Do you like the other boys? Do you like the classes there? Do you like your housemother, Mrs. Smiley? What do you do all day? Do you like it?"

"Fine."

It wasn't the fake in "fine" that finished me off. It was the emptiness in his voice, as if whatever was left of him had disappeared. I heard it grow—each time I called—this vacuum, sucking my son out of himself, away from me.

"Can I talk to Mrs. Smiley please?"

"OK," he said.

Mrs. Smiley was the housemother for eleven-year-old boys. Ben was an eleven-year-old boy, which meant—didn't it?—that Mrs. Smiley was Ben's stand-in mother. So why did her voice sound like Ben's did—so empty, so faraway and vacant? Why were the words she spoke, every time she spoke them, the same, like the tired monologue of a bored actor, stuck in the only role she would ever play? Why did it take her so many minutes to reach the phone?

"Fine, Mrs. LaSalle. Just fine." But I hadn't asked her about herself. I'd inquired about my son.

"*Ben* . . . Mrs. Smiley, I'm asking about Ben?"

"Just fine, and how are you, dear?"

"Well, he doesn't *sound* fine. He sounds awful."

"I'll have a talk with him, dear. Don't you worry about anything."

How reassuring.

After so many weeks of pretense, after begging Steven for permission to visit, after being told, "The therapist said it's not a good idea, the court said it's better if neither of us visits, Ben will be fine, he just needs time to adjust," followed by, "You just have to let go," I decided to find out for myself.

That's when I discovered why Mrs. Smiley walked so slowly. She was a roly-poly little woman who spent her days in a fluffy white room with teddy bears and tiny glass bottles of perfume. Her room had its own bathroom and was separated from the boys' rooms by a long, narrow hallway. Maybe sounds didn't travel down that hallway, especially the sound of a gang of slimy boys molesting a harmless, innocent boy. Or maybe Mrs. Smiley was too round to leave her fluffy bed and walk down the hall and see where the sounds were coming from. Or maybe she had heard these same sounds over the years from other slimy boys, and maybe she thought, *Boys will be boys, and I'm not getting paid enough anyway.* Or maybe by now she was as dead as Ben was.

But I didn't know then that Ben was being sexually molested. I knew he was being teased, even hazed, but I didn't know *that.* I wouldn't know it for fifteen years, not until Ben was twenty-six years old. Because it took that much time for Ben to understand that what happened to him in boarding school wasn't his fault. It took that much time for him to talk about that year of his life, and to this day, when he does talk about it, it's only in shadows, it's only in fragments, as if putting the experience into words could penetrate him still.

But back then, that year when Ben was eleven, I knew only the sound of words that went unsaid. Unspeakable words. I knew only the reek of shame that filled his room when I went to visit. I knew only what I saw with my horrified eyes, in my son's closet, and in his drawers and behind his desk.

I was more desperate to help him than I had ever been before. But how could I help him, when each mound of feces created another hill of shame, until the shame had grown into a mountain, even greater than the feces, and he didn't understand what was happening to him? How could he know that the bowel movements he couldn't hold long enough to make it to the toilet were part of his first episode of Crohn's disease, just one more chronic autoimmune illness he couldn't control? We didn't know it, and neither did he. All Ben knew was a shame that surpassed all the embarrassments of the past. It was one thing to carry a yellow plastic inhaler in your pocket, and quite another thing to carry a load of shit in your pants.

When your bowels betray you, and your lungs constrict, and you look around and see other kids who can make it to the bathroom in time and who don't carry pockets full of yellow plastic inhalers, you wonder what is wrong with you. When you're incapable of understanding the unwritten rules of social behavior, and you'd rather read by yourself than play ball with your friends, when you love information and commit it to memory the second you learn it, when you must have the same foods in the same order, when you jump out of your skin whenever you hear a loud noise, when you sound like a college professor whenever you speak—when in all these ways you are different from others you meet, you wonder what is wrong with you. And when even your own mother, whom you love and trust, gets mad at you for the ways you are, you begin to believe that whatever is wrong with you must be your fault, and you feel ashamed.

And so the year went on somehow with the nightly phone calls and my cheery voice and Ben's absent voice, and my pleading to Steven to let me see my son, and when he said no, my sneaking away anyway, time and again, against the judge's orders. What could they do to me that was worse than what had already happened? Ben was already lost to me, and I lost to him.

Somehow I managed to work those entire nine months Ben was in boarding school. I saw patients five days a week, from nine in the morning until eight at night. As I sat listening to couples argue about who was right and who was wrong, I didn't get sucked in: I knew they longed to drop the charges and simply love each other. I felt humbled and grateful for the trust placed in me, and I did not falter in how I listened or how I cared. During those long hours in my psychotherapy office, as I spoke the language of dysfunction with compassion and grace, I was a good person. I forgot I had an eleven-year-old son who couldn't make it to the bathroom on time and that I, his own mother, couldn't help him, or protect him, or even hug him, because he was six hundred miles away, and it was all my fault.

The worst times were the nights, after work, after my call to Ben. The pain was so great I ached for sleep—but I couldn't sleep, because when I closed my eyes, there was Ben alone in his bed, without me to tuck him in, too embarrassed to play with his persons, too bewildered to reach into his nightstand and take out his inhaler. He couldn't even comfort himself by going to the refrigerator for his slices of American cheese.

Ben was six hundred miles away from the refrigerator, and from me, the mother who put him there. So I drugged myself with two glasses of wine and an Ativan, just so I could get up the next day and do it all over again.

Steven relented on Christmas of that year. Or maybe the judge overseeing the case was in the holiday spirit and said yes, it was OK for Ben to come home for the ten-day school break.

I hadn't seen Ben since Thanksgiving, when we had sneaked a visit with him in Arizona. So all of us—John, five-year-old David, and I—waited at Burbank Airport for Ben's plane to arrive. There were lots of parents waiting with us, because it was Christmas break.

"Where is he?" asked David.

"He'll be here," said John.

"But where is he?" said I, when the last passenger had emerged.

"Is that him?" asked David, pointing to a very skinny light-haired boy dressed in an oversized man's jacket.

"Of course not," I said. "Ben doesn't even resemble that boy."

But the very skinny light-haired boy recognized us, because he was coming toward us and saying, "Hi."

"Ben, it's so good to . . . uh . . . see you. Are you . . . OK?" I said.

"Fine," Ben said in his faraway voice.

We didn't say much in the car driving home, because even the hollow standard questions like *How is school?* and *Do you have any friends?* and *How are your classes?* and *How are your grades?* were overshadowed by the only questions that mattered: *Why do you look like that? What happened to you? You look like a cadaver—what is wrong with you?*

We were not to discover what was wrong with Ben, why he looked like that and why he had lost forty pounds in a month's time, for many years to come. But right there, in the car driving home from the airport, I vowed to find out.

Crohn's Disease is an inflammatory bowel disease (IBD), the general name for diseases that cause inflammation in the intestines. Crohn's disease can be difficult to diagnose. . . . The inflammation can cause pain and can make

*the intestines empty frequently, resulting in diarrhea. . . . People with
Crohn's disease tend to have abnormalities of the immune system, but doctors do not know whether these abnormalities are a cause or result of the
disease. Crohn's disease is not caused by emotional distress.* *

Our house smelled bad during the Christmas break. Ben kept having accidents and John and I kept trying to figure out why.

"John, *you* talk to him," I pleaded.

"But what should I say? I don't want to embarrass him even more
than he's already embarrassed."

"But you're a man, maybe he won't be as embarrassed with you."

So John took Ben on walks and on car rides and to the movies and
asked him questions like *Do you know how to wipe yourself?* and *Can I
show you how?* He offered gentle encouragement like *Don't be embarrassed, because it takes practice—coordinating all the steps—taking your
pants down, bending over, folding the toilet paper, and getting your hand
around to the right place.*

"Did he do it?" I would ask each time the two of them emerged from
the bathroom after a practice session.

"Yes, he did it. But I don't think that's the problem," said John.

We thought Steven might have better luck finding out what Ben's
problem was. Maybe a visit with his father would be good for Ben.

The visit didn't work out. Ben was on his way to Steven's house, but
he didn't even make it that far. The dog hair in Steven's car was enough
to bring on a full-blown asthma attack. And so there he was—right back
home with me—coughing and wheezing.

If I only knew. Why he smelled so bad. Why he had so many accidents. Why . . .

"Ben, why have you lost so much weight?"

"I don't like the food there. They don't have American cheese or the
right kind of cereal or peas in the pod," Ben told us.

*Source: National Institutes of Health

"Then what do you eat, Ben?"

"Bread."

That's all you eat?

"It's OK. I don't care."

"Well, I care. I'm going to get to bottom of this, if it's the last thing I do."

"Please, Mom. Don't make a scene. The kids already think I'm weird."

"Don't worry. I'll talk to the doctor in the infirmary. The kids won't know."

So at the end of Christmas break Ben brought his mother back to school, and she walked into the infirmary and confronted the doctor.

"Look at my son, Dr. Feingold. Do you see anything wrong?"

"Like what?" asked Dr. Feingold.

"Like how thin he is! *What's wrong with you? Can't you see he's melting away?*"

Dr. Feingold couldn't see, because in order to see something was wrong with how Ben looked, he would have had to know what he looked like before. At the very least, he would have had to be notified by Ben's housemother, Mrs. Smiley, or the director of the school, or a teacher, or Ben himself. He would have had to consult the careful medical records Steven had provided. He would have had to care enough to call Ben into his office, sit him down, and look at him face to face. *He would have had to talk with him.*

But Dr. Feingold had done none of this, and now he was only worried about covering his ass. He was only worried I would go to the director and he would lose his cushy part-time job.

"We'll put him on Ensure," said Dr. Feingold. "That should do the trick."

"But that's milk. *You don't put a boy with asthma and diarrhea on milk!*"

"Oh. I didn't know Ben's asthma was that bad, and I didn't know about the diarrhea."

"Well you should have, shouldn't you?!"

My outburst was met with silence from Dr. Feingold and his three nurses, but I didn't care. It felt good to blame, to spew out my frustration and powerlessness on someone else. It was a relief to finally be able to make something happen with the force of my rage. I accomplished nothing for Ben, but it did a lot for me. I had found a way to feel better for a little while. All I had to do was blow up.

Ben's mother had promised not to make a scene, but she had made one anyway. And now, added to the list of people who thought Ben was strange were one doctor and three nurses who thought, *No wonder the poor boy is strange—look at his crazy mother!*

I may have been crazy, but I knew one thing. I knew that this boarding school idea was crazier than I was. It wasn't making Ben healthy or happy; it was only making him worse.

I wanted to bring Ben right back home to Los Angeles with me and put him in a school—any school—close to home; but I had agreed to let this crazy experiment last a year. That meant Ben had to endure six more months of loneliness and shame, shit from his classmates, and shit from his rebellious body.

All I had to do was wait.

16

HOW WAS YOUR DAY?

I had a lot of problems in North Hollywood High School. The reason I wanted to go there was because two "friends" I knew went there. Unfortunately, neither of them wanted anything to do with me. I felt like an absolute fuck-up, doomed to failure no matter what I did.

———

"You think *you* have problems?" said Mr. Marks. "Your problems are nothing compared to this lady's."

Mr. Marks was Ben's tenth grade biology teacher, and the "you" in his sentence was aimed at the large group of parents vying for his attention on Parent-Teacher Night at Ben's public school.

The boarding school experiment was three years behind us. Ben had come home from Arizona and returned to the Rudolf Steiner school where he felt at home. "His friends" and "his teacher" were waiting for him. He knew the routine of make-your-own-notebooks, the long pants, the collared shirts, and the morning greeting, with smiling Mrs.

Kilmore standing at the doorway of her classroom, shaking each child's hand.

"Good morning, Zachary . . . good morning, Cynthia . . . good morning, Benjamin." Only full names were allowed, never nicknames—but who cared about that anymore, after what had happened in boarding school. Ben had spent his entire sixth grade in a place that allowed nicknames, but look what else they'd allowed. Now he was back where he was safe. His old school was waiting for him.

His old school was glad—or at least willing—to welcome him back. There, even though his notebooks weren't as lovely to look at as they were supposed to be, the teacher was used to them that way. She was used to Ben. And at Open School Night, when his parents peered into his messy desk and all his crumpled old notebooks, the ones he "forgot" to bring home, came tumbling out for all the world to see, his parents were used to that too.

But after ninth grade, Ben had a choice to make. Should he continue in the Rudolf Steiner school, with "all his friends" and "his regular old teacher," or should he begin tenth grade where the action was: in public high school? Public high school, where kids wore backpacks, blue jeans, grungy old sneakers, and T-shirts with the names of heavy metal bands written in big black letters on the front. Public high school, where kids walked up and down hallways high-fiving friends, snuck into bathrooms to smoke cigarettes, and went to Friday night football games. Public high school, where the regular kids went.

Ben chose to be regular. I wanted him to be regular. Ben went to public school.

"You think you have problems?" And all the mothers and fathers who had been vying for Mr. Marks's attention turned en masse and looked at me. Yes, I had problems; Mr. Marks said so. But even if he hadn't, they'd still be there—waiting for me at home in Ben's vacant eyes. Sure, I had problems, but weren't they personal? Wasn't I entitled to keep them to myself?

"You think *you* have problems, you think *your* kid's trouble, you think *you* need help, you think *you* need to talk to me. . . ."

I couldn't do anything about the color of my beet-red face, but I could still talk. I could still stand there and remind Mr. Marks that, after all, "My son . . . uh, Benjamin . . . you know . . . your assistant. . . ."

Mr. Marks blinked twice. The first blink came after the mention of Ben's name and the second came after the word *assistant*. I could understand the first blink, but not the second, because Ben was—*wasn't he?*—Mr. Marks's assistant.

"Guess what, Mom?" Ben had announced the second week of school. "You know my teacher, Mr. Marks, my biology teacher? Well, guess what! He asked me to be his assistant."

"He did? Why?"

"Because, Mom, he said I'm the best reader he's ever met and would I be his assistant."

"But Ben, you've never even taken biology before. Why would he do that?"

"Like I told you, Mom. It's not because of biology, it's because of what a good reader I am."

"Oh."

It could be true, couldn't it? After all, Ben *was* a good reader.

"He asked me to grade papers."

Anything can be true if you want it hard enough. Especially if you train yourself to look at only the parts that *could be true*. I was good at doing that, as good as Ben was at reading. Plus, I had been at it—lying to myself—as long as Ben had been lying to himself. We were old troopers—Ben and I—so who was I to say it wasn't true?

"No, Mrs. LaSalle. Ben is not my assistant. He's failing my class."

"Oh."

David was eight and Ben fifteen the year Ben went to public school. David was as good at throwing, catching, diving, putting, batting, shooting, lobbing, kicking, and punting as Ben was at reading. Balls, bats, rackets, and books—our home overflowed with them. But they did not mingle, these objects of affection. They remained forever divided and irreconcilable.

"Come on, Ben. You *promised*. You said only *one* more chapter and then you'd shoot baskets with me."

"OK. In a minute."

"That's what you *always* say," whined David.

"Leave me alone."

"But you promised!"

"*Mom!* Tell David to leave me alone," Ben appealed to me.

"But he *promised*, Mommy. *Ben promised*," David appealed back.

Ben was not David's idea of what an older brother should be. What David wanted was an older brother like his friend Jason's older brother, Robert, the football hero, who sometimes let Jason tag along with him to practice. Or a brother like his friend Alan's older brother, Tony, the boy with the Saturday night parties, even though the loud music made his mother angry. If he was going to have a brother, and especially if he was older, he should *act* older. He should be *better* at ball, not worse. He should have *more* friends, not fewer. He should be cool, not a nerd with his nose in a book.

Just like the balls and the books, I was divided, too. I wasn't one mother with two sons. I was one mother with one son, and another mother with the other. One of the mothers worried about her son playing kickball in the street, and the other mother worried about her son reading books on the bed. But I worried more about the books on the bed than the balls in the street. There were houses full of ball-playing boys on the street, but only one house with a fifteen-year-old, all-day-and-all-night-book-reading boy on the bed.

If only Ben were a little more like David, the boy with a soccer game to play every Saturday and a birthday party to go to every Sunday. It would be OK too if David were just a little more like Ben, the boy who liked to read. But somehow I knew that even if David never liked the written word as much as Ben, if he failed to memorize even half his older brother's information, he would still be all right. David had friends.

"Ben, did you promise David you'd shoot baskets with him?"

"Leave me alone, Mom."

But I wouldn't leave Ben alone, not any more than his annoying little brother would.

Nor would his stepfather, John, leave him alone.

"Get up, Ben. Come on outside, there's a whole gang of kids outside playing ball." John was the neighborhood dad, the father who taught Scott across the street how to hold a glove and Tommy down the block how to punt. He loved his role as coach for all seasons, for boys with their bats and balls, and he thought if he just tried harder, Ben could become a boy with a bat and ball too.

But he never did, not really. From time to time Ben did go outside. But when he got there, he'd just stand around, watching, or staring off into space, with a glazed look on his face.

"What the hell is *wrong* with that kid?" John would ask when he'd come back inside.

"You know. That's just the way he is."

"*But why?* He's so peculiar. Something's just not right."

"I know, John. A lot of things aren't right, they've *never* been right. But we can't make him play ball, we can't make him stop reading . . . we can't make him regular."

"Maybe we could if we tried harder. Maybe public school will be a good influence."

"Maybe."

But I didn't have much hope. I came home sobbing after the fiasco with Mr. Marks, and I asked John the same question he'd been asking me: *What's wrong with Ben?* It was the same tired question I'd always asked. I knew Ben was different from other kids and I knew *how* he was different, but I didn't know why.

It was Mr. Marks, the teacher who had embarrassed me, who was the first to suggest there might be a way to find out.

"He's obviously a smart kid, Mrs. LaSalle. He stores more information in his head than a library, yet . . . I don't know . . . something's not right."

"I know . . . but—"

"Has he ever been tested?"

"For what?"

"For learning disabilities."

"*Learning disabilities?* He learns everything the minute he reads it!"

"But that's just the point. He can't perform. He fails tests. His reading is out of the ballpark, but he can't add, he's a terrible speller, and his penmanship is barely legible. *Something* isn't right."

So Ben was put through a series of neuropsychiatric tests. The findings were consistent with Mr. Marks's observations, and mine, and the nursery school's, and the Rudolf Steiner school's.

Academically, the results of the WRAT-R-2 indicate that Benjamin's reading skills are beyond the twelfth grade level, placing him within the superior range of academic competency. His arithmetical skills are at the beginning of the sixth grade level, placing him within the lowest range of borderline academic competency.

Following this, Benjamin was administered an individualized educational plan (IEP). Besides special help addressing his deficits in arithmetic, he would receive help in writing and spelling.

His spelling skills are at the beginning eighth grade level.

On top of all this, Ben would be going to a social skills program to improve his nonverbal and adaptive/social functioning.

According to the Vineland Social Maturity Scale, Benjamin is presently functioning similar to an 11-year, 6-month-old young adolescent, placing his adaptive skills within the low borderline range of adaptive intelligence.

It was a relief to receive an authoritative piece of paper document-ing what I had known all along—that something *certifiable* was wrong with Ben. It wasn't my imagination, and it wasn't me. It was real. Finally I had an official answer to the question, *What is wrong with Ben?* My son was severely learning disabled, and he was socially disabled on top of that. At last—with the help he needed— it was going to be all right. At last, after all these years, Ben was going to be all right and so was I.

But of course I was wrong. We didn't have the answer to the ques-tion, *What's wrong with Ben?* We had part of the answer, a small piece of the puzzle. Getting the full answer would take another decade.

A piece of paper, despite its good intentions, can only go so far. Even special help in math and spelling and a social skills group encouraging friendship and sharing can only go so far. Special classes and teachers and tutors and therapy and all the good intentions in the world could go only as far as Ben could go. And that was hardly far enough.

"BEN, IT'S YOUR TURN to tell about your day," I said each evening as our family sat around the dinner table.

"It was fine."

"What did *you* do in school today, David?" John would ask.

"Nothing. Can I be excused please? Scott's coming over to do home-work."

"No," I said.

"No," John said.

"This is boring. Why do we have to sit around every night telling about our day?" David complained.

"Yeah, why do we?" Ben chimed in.

"Because we're a family and we're interested in one other."

I said a lot of things in those days that weren't true. Maybe I thought they were true, these hopeful, happy picket-fence-family images I tried so hard to sell to my husband and sons. Maybe I thought I could make them true, by acting as if, by directing the LaSalle family dinner table show.

And how was your day today, Ben?

Really?

And then what happened?

And how was your day, David?

You don't say?

And then what happened?

But it wasn't true, what I said about being a family and being interested in one another. We were a family, but only some of us were interested in one another. I was interested in Ben. John was interested in David. David was interested in his friends, and Ben was interested in being left alone.

I was also interested in how John behaved at the dinner table. More precisely, I was interested in evaluating how he behaved. I did this by keeping a tally of how many times John directed his conversation toward David and how many times he directed it toward Ben. Also, I was interested in the tone of John's voice when he spoke to David and the tone of his voice when he spoke to Ben.

"Ben, don't just eat the meat, you have to have at least one bite of vegetable," said John.

"OK," Ben would say, putting a forkful of broccoli into his mouth and keeping it there, chewing, until John looked away. Then he'd spit it into his napkin.

This wasn't so bad—a teenager who hated vegetables. A teenager who couldn't stand sitting at the dining room table, answering inane questions about his day. A teenager who wanted to get back to his room.

That's what was bad. Ben's room.

The problem wasn't in the dining room.

Most teenagers consider their rooms off limits to their parents. Ben was regular in that regard. His room was his refuge—from us, from school, from his brother, from reality. He didn't want us in there.

Fine, I thought. *I don't want to go in there. Give him his privacy.*

Ben's room was a kingdom of chaos. The walls were covered with bloody, brutal posters. The music he listened to was frightening. Violent, hateful, full of despair, all about revenge.

Gone were "The Wheels of the Bus" going round and round.

Gone were the cities Ben used to build for his beloved persons.

Gone were Ben's persons.

Gone was his grasp on reality.

Ben's mind was in chaos, and so was his room. A trail of dirty laundry tossed over a pile of freshly folded clothes; a lane of sticky American cheese wrappers; a path of empty notebooks, album covers without records, records without album covers, last year's books, this year's books, next year's books; mounds of snotty tissues; and behind, beneath, and between everything, Ben's underpants stinking of stored-up shit.

"I hate everyone, everyone hates me, I'm gonna kill everyone, I'm gonna kill myself," blared out of the stereo, speaking the only words Ben seemed to care about. He didn't care about me, or John, or David. He didn't care how he looked or how he smelled. He didn't care about school, or making friends, or what his teachers thought. He didn't care about anything.

My son was falling apart in front of my eyes, and I was asking about his day.

"I heard this great song about a Joan of Arc thing, people burning at the stake, and I got this idea for a video."

"Really, Ben? That sounds interesting. Tell us about it," I'd say.

Ben was smart, creative, and talented. One day he was going to do great things. Somewhere I read that Steven Spielberg got his start as a teenager, making home movies. Why couldn't Ben do that?

"*People burning at the stake, Ben? What the hell's wrong with you?*" John yelled.

What was wrong with Ben was the pain and humiliation he felt every day. What was wrong with him was his growing sense of paranoia, his suspicion, his inability to understand that others have thoughts differ-ent from his own. What was wrong with him was his growing awareness that he was different from others, though he didn't know why or how. What was wrong with him was wanting friends, but not knowing how to make them. He'd try to make them by demonstrating how smart he was. So he talked and talked, he told and told. But that didn't work—it only made them laugh. What was wrong was how depressed and self-hating he was becoming.

"Let him speak, John. Let him tell his video idea."

"No, I certainly will not! *A video about people burning on the stake? Ben, what the hell are you thinking about?*"

Now this was definitely *not* a pleasant tone of voice. It was challeng-ing—anyone would say it was. Why was John treating Ben like that . . . so hostile, so mean? He didn't speak to David that way.

"You don't like Ben—it's obvious you don't," I'd say to John each night after dinner.

"I don't like his behavior. I don't like his crazy stories. I don't like his lies."

"But maybe if you treated him better, if he felt more encouraged by you, he'd be different."

"*Why is it always my fault?*"

"I'm not saying that. I'm saying why can't you just be nicer to Ben?"

"I'll be nicer when Ben is nicer. I'll be nicer when I can trust him."

"You don't trust Ben?" I asked.

"*Do you?*"

BEN HAD TAKEN TO CUTTING SCHOOL, forging my name to truant slips, and making sure to be close to the phone when the automated truant line ("This is to let you know that your son or daughter was absent from school today") placed its 6:00 P.M. call.

One day he cut school after lunch, thinking that no one would be home at twelve-thirty on a Wednesday afternoon. Ben was in luck for the first half-hour, but then he heard a car pulling up in the driveway. It was John. What should he do? Years later he told me he thought to himself, *I know! I'll hide in the downstairs closet.* It was empty at the time because we were about to remodel the house, and Ben thought he'd just stay there, waiting for John's footsteps to disappear. But every time he thought the coast was clear, John's footsteps would return. Finally, when he could wait no longer, he stepped out of the closet, scaring John half to death.

"*God damn it, Ben! What are you doing?*"

"Hiding in the closet. I'm hiding in the closet."

"I can see that! *Why the hell aren't you in school?*"

"It's boring. It's dumb. It's a waste of my time."

"Well, you're going right back. Get in the car, I'm taking you right back. And don't come home till school is over!"

That evening at dinner I didn't ask Ben about his day. John did.

"So, Ben," John said, "do you want to tell us why you cut school today?"

Ben didn't answer.

"Ben?"

"John," I said, "maybe Ben doesn't feel like—"

"Barbara, I'm trying to understand what's going on here. Why do you cut school, Ben? Turns out you're cutting school a lot. I mean *a lot.* What's going on?"

I could tell John was trying to keep the threat out of his voice, but it wasn't working.

"Huh?"

Ben said, "I don't want to get killed. I'm going to my room." He stood up and left the table.

"I'm going to my room, too," David said.

"So am I," I echoed. The whole family, if you could call it that, left the dining room, except for John, who remained at the table, fuming.

An hour later John came into our bedroom. There were tears in his eyes.

"Where have you been?" I asked.

"Ben's room."

"He let you in?"

"He didn't have a choice. I don't care about his privacy anymore."

"John—"

He brought his hand from behind his back and dropped two large kitchen knives on our bed. "From under his pillow," John said. "And a baseball bat under the bed. Ben doesn't play baseball. I know that for a fact."

"What did he say?" I asked.

John shook his head. "He's not talking to me." He sat down on the bed and buried his face in his hands.

17

DRIVING FOR EVERYONE

I had been told from an early age that I was special. Yet I couldn't accomplish anything.

———

BEN WAS THROWN OUT of the regular public high school, with the regular kids, for telling his history teacher off. It happened the day she was lecturing on the Know-Nothing party, a group, Ben tells me, of political isolationists. Of course Ben knew everything about these Know-Nothings. It was his teacher who didn't. So why shouldn't he tell her? "This is a perfect topic for you to teach, Mrs. Brighton," he said one sunny spring Wednesday morning.

"Oh?" inquired Mrs. Brighton, eager for the compliment.

"Yes," said Ben, "because you know nothing."

So Ben went to yet a third high school. This was a "special" school for special kids with special challenges, like learning disabilities, attention disorders, and emotional problems. According to Ben's latest neuropsychiatric tests, he had all three.

He was placed in a small class where he was given help in reaching the goals he had set for himself. His days, like his brain, were divided into two parts. In the morning he received help for his deficits, and in the afternoons he received appreciation and stimulation for his gifts. Mornings were spent in the special school for kids who couldn't count backward from seven, alongside those who might be able to if they could sit long enough to bother. Afternoons were spent across the street on the campus of UCLA, a university for elite achievers, those with the highest grade point averages and SAT scores. In the fall he was granted permission to take a course in Western civilization, followed in the spring by a course in communication. He got As in both.

But then the special school announced it was closing. Ben still didn't have a high school diploma, so in what would have been his final year of high school, he took the high school proficiency test. He passed. So Ben set off to Valley Community College, where he registered for two classes, one in philosophy and the other in film.

"One day I'm going to be a famous director of films," Ben told me the first week of school.

"Oh?"

"Yeah. I've been writing films in my head all my life." And then, when I failed to respond, he added, "Well, haven't I?"

"I guess so, Ben. Counting your cities and your weather reports and your Joan of Arc video."

"Oh, that? Forget that, Mom. That was an aberration. That was just me being crazy."

"And you're not crazy now?" Up to now, John was the only one who'd used that word. Now Ben was claiming it for himself.

"Not in the least. I'm not even a little bit crazy."

"Oh?" It was an expression I was accustomed to assuming. A question I used with patients all the time. Open-ended, probing, without being overly intrusive.

"Yeah, and *you'll never guess* what I'm gonna be doing."

"Tell me." But I didn't mean it. I didn't want to catch the ball Ben was passing to me. I didn't want to play the guess-what game. "Guess what, Mommy? Guess what, Mom? Guess what, Mother?" How could a question, two simple words, have changed from being so dear to bringing so much dread? "Guess what? I'm on the football team. Guess what? Josh and I went to a movie." Guess what? I'm a regular kid, which makes you a regular mother, and isn't it fine, isn't it great, isn't it what you and I have always wanted?

"I applied for an internship at this film production company, Indian Neck Productions, and *I was accepted!*"

"You mean you have an internship at a film production company?"

"And not only that! It's a *paid* internship. *I'm getting paid!*"

"Baloney, Ben. You expect me to believe that you're getting paid for a junior college internship? I'm not *that* naïve."

"It's true, Mom. You'll see."

But when would I see?

"Ben, I want to believe you, but I can't. Why should I? Everything you say is a lie. . . ."

"Well, this time I'm telling the truth. I swear I am."

"OK then. When is payday?"

"Every other Friday."

"Show me the check, and I'll believe you then."

"It's a deal."

Not one question passed between us that day, sixteen years ago, about *what* Ben would be doing in his position as intern, because I no longer cared *what* Ben was doing. I only cared *if* he was doing it.

"So Ben? It's Friday, the second Friday of the month?" I said fourteen days later.

"What about it?"

"Where's your paycheck?"

"Oh, that. They were short on cash flow this month. They asked if it would be OK for the staff to wait till next week."

"*But Ben, you swore it was true! You stood right here and swore.*" I was swimming in a sea of purple.

"It is, Mom. You'll see it is."

"*When?*"

"Like I said. Next week."

I saw no paycheck next week, or the week after that, or the one following. But I heard a lot of excuses, and I witnessed a lot of sworn testimony. "It's coming, Mom, I swear on my life it is."

It was only fifteen years later, when I asked Ben about this period of his life, that I learned the true story of his internship at Indian Neck Productions.

Although it was not a paid internship, it *was* an internship. That part was real. And although Ben did not, as he'd thought he should, qualify for a private inner office with a big fancy desk, he did in fact sit in an outer office with a plain one. He didn't, as he'd thought he should, stand behind the camera and say "Cut!" and "It's a wrap!" But he did take phone messages. He did use the copy machine. He did file. And once, he even attended a story meeting.

This is the true story of my internship at Indian Neck Productions.

As you know, I was going to be a famous director of films. I had lots of stories and creative talent, so why shouldn't I become famous? The only problem was, I had no idea what a director did. I just knew he bossed people around.

So I applied for an internship at Indian Neck Productions, and when I got it, I figured it was my big break. I focused all my energy on becoming a famous behind-the-scenes player in Hollywood.

But I had no idea how to conduct myself in an office setting. I couldn't relay phone numbers because I'd turn the numbers around. I couldn't take down phone messages because I couldn't write fast enough, and I was embarrassed to ask, "Can you spell that, please?" I couldn't file because I can't put things in order, and I couldn't log in the scripts properly.

I wanted to be in one of the private offices and couldn't figure out why I didn't have one. How could I be a famous film director without a private office?

Indian Neck shared office space with a film publicity firm. The people there hated me so much they actually put down a strip of tape between their office and Indian Neck and told me never to set foot over into their side. I don't know why they hated me.

Making copies was the worst. Once I was asked to make five copies of three separate scripts. But how could I? I didn't even know how to run the machine. It took me all day to do that job.

Sometimes I was allowed to read scripts and do "coverage." Once I even sat in on a story meeting. It was a disaster. I had just eaten a huge lunch and fell asleep in the middle of the meeting.

Indian Neck had a large glass pig filled with candy sitting in the lobby. I ate candy by the bagful. They also had a petty cash drawer, which I stole from regularly. One day I found it locked, but I knew where the key was kept, so I went across the street and had a copy made.

The final straw in my career as a famous film director happened the day I lost a script. The boss yelled at me for ten full minutes and told me never to set foot in the office again.

After the fiasco at Indian Neck, Ben didn't bother returning to classes at Valley Community College. Instead, he registered at Santa Monica City College.

"It has a good learning disability program, Mom. And the campus is cool! Just like a real college campus. And when I get my driver's license I'll be able to drive there!"

"Ben, you can't drive," I told him.

"I can take driving lessons," he said.

"Ben," John said, "you can't drive. *You cannot drive.*"

"But *why* can't I drive? Why can't I take driving lessons like everyone else?" Ben pleaded. "I'm sixteen."

"You know why, Ben," John said, turning away. It was an old argument and John knew where it was headed. It was headed nowhere, but first, before it ended, it would swerve, causing a second collision. Collateral damage.

"But *maybe* he could. Why can't we at least give him a chance?" I'd say to John when we were alone.

"*A chance?* A chance for what, Barbara? A chance for him to die in a car crash? A chance for him to cause someone else to die? *Exactly why should we give him a chance?*"

"Because he needs to feel good about *something*. What does he have? He has no friends. I don't hear a word about his classes . . . I doubt he's even going anymore. Maybe a car and a driver's license would make him feel better—"

"*Feel better?* Oh, Barbara. . . ." This time John's back was toward me. The irritation in his voice was mixed with a sadness, a tone of resignation I had never heard before. "Oh, Barbara . . . when will you ever see what's in front of your nose?"

"Never! Not if it means acting like *you*. Not if it means giving up on him. Not if it means giving up on him like *you have*. You don't even bother to hide it. It's written all over your face—"

"Barbara, don't say that!"

"*I will say that!* I'll say any damn thing I please! How could you do that to him? Give up on him? *I hate you for it. I hate you!*"

That's where the argument was headed. That was the collateral damage.

"OK, NOW CAN I DRIVE?" Ben asked on his seventeenth birthday.

By this time John was tired of fighting with me. I refused to see what I knew was true, what John knew was true. Ben shouldn't drive, because he couldn't. No matter how much he begged—a car would make all the difference, a car would make him regular, a car would bring friends and interesting places and parties and. . . .

I searched the yellow pages for a driving school that catered to people with special needs. "Look at this one, John. This ad says they work with the elderly and the handicapped."

"Of course they say that," John said, but he wouldn't look. He was busy reading the sports section.

The man from Driving for Everyone said he could meet with us on Thursday night. "With just us?" I'd asked when we spoke on the phone. "Or do you want Ben to be there too?"

"Is Ben the driver?" the man asked.

"Yes, but—"

"Well, then, of course. Of course he should be there."

How could I explain about Ben if he was present? Would the man from Driving for Everyone understand about eye patches in all colors, or jumping on trampolines while counting backward from ten, or talking before walking, or terror on jungle gyms? Would he understand that for this seventeen-year-old, and for this seventeen-year-old's mother, the man from Driving for Everyone was Ben's last chance?

"We'll start him on a Toyota Camry. He'll do just fine. Won't you, Ben?"

"When do we start?" asked Ben.

"How many lessons will he need?" asked John. "And how much do they cost?"

"It depends. Most people learn enough to take their driving test in a single series. That's eight two-hour lessons for 160 dollars."

"Most people—"

"John! Not in front of Ben."

"Look Barbara, this isn't something we can pussyfoot around. This is serious business. It's about driving, for Christ's sake!"

Ben interrupted, "Don't worry. Eight lessons at two hours each is a lot of time. I can do it. It was different with the eye patch, Mom. That was boring. And don't go by Miss Reed, either. I didn't care about all that stuff, but I care about *this*. I care about driving and having my own car.

I care about not having to take two buses all the way to Santa Monica City College. It'll save time. I'll get a parking pass from the student office. You can deduct it from my allowance. You can—"

Ben started his first series of eight two-hour lessons in February of his eighteenth year, and his second series in April. On the last day of his time with the man from Driving for Everyone, Ben drove to the DMV and took his driving test.

He passed.

We would give Ben our old Ford Galaxie four-door sedan, the one stored in a parking garage twenty-five miles away. It was big. It was sturdy.

John and Ben drove the twenty-five miles to pick it up. Then John followed behind Ben as he drove the Ford home. "I've spent this whole last week assembling my tape collection, Dad. I've finally decided."

"Decided what, Ben?"

"On Springsteen. The rest of my collection stays home."

"What are you thinking Ben? The first day driving and you're worrying about tapes? What's the matter with you?"

Ben was silent.

"Don't even bother bringing them. If you're going to drive, you're going to pay attention to driving."

John followed Ben home. All twenty-five miles.

"When he's going straight he's absolutely fine," John said when he arrived.

"That's great, John!" The trip back and forth had taken two hours. It was a long time to hold my breath.

"Did you hear what I said, Barbara?"

"Yes. You said he drives absolutely fine."

"I said when he's going straight he's absolutely fine."

"Oh."

"Absolutely fine except for the rolled-down window and the arm out the door—all hip, slick, and cool. Absolutely fine, except for changing lanes. Absolutely fine, except for left turns. Except for backing up, except for—"

"Oh."

"Yeah," said John.

"But he passed the driving test. He took sixteen two-hour lessons. What should we do?"

"Forget the *we*, Barbara. There's no we in this driving thing. There's only you wanting to pretend everything is fine. There's only Ben wanting to pretend everything is fine. *Leave me out of it!*"

NEWSPAPERS, NICKELS, NOTEBOOKS, soda bottles, gum wrappers, pennies, pencils without points, points without pencils, sweaters, T-shirts, dirty socks, and crumbs. That's what Ben's car looked like. Just like his room. Just like his life.

"Clean it up, Ben," I'd say.

"Clean it up right now," John would say.

But Ben couldn't clean up his car any more than he could clean up his room. Or his life. He'd begin, though; he'd always begin. He'd pick up the week-old newspaper and bring it to the trash can. But before he'd throw it in, he'd read the headlines. "Hmm . . . that's interesting," Ben would say to himself while I watched from the window. "I don't remember reading this. . . ." And then Ben would sit down on the back stair, where he used to sit when he read his *Child's History of the World*, when drool still dribbled down his shirt, and read last week's newspaper.

BEN WAS PROUD TO GO to Santa Monica City College. Or maybe he was proud of the blue and white parking sticker hanging from the windshield of his gray Ford. There was just one minor problem.

The first day I took the car to school I found a parking space in the student parking garage. It was between two cars. But I couldn't back up. So when I tried to straighten out my car, I'd ram into the car on my left.

But I kept trying. And every single time, I'd ram that car again.

So along comes this guy. He's standing behind me and he says, "What are you doing?"

"I'm trying to back out," I say.

"But you're destroying someone else's car."

"I know I am. But I can't back out."

"But what's the problem? Just back it out straight."

"I'm trying. . . ."

"Do you want me to do it?" asks the man.

And I say yes and let him back it out. But when I go to get back into the car, the man stops me. He says, "Where do you think you're going?"

"Home," I say.

"No, you're not," the man says. "You're not going anywhere till you leave your insurance information on the windshield of that poor guy's car."

"But I'm afraid," I remember telling him.

"I don't care," the man says. "You destroyed that car and you have to pay for it."

That was the end of my driving career.

18

FIRE!

I had a feeling of separation from the rest of the world. I felt so powerless. This led to an intense desire to change how I was treated and perceived by others. I began to hate people. This feeling, combined with fear and paranoia, along with a general lack of understanding of the world and other people's experiences of it, led me to completely break with reality when I was eighteen years old.

―――――

BEN'S EYES HAD ALWAYS BEEN faraway, as if they had better things to do than focus on the eyes of another. But now they were dead. Now Ben's eyes had nothing to do. Their light, the focused inner sparkle that had twinkled with so much imagination—rich with cities and streets and trains and commercials and play-by-plays—was gone.

"How was your day, Ben?" had switched to "Ben, what's wrong?" Why are you sitting there all alone doing nothing? Why don't you talk to me? Why, when you do talk, do you say things that scare me? "Ben, what's wrong?"

"I'm sitting here planning a video."

By now Ben weighed over 250 pounds. His three slices of American cheese had grown to three pounds of American cheese, and his peas in the pod were replaced by Big Macs, malts, and French fries. Ben ate all the time—early in the morning before anyone else in the house was awake, in the middle of the night, and throughout the day.

"Ben, there's a trail of crumbs from the sink to the kitchen table and all around the floor. It's only 7 A.M., and already the kitchen looks like it was hit by a cyclone."

"I just had some cereal."

"*When* did you have cereal? And *where's* the loaf of bread I bought yesterday? And *where's* David's lunchmeat? Where's David's cheese? Where's the peanut butter? Where are last night's meatballs and spaghetti I was planning to serve tonight?"

"I don't know. Why are you blaming *me*?"

"OK, Ben. From now on I want to see a receipt for every lunch you buy. Even if it's under three dollars. If you can't control your food intake, and you refuse to go on a diet, I'll just have to start monitoring what you eat when I'm not with you. I'll just have to start locking up the food."

"Whatever."

I found it hard to look at Ben or even get close to him. Here he was, sitting all alone, "planning a video," with not a friend in the world, while I, his own mother, couldn't bear the sight of him.

He smelled bad. When he bent down to tie his shoes he could hardly reach beyond his stomach. When he leaned forward, his shirt would hike up, exposing tire treads of stretch marks running across his butt and his back.

I was his mother. My son was forlorn, a failure in school, a failure at home, the precocious promise of his boyhood ruined.

I was his mother and I couldn't even hug him.

"What's the video about?"

"Fire."

"What do you mean, fire?"

"It's about fire and people burning."

"You mean like your Joan of Arc video? With people burning at the stake?"

"No this one's about burning down the Galleria Mall."

"*What?*"

"You heard what I said."

"But, Ben, *why? Why do you want to do that?*"

"Because I hate all those people who go there. They're just like the kids in every single school I've ever been to. Every single fucking kid in every single fucking school."

"*Ben!*"

"Leave me alone, Mother. Just leave me alone. You ask, and I tell you, but you don't like what I tell you. You don't like what I say. You don't really want to know, so why don't you *just damn leave me alone.*"

Ben was right. I didn't like what he told me. If someone else had told me a fantasy about burning down a mall—a friend, a patient—I'd understand what he was really saying. That he felt powerless, totally impotent, and that feeling this way made him angry. So angry he had to *do* something. Something big enough to change him from powerless to powerful.

"Is that why you've stopped going to the mall, Ben? You used to always go to the mall."

"The mall sucks."

"*Ben!*"

"You know it sucks. All those people who think they're so cool—"

"Is that why you're so angry? Because of the people? Because they think they're cool and they don't think you're cool?"

"I hate them!"

"Ben, what happened at the mall? You used to beg to go there, you always asked for a ride. But now you hate it? Why? *What happened?*"

"I always hated it. The stupid people who think they're so cool. They eat at the fancy tables near the video arcade, in their cool clothes, laughing as if they're so cool."

"Where do *you* eat, Ben?"

"At McDonald's with the other losers."

Ben was no longer seeing Dr. Morris, the therapist who thought his lies were fantasies. For the past year he had been seeing Dr. Carter, a psychotherapist referred by the learning disability clinic he was going to for special help during his year at Santa Monica City College.

"Dr. Carter, this is Ben's mother. I know you can't talk about Ben, but I need to tell you something," I said into Dr. Carter's answering machine. "Please call me back. Right away." But then when he didn't, when an hour had passed and I still hadn't heard from him, I called his number again and wrote down the second number listed in the announcement, the one to call "in the case of an emergency."

Dr. Carter listened to the story about burning down the mall. He listened to what I told him about hating people because "they think they're so cool."

Then he said, "Mrs. LaSalle, I think it's time for Ben to take the MMPI."

"You meant the personality test? The psychological profiling inventory test?"

"Yes, that's the one."

"But isn't that used for special cases . . . I mean for criminals and psychotics and—"

"Mrs. LaSalle, according to what you just told me, Ben is indicating some serious ideation."

"Oh God. I know he is. Do you administer the test?"

"No. I'll call right back with a referral."

"EVERYTHING IS FINE," Ben told the psychologist who administered the test. "I'm depressed, but OK. I have a lot of problems that make me depressed. My impulse control is a definite problem. I eat all the time. I spend money. I have no real life skills. I cut myself shaving. . . ."

MINNESOTA MULTIPHASIC PERSONALITY INVENTORY (MMPI): *Administered February 5, 1987, to Benjamin D. Levinson, male, eighteen years of age*

The profile indicates severe distrust, emotional distancing, and estrangement. Under stress his behavior is likely to become seriously inappropriate if not borderline psychotic. Others are apt to see him as unpredictable and changeable and as very difficult to understand. Projecting and rationalizing of his own behavior, his understanding and empathy for others and awareness of how he hurts and alienates them appear seriously distorted. . . ."

The MMPI validated Dr. Carter's concern. Ben was manifesting psychotic thoughts and was in need of an inpatient diagnostic evaluation. He was placed at UCLA's Neuropsychiatric Institute. Ben's ward was 2-West.

It was locked.

"This is the story of a little boy who loved to do all kinds of things . . ." Ben wrote when asked to compose a story about himself during that first hospitalization.

First of all, he loved to read. He read everything he could get his hands on, from matchbook covers to Shakespeare. He also loved to listen to the radio and play with his persons. He spent hours playing and laughing and staying in his own little world. . . .

This is the first psychiatric admission for this eighteen-year-old Caucasian male who presented with a long history of behavior, school, and peer relationship difficulties. . . . The parents were concerned about his ability to distinguish truth from fantasy. In addition, he has become a compulsive eater and spender. He is morbidly obese. . . . In addition, he has been socially isolated and never able to have friends. . . .

One day it was time to go to school and he had to leave behind his radio and his persons and learn things. He had to learn how to tie his shoes and comb his hair. He had to learn to play football and baseball with the other kids. The little boy didn't like to play with other kids. He thought he was too smart to be playing football, and he wasn't very good at it anyway. The little boy learned that he'd rather stay in his room and play with his school bus and persons than play with the other children. . . .

In addition, he describes having violent fantasies. He says these fantasies occur when he is angry. He has denied being paranoid, but in social situations, such as in a club, he feels that people are watching him and don't want him around.

Then the little boy went to high school, and it was time to think about going to college. All his teachers told him he was brilliant, but that he was also stupid and lazy and a failure and would never be able to perform in college. This made the little boy very confused. If everyone said he was brilliant, why couldn't he go to college?

While he was on the unit he was very cooperative and, although he became angry, at no time did he act upon his anger. . . . Ben had a very difficult time structuring his time on the unit. He became quite upset about not being able to leave the unit and not participating in activities such as school because he is eighteen years old.

The little boy learned that he was different from everyone else because he was smart but didn't know how to put his smartness on paper. This made the little boy very angry and frustrated because . . .

The WAIS-R shows more than a 30-point difference between the Verbal and the Performance scale IQ scores. Academically, the results of the WRAT-R-2 indicate that Benjamin's reading skills are beyond the twelfth grade level, thereby placing them within the superior range. His arithmetic skills are at the beginning of the fifth grade level, therefore placing them within the dull-borderline range. . . .

More than anything, the little boy wanted to tell and show people what kind of person he really was. He wanted to express all the dreams and stories stored up in his head.

On the Benton Facial Recognition test, his performance reflected significant impairment. . . . All in all, it was felt that the clinical picture was most consistent with an atypical psychosis. It was felt that a trial of a low-dose neuroleptic may help contain his anxiety and organize his thoughts. He was begun on Navane and Cogentin.

This little boy is me. I want you to know what it is like to be me, although it is just as hard for me to imagine what it is like to be you. Perhaps one day I will be able to communicate what it is like to hear what I hear and see what I see. But it is going to take some effort on your part to understand.

19

THE NUT HOUSE

I wasn't surprised when I was told I was going to a psychiatric hospital. I always knew one day I'd end up in a nut house.

———

"Excuse me? Would you know which elevator goes to 2-West?" I asked the young man in the white jacket waiting for the elevator.

"The locked ward or the other one?" said the man.

Maybe the young man in the white jacket waiting for the elevator belonged to this place with the shiny floors and the corridors going in all directions with their bays of elevators going in all directions, because he said the word "locked" as if he were talking about the weather. Is the day sunny, or is it overcast? Are you happy, or are you sad? Do you belong here like I do, with a microscope and a test and a degree in psychiatry, or are you one of them?

"Locked, please."

Please? Why did I say please, as if the young man in the white jacket were taking my lunch order? Medium-rare please, light on the salt.

Please! Get me out of here.

It was Friday, and we had brought Ben here Thursday, and the following day would be Saturday, and then comes Sunday, and all the days after—one running into the next—a singed page in *A Child's History of the World*, charred, now burning, now up in smoke. A mother, her days—one running into the next—her dreams once hopeful, then worried, now up in smoke.

"Take the number three elevator, get off on seven. Switch to number four and press 2-West. It will take you there."

"Thank you."

Thank you? Thank you for setting me straight.

Now I can find my way to my son.

I'm riding up the elevator. I'm walking across the hall. I'm pressing the button. I'm riding up another elevator. I'm finding my way to my son. He is locked up, you know. He is on the inside and I am on the outside. He cannot walk out from where he is to where I am, but I can walk in to where he is.

But first, I must ring the bell. The sign says so. "For admittance, please push the red button." I push the red button and the bell rings. Through the glass I see three nurses. They look up. One nurse is writing, one nurse is talking, and one nurse is laughing. I watch them from behind my side of the glass. But the nurses do not stand. They do not walk over to the door. They keep writing and talking and laughing. I push the red button again. I look through the glass. Now I see the laughing nurse stand up. She is coming toward me. She is talking to me through the tiny window in the glass. "Yes. Can I help you?" she asks.

Can you help me? How exactly would you manage that?

Can you get me out of here?

No, I came here of my own free will. If I decided, I could turn around right now. I could retrace my steps and find my way back to the lobby, back to the parking lot. I could get into my car and drive it up to the parking booth and the man would say, "Three dollars, please," and I would give him a five and he would give me two dollars back. Then the man would push the parking lot button and the black bar would lift and I could drive anywhere I please.

But where would I go?

"Yes. I'm Benjamin Levinson's mother. I came to visit him."

The laughing nurse pushed a button on her side of the glass and the door opened. "Benjamin Levinson? Oh . . . yes. . . ." and she looked at me. Not at my face, but at my body. Up and down the length of it, as if to ask, "Your son is fat—are you fat, too?"

"Where can I find him, please?" And how will I find him?

Will I find him as I left him? "Mom! Why do I have to stay here and how long do I have to stay and why can't I leave and why are they taking everything out of my suitcase? Why are they taking my radio apart? What are they looking for? Why are they taking my razors away? How can I shave without razors? *Please, get me out of here!*"

To which I calmly replied, "No, sweetie, you can't leave just yet. This place is going to help you. You'll feel better after you leave."

You'll feel better after we sing "The Wheels of the Bus," after you eat your American cheese, after you read *This Is Brazil, This Is London, This Is San Francisco*, after you tell me everything about the train diorama, after you learn to ride a bike, after you do one more set of eye exercises, after you have one more playdate, after you talk to Dr. Morris and Dr. Carter and tell them what is bothering you, after you jump on the trampoline and count backward from ten, after you get back from boarding school, after you go to a regular school, after you go to a special school, after you take driving lessons, after you get your driver's license, after you go to college, after you drive to college, after you take one more test to see what is wrong with you, after you clean up your room, after you clean up your car, after you tell the truth. You'll feel better then.

20

TRANSITIONAL LIVING

The diagnosis of atypical psychosis is simply a scientific way of saying "He's screwed up, but we don't know how."

THE PSYCHOTROPIC MEDICINE made Ben less screwed up, but it also made him numb and spacey and hardly there.

Ben had been there. With me, with Steven, with John and David. For eighteen years. Now he was gone.

Ben was eighteen, the age when kids leave home. But while the other eighteen-year-olds were looking forward to college, Ben was shopping for a place to take care of him. And while the kids from his preschool playgroup, Heather, Griffin, and Matthew, were looking at college brochures and being interviewed by college admissions officers, Ben was being interviewed by intake officers from transitional living programs.

Ben's interviews were conducted in the hospital. The first place that came to call was Concerned Living. I liked the sound of that one.

Ben liked it too.

"But why, Ben? What did the man who came to visit say about the place that made you so impressed?" I asked Ben at the end of his six-week stint at UCLA's NPI.

"They told me I could live in my own apartment with just a little bit of supervision."

"What does that mean?"

"You know. They teach independence. They want you to learn to live on your own, so they teach you how."

"But how? How do they teach you?" They must use some secret formula, because whatever it was, God knows it wasn't available in books, it wasn't printed in therapists' manuals, it wasn't to be found in self-help classes or tough love seminars or anything else I'd tried.

"I don't know. Probably like they do it here in the hospital, with groups on hygiene and grooming, and money management, and cooking and cleaning, and shit like that."

Shit like that. Uh-huh, I knew about shit like that. I'd learned everything I ever wanted to know about shit like that in the last six weeks. It was all there, hanging on the wall. In bouncy spring colors:

SCHEDULE OF ACTIVITIES
9:00 A.M. Hygiene and medications
10:00 A.M. Free time
11:00 A.M. Medications and behavior modification
12:00 P.M. Lunch
1:00 P.M. Free time
2:00 P.M. Medications and group therapy
3:00 P.M. Money management
4:00 P.M. Free time
6:00 P.M. Dinner
7:00 P.M. Board games in the Social Hall
9:00 P.M. Medications and occupational therapy
10:00 P.M. Lights out

Ben and his fellow inmates marked time from meds to meds. "Meds! Morning meds. Please line up in single file."

I saw it with my own eyes, the spacey, numb, shuffling men and women with their eyes facing down and their feet barely moving, waiting for the one in front to get his paper cup with his one, two, or three white pills. "No, you can't take it later. Here's a cup of water. You must take it now. No, you can't take it to your room. You know the rules. You must take it right here, while I watch."

The Shuffling People, that's what I called them. And Ben was one of them.

"What else did they say, Ben?"

"Nothing. Except it's in Beverly Hills. The apartments are in Beverly Hills!"

"Ben, is that why you like it? Because it's in Beverly Hills?"

"So? What's the matter with that? It's a perfect location. Maybe I could even get my car back."

So Ben went to Concerned Living and was placed in an apartment with five other mentally ill young men. The apartment was furnished. It was a spacious old Spanish-style place on a three-quarter square courtyard. The fourth side opened to the street.

"Oh, this is nice," I said the day we moved Ben in. The living room had hardwood floors. Oh, this is nice. There were two recliners, one couch, and a giant TV. Past the living room was a formal dining room. Then came the kitchen and a small breakfast nook. That was downstairs.

Upstairs were three small bedrooms housing two young men apiece. They were assigned randomly, or maybe by first initial—Ben to Brad, Doug to David, and Neal to Nevil. Six men suffering from various forms of mental illness: schizophrenia, schizoaffective disorder, bipolar disorder type I, and plain old antisocial personality disorder with a touch of obsessive-compulsive disorder (OCD).

Brad, Ben's roommate, suffered from antisocial personality disorder with a touch of OCD. Or maybe it was the other way around. Maybe

Brad's primary diagnosis was OCD with traits of antisocial behavior. Ben's diagnosis was atypical psychosis. But Ben was just as antisocial as Brad and had his own obsessive-compulsive behaviors. Both men were creatures of habit, which could have been good, but in their case was bad, because Brad made hospital corners and Ben made messes.

On their first night together, Brad said, "Don't tell me anything about you and don't ask me anything about me."

To which Ben replied, "Why not?"

"Didn't I tell you not to ask me anything? *Didn't I just say that?*"

So Ben agreed and listened to his records instead. Brad, on the other hand, favored television, which he watched obsessively till three in the morning.

Notwithstanding his own prohibition against talking, Brad himself did talk. Rather, according to Ben in our nightly phone conversations, he yelled.

"But why, Ben? What is he yelling about?"

"I don't know. He just yells."

"But he must be yelling about *something*? Are you doing something he doesn't like?"

"He doesn't like the way I keep my side of the room. He doesn't like my underwear on the floor, which is not my fault because I don't have a clothes hamper, and he doesn't like the records separated from their album covers, which I can't help because I'm making tapes and I don't have time to put the records back into their sleeves because I'd just have to take them right back out again."

"Oh."

My days at Concerned Living were spent at a day program right behind Seven-Eleven and Jacopo's Pizza Place. We were encouraged to eat there, and often I would have lunch or dinner with my counselor at Jacopo's. I don't know why he thought pizza was good for me. Maybe he thought he was making me happy because I could eat a whole pizza all by myself.

On Fridays they would have a major cookout with tons of food. Once I was allowed to cook the meat. I liked that, because that way I could eat more food. But I nearly blew the place up and I burned the meat to a crisp.

The only useful thing I learned at Concerned Living was how to shave properly. No one ever told me I had to find a job or go to school, but I ended up finding a job anyway. It was in a record store, which I liked because everyone who worked there looked so cool. I thought if I worked there I'd be cool too. No one helped me, though. No one took me to the interview or told me what to expect or how to behave once I got the job.

"But Ben," I asked fifteen years later when we were talking about that period of his life, "isn't that where you first met Kathy? Wasn't that another good thing about that place . . . you know, meeting a girl?"

"But, Mom, you know Kathy was nuts. Nuttier than me."

"Yeah, I knew it. But I didn't think you did."

"Sure I did. Don't you remember, Mom? Kathy used to spend whole days cleaning her apartment. Every nook and cranny. She moved all the furniture so she could scrub each piece."

"So why did you like her, Ben?"

"Because she was a girl. She liked me."

"Guess what, Mom. I've got a girlfriend!"

Here we go again, I thought.

"What's her name?" I asked. *And what girl's going to pay attention to a four-hundred pound loser?* I wondered.

"Kathy," Ben answered. "She really likes me."

"And when do I get to meet this Kathy?" I asked. *Show me the paycheck, Ben. Show me the paycheck.*

"Today. Right now. She's in the apartment next door."

And lo and behold, there was a girl and her name was Kathy. A skinny little thing, a mouse of a girl next to this mountain of a man. She didn't have much to say, though she smiled a lot while I tried to make conversation. And she seemed to like Ben. But why? Why did she like him? Did they have a sexual relationship? How could they? I didn't know. I didn't want to think about it.

All I could see was that Ben was Kathy's hero, her superman. He was smart, he knew the names of states, he read the newspaper, he knew how to put gas in the gas tank, he liked foreign films, he talked a lot, he made her laugh, he was nice to her. Kathy, on the other hand, didn't know the names of states, she didn't read words, she couldn't put gas in the tank because she didn't know how to operate the pump, she only liked cartoons, and she talked a lot about clothes and makeup and how she would look on her wedding day.

Kathy didn't seem to notice what I noticed. That Ben weighed four hundred pounds, that he smelled bad, that when he breathed he whistled. Or she did notice, but she didn't care. She loved Ben's girth because there was lots of room for laying her head on his chest, on his belly, on his thigh. She could do it while he read the newspaper. She could do it while he talked. She could do it while he read the subtitles.

Kathy needed someone big and smart. Ben needed someone who thought he was just fine. God knows, I didn't.

Ben remained at Concerned Living for six months. He would have stayed longer if it weren't for a problem with his health insurance.

"Mom," Ben told me in one of our nightly phone conversations, "they just told me that in two weeks my insurance runs out and I'll have to find another place to live."

"Aren't they going to help you *find* another place?"

"They didn't say anything about that part."

The next place Ben lived was Your Neighbors. I liked the name of that place too.

In that place people lived in unsupervised coed apartments. "Here they are encouraged to live as *normal* a life as possible," read their brochure.

In Your Neighbors, each participant had to sign a contract stating that he or she would be compliant with their meds. They had to agree to go to their doctor's and therapist's and psychiatrist's appointments. They had to agree not to abuse drugs and to practice safe sex. They had to follow an established course of treatment agreed upon with their case managers. If a person was in a day program, he had to continue. If a person was working, she had to keep doing that.

When I moved to Your Neighbors, I kept working at the record store. But I had problems at work and at Your Neighbors right from the start. I detested taking showers and I couldn't wipe myself properly. I smelled awful. My roommates wanted nothing to do with me.

I was eventually fired from the record store because no one wanted to work with me. I lied. I smelled bad. I stole records. I stole money.

I hated my roommates and they hated me. Add to the mix that I still was not right mentally and neither were they. It's rather amazing that no one was killed in that house.

Amazing, indeed. It was not surprising that Ben failed to comply with the agreements stated in his signed contract. He was not compliant with his meds, neither those for his mental health nor those for his physical health. His asthma was out of control and he ended up in the emergency room at least once a week. Also, he stopped taking his psychotropic drugs, and . . .

My mental problems came back with a vengeance. After a year in Your Neighbors in which I actually went backward, not forward, I ended up back at UCLA-NPI.

"This is Mary from Your Neighbors, Mrs. LaSalle. I'm sorry to have to tell you, but . . . Ben is back in the hospital."

"Oh my God! What happened?"

"Well, according to his roommates, he started keeping knives under his bed because he thought he was in danger of being killed."

"Oh."

"Yes, and I'm sorry to have to tell you . . . but his roommates couldn't live with him. Last night they put him in a taxi and told the driver to take him to UCLA's emergency room."

"Where is he now?"

"I'm sorry to have to tell you . . . it was decided he needs to be hospitalized."

"Locked or unlocked?"

"I'm sorry to have to tell you . . . it's locked."

21

REQUEST DENIED

You didn't care about how I felt. All you cared about was getting answers about what was wrong with me. I didn't care about getting answers. All I wanted was to be told nothing was wrong with me.

———

"John, Mary from Your Neighbors called."

"What now?"

"Ben's back in the hospital. NPI 2-West. Same as last time."

"*What the hell happened?*"

"Knives under his bed. Roommates sent him to the ER. ER sent him to 2-West."

"Will this *ever* end?"

No, it never will, I thought. Not as long as I'm Ben's mother. Which means, forever. We're stuck with each other—Ben and me—but which one of us got the worst end of the bargain? Mother or son? Son. This was the ugly truth. No matter what John said to try to reassure me—"You've done everything a mother could"—no matter what my friends said to try to assuage my guilt—"I don't know how you do it"—it was there day and night, burning a self-hating hole in my heart.

Ben was entitled to a mother who accepted, loved, adored, and delighted in him, no matter what. But the terrible truth was—I didn't. Nor could I remember when I had.

"Look, Barbara, we're not getting anywhere. We're going in circles. Ben's going in circles. We have to look somewhere else. We have to try another avenue."

NEUROPSYCHOLOGICAL EVALUATION: *UCLA Neuropsychiatric Institute*
DATE OF BIRTH: 01-31-69
DATE OF TESTING: 12-01-88

Benjamin Levinson was referred for neuropsychological assessment by Dr. Joanne Eisen of UCLA Psychiatric Hospital (2-West,) where Ben was an inpatient. Ben's stepfather, John LaSalle, personally requested that Dr. Satz meet with his son and assess his son's neuropsychological functioning. . . .

Benjamin Levinson is a nineteen-year-old left-handed male with a history of learning disabilities and severe emotional and behavioral problems. . . . This is his second psychiatric hospitalization. . . .

We knew the drill. We knew 2-West, the locked ward with the Shuffling People. We knew the meds that made the people shuffle. Ben had taken these meds all through his months at Concerned Living and Your Neighbors. The meds made him shuffle, but they didn't make him a better neighbor. So this time we tried a different route—a different battery of tests—ones that examined a broader set of questions than the standard psychological tests.

Standard tests ask the questions, *What is wrong with this patient? Is his behavior normal or abnormal? What kind of personality does he have?* They do not provide insight into how different regions of the brain and their connections to other areas may be responsible for the formation of personality and behavior. Merely asking what type of personality one has and determining whether it is normal or abnormal may provide the label, but not the reason.

"Here I am, hospitalized again," Ben said the day he arrived at 2-West for the second time in his almost twenty years of life. "Here I am locked up again. Here I am back without a razor, without a radio, without the right to do what I want, when I want. Here I am again in this loony bin. I'm not crazy. Why does everyone think I'm crazy? *I hate it here. I hate you. I hate everyone.*"

Back again in his orange hospital gown. Orange for crazy, orange for watch out, here comes 2-West. Orange for locked up, muttering, shuffling, staring, smoking, drooling, crazy. Ben's gown was smeared down the front with drops of noodle soup, the six-pack pacifier John and I had stopped to buy on our way to the hospital. His hair was uncombed. He smelled worse than ever. He stared at the polished floor when he spoke, and when I tried to touch him, he shrugged me off.

"I know, sweetie, it's a bummer. But . . . you know—"

"*Know what?* I'm sick and tired of taking tests. I'm not a guinea pig. I'm a person, I'm a—"

"Of course you are, sweetie. But this is a new kind of test . . . maybe this one will help with—"

"*What?* Knowing what to call me? Giving me a label? Don't you know *anything* about me? I don't give a damn *what* they call me. *All I want is to be normal.*"

"I know, sweetie . . . but. . . ." What are my lines now? What am I supposed to say? These pages—son in hospital, son in psychiatric hospital, son taking tests, son taking more tests—are missing from my script.

"All I want is to be a regular person. But they keep telling me I'm not. That I'll never be regular. I'll never be normal."

"*Who* said that?" Oh God.

"What do *you* care? *You agree with them.* You've always agreed with them. *Why don't you admit it? You think I'm as weird as they do.*"

"Not weird, sweetie. It's not that . . . it's. . . ."

"Liar! Fucking liar! You're just like everyone else. *Just go away and leave me the fuck alone!*"

Ben took the tests. He took them in between trips to the hospital cafeteria. One test, one doughnut. Another test, another doughnut.

The findings of the neuropsychological workup were delivered to us the second week of January 1989. In two more weeks Ben would be twenty. *How old*, I wondered, *was the psych intern in her miniskirt and leather boots, reading Ben's chart as if it were just another boring assignment in her race to Ph.D.?*

"I see," she began, "from Ben's previous records that he has taken the Wechsler Intelligence Test several times before."

"Yeah," said Ben. "He has."

It took a few seconds for the intern to realize that Ben was mocking her.

"Ben," she said, "if this is too hard for you, you don't have to stay."

"*What?* And leave my parents here to decide my life? I may be crazy, but I'm not *that* crazy."

"All right, then, Ben. Please remain silent while I read these findings."

"Yes, ma'am," said Ben, turning his chair to face the window.

"It says here that Ben shows a significant difference between his Verbal scores and Performance scores. In fact, the report notes, this is one of the largest discrepancies we have seen in twenty-five years of practice." This must have impressed the intern, because she paused for a moment to look at the prior page. Then she gasped.

"It says here that Ben's Perceptual and Organizational scores indicate that his visual-perceptual skills are grossly impaired. And his ability to recognize faces is severely impaired, placing him in the point-five percentile."

"No shit," said Ben, still facing the window.

"It says here," she continued, "that verbally, Ben places in the ninety-first to ninety-ninth percentile. As for his nonverbal score, it's in the first percentile." Another gasp.

"I've made three copies of the Summary and Impressions. Feel free to read them," she said, handing each of us—Ben, John, and me—a copy.

SUMMARY AND IMPRESSIONS: *Descriptively we see a young man with a profound neurological-cognitive impairment that involves appreciation of visual experience and execution of visually mediated actions and social interactions. . . .*

In our experience, cases who show this disturbance uniformly have major defects in the modulation of affect and bonding with other people. From a developmental standpoint, it has long been recognized that in order to appreciate and react appropriately to subtle social visual cues (often facial), the child must be able to perceive and learn the meaning of these stimuli. As Jerome Bruner and others have pointed out, visual experience plays an extremely important role in social behavior and bonding. . . .

It is very clear that Benjamin was deprived of a major modality of learning during his developmental years. Unable to clearly perceive, under-stand, or integrate much of the visual experience he was presented with as a child, he relied heavily upon auditory cues. . . . Note further that Ben-jamin still reports difficulty in shaving, grooming, combing his hair, and dressing. . . . Furthermore, although Benjamin's language is fluent, it is often disconnected from affect. Difficulty in modulating affect also frequently accompanies profound visuospatial impairment.

Ben finished reading his copy first. "So bullshit fucking what!" Ben screamed. "You don't even know who the hell I am. You don't know me at all. I'm smarter than you, with your fancy degree and your stupid white jacket. I'm smarter than every one of you! You may have the keys to this wacko place, but you don't have *half* the brains I do."

"Ben!" I said. "She's only doing her job."

The intern didn't blanch. "That's OK, Ben. I know this is upsetting. And you're right, you certainly are smart."

"Fuckin' A, I am. *I read before I walked. Did you know that?* Did they tell you that? I read everything. I know more stuff than you'll ever know. I know all sorts of stuff!" Ben said. But before he could finish, he began to sob. He sobbed and sobbed and sobbed. And in between each sob, he wailed, "Just leave me alone. Leave me the fuck alone. Why can't you leave me alone . . . ?"

I was sobbing too. And so was John. Both of us dropped to the floor where Ben lay in a heap—a giant wet orange blob.

Somehow we got through that meeting. But not without multiple trips, walking Ben up and down the hospital corridor—first John, then me. And not without multiple rides up and down the elevator to the hospital cafeteria. Who cared about calories now? Who cared that Ben weighed a ton? My son's heart was broken. It was heavier than all the years of eating, all the pounds of food he had ever stuffed down his throat to make the pain go away. But the pain hadn't gone away. It had only gotten worse.

The test data didn't describe anything I didn't already know about Ben's behavior. But it did provide an explanation. For that, I felt relief. It wasn't my fault. It wasn't Ben's. All it was, was tragic.

For almost twenty years I'd expected my son to behave in a way his brain could not accommodate. For almost twenty years I'd wanted Ben to be one way—mine—but he couldn't. He could only be his way.

What should I do now? Now that I knew that "a great deal of Benjamin's emotional and behavioral problems undoubtedly stem from the frustration he must feel in not being able to interpret much of the social concourse (often visually mediated) around him."

Ben's mental problems were developmental in origin, yet he was stuck in the mental health system, traveling from psychiatric hospital to transitional living center and back again to psychiatric hospital.

He was a foreigner from a different culture trying to make sense of ours, where "gestures and facial expression convey subtle meaning that eludes even the visitor who speaks the language fluently." Ben spoke the language fluently, but what good did that do?

Furthermore, the report said, "many have reported this to be an extremely frustrating and depressing experience, which leads to feelings of being on the 'outside' in every social sphere."

No playdates, no buddies, no invitations, no weekend sleepovers, no parties.

The report made a recommendation. It said he "should be placed in a structured environment where he could be taught fundamental daily skills such as personal grooming and hygiene, housekeeping skills, budgeting, and social skills, which will help overcome some of his developmental deficiencies."

"But wasn't Concerned Living such a place? Wasn't Your Neighbors?" I asked the intern.

"Not exactly. Those places lack the structure Ben needs."

"What she means to say," Ben said, "is that those places let you make your own decisions. They don't tell you what to do every minute of your life. Isn't that what you mean? *Why don't you just say what you mean instead of beating around the bush? Why don't you just the fuck say it?*"

This time Ben remained in the hospital for only two weeks. I visited on Monday, Wednesday, and Friday. John visited on Tuesday and Thursday. We both visited on weekends. One Saturday, we brought David.

"Ben's in the hospital, David. Would you like to pay him a visit?" Better to say, "Ben's in summer camp, David, would you like to pay him a visit? Ben's in college, David, would you like to pay him a visit?" But I didn't get to say what was better; I got to say what was true.

"*Again?* Why *again*? Why does he have to be in there with all those strange people? Can't he come home and live with us? Can't he just come home and live here?" David was wearing his little league uniform, number three. His lucky number. He had just pitched his third straight no-hitter.

"Because, sweetie. . . ." Because what? Because why? Why couldn't Ben just come home and live? Because he spent all his time alone in his room? Because his room was always a mess? Because he ate too much? Because he didn't play ball? Because he's not like you, David?

"Because, sweetie, Ben is having trouble. We need to find a way to help him—"

"But why does he have to be in the hospital? He's not sick, he's just . . . different."

"Does Ben belong in the mental health system, or somewhere else?" I asked the social worker at the time of his discharge from the psychiatric hospital.

"You could try Regional Center, but I doubt that they'll agree to service him," she said.

"Regional Center? What's that?" I asked.

"It's an agency that provides services for people with developmental disabilities like mental retardation, cerebral palsy, and autism," she said, scribbling something on Ben's chart.

Ben was at that meeting too. "Yeah," he said. "That's what they told me. An institution. With retarded people."

"Did they say you were retarded?" I asked.

"No. But they might as well have. They said there's something wrong with my brain. That I'll probably need help for the rest of my life."

"They said that?"

"Yes, they said that. But they didn't have to—I read the report. It's stuck right here between the hemispheres of my big fat useless brain," Ben cried. He was holding his head and reciting the memorized words in between sobs, "He will probably never be able to handle his affairs independently because of his neuropsychological disorder. We recommend that Benjamin be placed—"

"Ben, I won't let anything bad happen to you, I promise. I promise, sweetie—"

"Bullshit! Bad things have always—"

"But Ben, don't you want to learn to take care of yourself? Maybe you can go somewhere for a little while where they teach you how to take care of yourself and then you can live on your own."

"*No!* Just because I can't shave doesn't mean I can't live on my own. Just because I'm fat doesn't mean I can't live on my own. I'm not retarded. I'm smart. That's what's wrong with me. I'm fucking smarter than all of you!"

"Yes, Benjamin, you are smart. Nobody's saying you're not," said the social worker. "Nevertheless, the tests indicate you need help with basic self-help skills. Can you control your eating on your own? Can you manage a checkbook? Can you hold down a job?"

"So what if I can't? So what? I'm still smarter than you!"

"Oh, Ben. It's not your fault. Don't be ashamed. You don't have to be ashamed. It's not your fault."

"But I don't want to be like this," Ben wailed. "Why do I have to be like this? It's not fair! I don't want to be fat. I don't want to be different. I don't want to be a freak. I want friends. I want a job. I want a car and a normal girlfriend and cool clothes. I want to hang out in clubs and dance and stay up late and—"

APPLICATION FOR REGIONAL CENTER SERVICES

These are all the things you must show in order to establish Regional Center eligibility:

1. *The disability originated before age eighteen.*

2. *The disability continues, or can be expected to continue, indefinitely—that is, the disability is chronic and the applicant will require Regional Center case management services throughout his or her lifetime.*

3. *The disability constitutes a substantial handicap.*

4. *The disability falls within one of the following categories:*
   a. mental retardation
   b. cerebral palsy
   c. epilepsy

    d. autism

    e. handicapping conditions found to be closely related to mental
      retardation

    f. handicapping conditions found to require treatment similar to
      that required for mentally retarded individuals

    g. the disability is not solely physical in nature

Dear Mr. and Mrs. LaSalle:

*The Regional Center eligibility evaluation of Benjamin has been completed.
An interdisciplinary team staffing was held on 10/25/89 to review the results
of these evaluations. It was determined that Benjamin does not meet the
requirements for Regional Center eligibility. He is not mentally retarded.
He does not have cerebral palsy, epilepsy, or autism. . . . Your request for services is denied.*

If you do not agree with this decision, you have the right to an appeal. . . .

    Benjamin had been rejected by lots of people and places. Regional
Center was just one more place. So off we went again in search of
another transitional living facility and off Ben went again to another
facility with a happy, healthy, and wholesome name. It wouldn't be
the last.

22

FOUR-POINT RESTRAINTS

The biggest lie I told was the lie I told myself. That I was OK, that nothing was wrong with me, that nothing was bothering me, that I could handle it. Never say you're scared or sad. Only show anger, because then people will be afraid of you. Then they'll leave you alone.

————

FEBRUARY 12, 1989, 7 P.M.: "Hi, Barbara," said John. "I'm leaving Inglewood now. I just brought Ben his air filter. What? Yeah, I visited with him for about half an hour. . . . What? No, I wouldn't say he's fine. He's about as good as can be expected. In any case, I'm leaving now, so I should be arriving in Oxnard at about eight-thirty. Love you. See you then."

FEBRUARY 12, 1989, 7:30 P.M.: "Hello, Mrs. LaSalle? This is Miss Grier from Transitional Living. Ben just fell and hurt his ankle, or leg, or calf, or something. In any case, he can't stay here. Please come and pick him up. Right now."

"*What?* But Miss Grier, my husband just called me a half-hour ago. He was just there to drop off Ben's air filter. He's driving out to Oxnard right now. The distance is at least sixty miles. It'll take him at least an hour and a half to get here. There's no way I can reach him now. He'll be exhausted when he gets back. Can't you keep Ben overnight? Just overnight? We'll pick him up first thing in the morning. I promise."

"Absolutely not. Ben must be picked up this evening. His bags are packed. He'll be waiting for you in the lobby. Good night."

The awful thing still hadn't happened. There were three down, three transitional living places and one to go before it would.

Three trips to the shabbiest sections of Los Angeles County. Three suitcases, each packed with seven pairs of size fifty-two boxer shorts, seven pairs of size fifty-four pants, ten size 5X T-shirts, one pair of tennis shoes, one pair of regular shoes, three packages of sweat socks, one package of dress-up socks, two Walkmans, one portable stereo, one clock radio, fifty tapes, three world maps, one *Thomas Guide*, and as many books as could fit into four doubled-up shopping bags.

The awful thing was waiting to happen. But first there would be yet one more place. One more transitional living program, with its posted schedule of activities, talking-to-themselves roommates, giant TV, weekday counselors, weekend counselors, free time, once-a-week disbursement of P and I (personals and incidentals) money, trips to the mall, movies, bowling alleys, locked knives, therapy groups, and medication lines.

It was a Sunday night. It was a Sunday night in April. It was Sunday, April 29, 1989. Ben had been in Friendship House for three weeks. It was seven o'clock at night, time for Ben's nightly call. It did not come. It was eight o'clock at night. Still no call. Nine o'clock. Ten o'clock. Eleven o'clock.

"John, something's wrong. I know it is."

"Why?"

"It's Ben—"

"What about Ben?"

"He hasn't called. Haven't you noticed? He hasn't called."

"So what? It's good that he hasn't called. Why does he have to call every night? He's twenty years old. Not calling is good."

Not calling *could* be good. But, of course, it wasn't. I knew it wasn't. Ben had called every single night since he was eighteen years old. Ever since his first hospitalization at 2-West, the phone would ring at seven o'clock.

"Hello. This is the operator. Will you accept a collect call from Benjamin?"

"Yes."

"Hi, Ben. What did you do today? How is your asthma? Are you taking your medicine? Do you like your roommate? Do you have any friends? What's planned for the weekend?"

Different operator. Different location. Same questions. Same answers.

"Nothing."

"Fine."

"Yes."

"No."

"No."

"Don't know."

Two years of collect calls at precisely seven o'clock every night. Ben had placed the calls, but it was I who'd waited for them. I who'd planned my nights around them. I who asked the questions. I who listened for the answers, both spoken and unspoken. I who hung up and cried. I who swallowed the Ativan. I who drank two glasses of wine. I who slept a drugged and dreamless sleep.

"It's *good* that Ben hasn't called. Don't call him, Barbara. I'm sure he's fine. Just go to sleep."

So I did. It was April 29, 1989, the night I fell asleep on hope.

And then the phone rang. "Hello, Mrs. LaSalle? This is Bruce, Ben's counselor. Sorry to be calling so late, but something has happened."

"Oh my God! Is Ben all right?"

"Well, yes and no. You see, Mrs. LaSalle, I was off this weekend, and I just got the call."

"*What call?* What are you talking about?"

"Beth, the weekend counselor, called me. She said Ben had been cooking dinner when another resident came into the kitchen. The resident was drunk and yelled at Ben. Ben took a kitchen knife to Beth's office and pointed it at her. He demanded his P and I money. He wanted to leave the facility."

"Oh my God! *Where's Ben now? What happened then?*"

"He cried. He didn't know what to do. He said he was afraid. He put down the knife. He asked Beth to call me. But Beth was afraid. She called the police. She also called the Emergency Response Team. But the cops got there first."

"*Oh my God! Where's Ben now?*"

"In County Jail."

The next thing I remember is sitting on the bedroom floor. I must have handed the phone to John, because it wasn't my voice relating the news. My voice was not working. My body was not moving. My lungs were not breathing. My eyes were staring down at the carpet.

There were some light specks of brown in the beige carpet. The vacuum must have missed them. The carpet felt prickly under my night-gown. We should have chosen the office grade, the one without the plush. I heard a man's voice. It was saying hello and goodbye. It was hanging up. It was saying hello and goodbye again. Hello. Goodbye. Hello and goodbye, five times.

The doorbell rang. It was three o'clock in the morning. "It's the bail bondsman, Barbara. Put on your bathrobe and come downstairs. We have to sign papers."

"OK."

"I called Mike, the cop. I called Sam, the lawyer. I called Ellen and Phil and Grace."

"OK."

The bail bondsman had red eyes. He smelled of alcohol. He showed us the papers. The last one said, "Parties responsible." We signed our names.

Then the phone rang again. John took the call, talked for a few minutes, then hung up. "That was Bruce," he told me. "He said not to bail Ben out just yet. He said County Jail has a good forensics department. He said Ben will receive mental health treatment.

"OK."

IT WAS THE MORNING OF APRIL 30, 1989, and the birds were singing. It was spring. My son was in jail and he hadn't called me. But why hadn't he called me? Didn't everyone who went to jail get one phone call? Who else would Ben have called?

It took four days to discover what kind of mental health treatment Ben was receiving. I found out from a stranger, an angel-stranger who called me the next day.

A jail *trusty* is an inmate. He is locked up, like all the other inmates. But he has earned privileges because he is good or because he has been in jail a long time, long enough to have washed many loads of dishes and folded many uniforms, long enough to have repented and found God and want to do good. Ben's trusty's name was Rocky. He did not tell me his last name. But if he had, I would find him and say, "God bless you."

I don't remember if I said "God bless you" when Rocky called. I only remember *four-point restraints*, *fouled pants*, and *cleaned him up*. I only remember sobbing. I only remember David's arms clutching my legs. I only remember David's words, "Don't cry, Mommy. Don't cry."

I had been told by one of the staff people at Friendship House that I would not be going to jail, that I would be going to a hospital. When the police showed up, I wasn't scared, because I wanted help. When they put the handcuffs on me and put me in the police car, I was too numb to feel anything.

I was taken to the police station, where they asked me some questions: Was I taking medication? Was I suicidal? Did I hear voices? I said yes to all three, thinking that I would be put in the hospital rather than jail. I was told I would have to go downtown to the Men's Central Jail because that was the policy for people who took medication and were suicidal. I was still numb. They put my hands behind my back and put handcuffs on me. It was so uncomfortable. I almost cried. I asked them to please let me wear the handcuffs in the front, but they told me they couldn't do that and put me in the back of the police car.

The policeman driving me asked me if he could stop on the way to get something to eat. I said, "Sure." He went into a drive-through and got something to go, and then we headed toward jail.

On the way to jail, the policeman struck up a conversation with me. He asked me if I thought I was crazy. I said no. He said he didn't think I was crazy either. I didn't know that he was trying to set me up to deny me an insanity plea. When I did go to court, that same policeman testified that I said I wasn't crazy. He said I knew exactly what I was doing. I was defenseless. If they had asked me if I'd wanted to kill someone, I would have said yes. I would have confessed to anything. My brain was not functioning.

Once we got to jail, I was taken to a holding cell. I was told to strip naked and get into a blue jumpsuit. I couldn't fit into the pants, and the deputies made fun of me. One of them went to get me a bigger pair of pants, but even those didn't fit. The deputies told me I was going to have to make do with that pair since they were not equipped to deal with a fat prisoner.

Then I was handcuffed by one hand to the wall. I sat there, waiting for someone to come and get me. It seemed like hours. Finally two deputies came to take me to the jail hospital. They made fun of how fat I was the whole way there. By this time, I was having an asthma attack and needed a breathing treatment. Fortunately, the nurse took pity on me and allowed me to have some puffs of an albuterol inhaler. The deputies wanted me to wait until sick call and stand in line with the rest of the inmates. But the nurse told them I wouldn't last that long.

When I arrived in the hospital, I was taken to a bench in a hallway somewhere in the jail and told to handcuff myself to the wall. I waited there—all day—handcuffed to the wall. Sometimes prisoners would come by, escorted by deputies, and they would point and laugh at me. The deputies paid no attention to me; they acted as if I wasn't there. I began to think I would spend the rest of my life handcuffed to that wall, sitting on that bench. One time I tried to stand up and a deputy told me to sit down or he would break my legs. That was the last time I stood up.

I saw other prisoners eating, so I asked a deputy if I could have something to eat. He told me I could eat flies.

I was taken up to the jail hospital ward by a green-suited trusty. I was put into a small room, about five feet by ten feet, which had an examination table in the middle, a steel toilet, and a sink. There was no window and the light was on the entire time. About an hour later, four deputies and a trusty came in the room and told me the doctor had ordered a shot of Thorazine and four-point restraints. I was told to take off my pants, and the trusty put a diaper on me. Then I was told to lay on the table while the deputies put me in four-point restraints. Then a male nurse came in and gave me a shot of Thorazine. After that, I was left alone. I fell into a deep sleep because of the Thorazine. One of the side effects of Thorazine is uncontrollable bowels, so I ended up pissing and shitting all over myself while I slept.

When I awoke, I was insane. I couldn't move. I couldn't move my head because it was locked in place. I didn't know if it was day or night. I began to scream at the top of my lungs. I screamed to God to let me die. I screamed and screamed and screamed. No one came to help me. I screamed some more.

All of a sudden the door opened, and a man came into the room. He was dressed in the green jumpsuit of a jail trusty. He was bald and covered in tattoos. He seemed like a giant.

"Why the fuck are you screaming?" he shouted.

"I'm in pain. I need help. I've shit all over myself," I said.

"Shut the fuck up. If you scream anymore, the deputies are going to come in here and kill you."

"I need help. Someone, please help me," I sobbed.

"If you stop screaming, I'll help you. But you need to stop screaming because the deputies won't have any sympathy for you. Tell me what you need."

"I've shit all over myself. I can't move and I'm in pain," I said. "Could you take these restraints off me?"

"I can't do that," said the giant. "I'll clean you up, though. Let me go get some gloves and some toilet paper. Don't scream anymore. I'll be right back." Then he left. A few minutes later, he came back with a bunch of things in his hands. "I'm going to clean you up now," he said. "If you can lift up your behind, it would help me a lot." Then he cleaned the shit off me. When he was done, he washed his hands in the sink and turned to me.

"I'm in here because I murdered someone," he announced. "I'm a neo-Nazi gang member and I'm going to be in jail for the rest of my life. While I've been here, I've found God. I've changed the way I think about the world and other people. I want to help you. But you can't scream anymore, because if you do, they'll come in and beat you up. I work on this floor in the evenings, and as long as you're here, I will make sure that you get the help you need. But I'm telling you, you can't scream. OK? If you scream, it will be out of my hands." Then he said, "Do you know when your court date is?"

"No," I said.

"Do you have anyone who can bail you out?"

"My parents."

"What's their number? I will call them and tell them you need to get out of here."

Whom do you call in County Jail when your son is locked up? Do you call the warden and say, "Hello, my name is Barbara LaSalle. My son's name is Benjamin. He is in your jail. May I speak with him please? Can you tell me how he is?"

Do you call the Los Angeles County Jail and press zero for information? "Hello, can you tell me whom to speak to if your son is in four-point restraints?"

Do you call the psychiatrist in charge of four-point restraints and beg him to remove the restraints because, you say, he doesn't know you, he doesn't know your son, but your son—the one in four-point restraints—is not a criminal. He is an innocent, very scared, very fat, very developmentally disabled, troubled young man. He didn't mean to scare that counselor. The drunk man was yelling and he was afraid. He had to get away from the drunk man because the drunk man yelled very loud. My son is afraid of loud. He's always been afraid of loud. The drunk man said mean things about how fat and ugly and useless and stupid Ben was. He had to get away from the drunk man, and to do that he needed his money. So he took the kitchen knife, the one he'd been using to cook with, and brought it to Beth's office, where his money was kept under lock and key. His own P and I, SSI money. He said to Beth, "Give me my money. I need to get out of this place." Then he cried. Then he put the knife down. Then he asked Beth to call Bruce, his weekday counselor. Bruce would help him. Bruce would know what to do. But the cops came first. And now he is in four-point restraints.

The psychiatrist of four-point restraints didn't have much time. "One minute, that's all I have. Tell me fast." So I said all my words in one breath, and the psychiatrist said, "One. I'll take off one. But if he makes any noise, if he yells, if he cries or causes any trouble whatsoever, it's back to four."

Was that the mental health treatment Bruce was talking about?

We called the bail bondsman back. "We made a mistake. Do you still have the paperwork? Can you go to the jail now? *Right now?*"

The bail bondsman could do anything for money. But the jail people didn't care about money. They cared about shifts and schedules.

Ben spent seventy-two hours locked up in Men's County Jail. I spent those same seventy-two hours locked up in my consultation room. My patients talked to me, but I couldn't hear them. I could see their mouths moving. I could see their tears. But what were they saying and why were they saying it? Didn't they know I didn't care?

All I cared about was the phone. The phone, which I could not hear if it rang, because therapists are not allowed to listen for the sound of ringing phones when they are behind closed doors for fifty-minute sessions. I was not allowed to pick it up and ask the only question that mattered: "*Ben, is that you?*"

So I did what I wasn't allowed to do. I moved the phone into my office. I turned it on, and through each fifty-minute session, I waited for it to ring.

It never did.

What I'd like to believe is that God heard me screaming and came down in a form appropriate to the setting. He came down to help me when I needed help, and he came as a bald, tattoo-covered neo-Nazi. I know there is a God, because I experienced his mercy when I was at my most powerless.

23

HOW DO YOU PLEAD?

Your Honor,

I am writing this letter in order to express my profound regret for what I did. I intended no harm, nor did I intend to rob my counselor, Beth, or anyone else. Rather, I was trying to protect myself against a threat, which at the time seemed real to me.

I am also writing this letter to plead with you to not send me back to jail. . . . Your Honor, my experience in the Los Angles County Jail was the worst experience of my life.

Yours truly,

Benjamin Levinson

———

BEN WAS TRANSPORTED to court in a black-and-white bus with bars on the window. His other bus was yellow and made of plastic. It was stored, along with his persons, and his *Child's History of the World*, and his first radio, and his giant *Atlas of the World*, and his unfinished knitting, in a huge box marked "Benjamin" in a brown wooden shed behind our house.

Ben's arraignment was on Wednesday.

"Sharon, can you pick David up from school tomorrow?" I asked my friend on Tuesday afternoon, as soon as we'd received the news that Ben was to appear in court the next day.

"Sure. What's up?" she asked.

What's up?

Oh, nothing much. Except my son is being charged with kidnapping and false arrest. He's been in jail since Sunday night, and I don't know what to say, or how to talk about it, or how he is or how I am. Everything I knew on Saturday is null and void. Who I was on Saturday is null and void. Tomorrow my son is going to court on a felony charge, and will you pick David up from school so I can be there?

Benjamin Levinson. Case number A12-987. People versus Levinson.

Ben's arraignment was at three o'clock on a Wednesday afternoon, but at nine, and ten, and eleven, and every hour till the hour we had to leave for court, I was on the phone. I was trying to reach someone, anyone, who could tell me anything about what to do now, what Ben needed at the arraignment—a lawyer, letters, records—what?

"What happens at an arraignment?" I asked my lawyer friend, Eileen.

"You get formally charged."

"With what?"

"The crime."

Somehow, amongst all those calls, while Ben was in the holding cell, I was put through to a deputy. The deputy had traveled on the same bus as Ben. His job was to guard the prisoners on their way to court and while they were in the holding cell.

"Benjamin Levinson?"

"Yes, sir. That's him."

"Is he fat?"

"Yes."

"Oh . . . that one. . . ."

"How is he, because he's not like the other prisoners, he's an innocent—"

"Innocent? How do you know he's innocent?"

"Oh . . . not that kind of innocent. I mean scared, unsophisticated, confused—"

"Yeah. He's in yellow—"

"What?"

"Yeah. Yellow for dings. Is he crazy?"

"No, I told you. Not exactly crazy. He's developmentally disabled, he's—"

"Look lady. I'm no babysitter. *What do you want?*"

"The trusty said he was having trouble with his bowels and—"

"You mean shit. He reeks of it. Had to segregate him. The other prisoners refuse to sit near him."

"Well, could you help him? Could you clean him up before he gets to court?"

"Told you, lady. I'm no babysitter.

He's in yellow. Yellow, the color of the jumpsuits for dings. *Ding* stands for ding-a-ling, which stands for loony-tunes, which stands for nuts, which stands for crazy. Dings wear yellow, not blue. Blue is for the regular jail population, not the men on Thorazine or in four-point restraints, who come from the streets or—if they're lucky, like Ben— from transitional living facilities. Men who have been diagnosed with developmental disability but have been denied services by Regional Center are dings; so are men with developmental disability who have not been denied services. Dings wear yellow, so the other inmates and deputies and the guards won't make a mistake and treat them like regular inmates.

In jail, regular inmates are in the top echelon because they're rough and tough compared to the dings. Dings are made fun of for being dings.

Fat dings are made fun of more because they are dings *and* fat. Fat dings with shit in their pants are made fun of the most because they are dings, *and* fat, *and* have shit in their pants.

The court was in Bellflower, California. Where's that? How far away? How long would it take to get there? We had to get there early, so we could get a seat in time to be there when they brought Ben in. When they called his name and case number. When they said, "People versus Levinson."

The courtroom had a front part, where the judge, the lawyers, the court reporter, and the bailiff sat. It had a back part for spectators. One by one, the bailiff called the names and case numbers. One by one, the prisoners came in from somewhere in back, from a side door where the holding cell was. Where they were confined, like pigs in a pen, till their number was called.

"Smith. Case number A678502. People versus Smith."

"Gray. Case number B98763. People versus Gray."

Gray wore a blue jumpsuit, and so did Smith. All the prisoners wore blue jumpsuits and all were handcuffed. Some of the prisoners smiled at the spectators; others smirked, as if they didn't care, as if these proceedings were all too boring, as if they could handle it, whatever it was, because they were tough, because they were proud to be tough and too cool to care. Some of the prisoners didn't smile or smirk or look up because maybe they were ashamed to look up, because they weren't too cool to care. They looked scared. But even the scared prisoners wore blue and stood up straight, despite their hands cuffed behind their backs.

Only one prisoner wore yellow. Only one prisoner didn't stand up straight. "Levinson. Case number A12-987. People versus Levinson."

Please, God. I was gripping John's hand. I was holding my breath. I was praying that Ben hadn't split the seams of his yellow jumpsuit, exposing his bare ass. I was praying there were no brown spots on his yellow jumpsuit. I was praying that the judge wouldn't grimace with disgust when Ben stood before him.

None of my prayers were answered. Not a single one. Ben's pants weren't only split, they were torn. His bare ass was exposed. And the brown spots were all over him. The judge gasped. The lawyers gasped. The bailiff and court reporter gasped.

Having his hands manacled behind his back forced Ben to walk bent over like he was crippled. He didn't look up, except for a fleeting second, and in that second I prayed that one of us would disappear.

While he was in the holding cell, Ben told me later, a deputy came in. "Do you want to tell me what happened? What you did?" the deputy asked.

"I want to go home. Can I go home?"

"Do you want to talk to me or not?"

"I don't know. What should I do?"

"Why are you asking me? I'm not your mama."

Ben was not supposed to be arraigned on Wednesday, I learned later. He was supposed to be arraigned on Tuesday.

SUNDAY, APRIL 29, 1989: *I'm arrested.*

TUESDAY, MAY 1, 1989: *My court arraignment is scheduled. But I'm incapacitated by the Thorazine. They stand me up, but I'm so drugged I fall down. My court date is postponed until the following day.*

WEDNESDAY, MAY 2, 1989: *I go to court to be arraigned. I'm still sitting in my own feces. The other prisoners and deputies make fun of me. The prisoners in the court holding cell tell me to "take a shower." They turn on the sprinkler system in the cell. Finally one of the deputies takes me out of the cell and gives me two minutes in a bathroom to clean myself up. It's not long enough.*

I go to the courtroom to be formally charged. I'm appointed a public defender and sent back down to the holding cell. A detective tries to talk to me about my case.

I am taken back to jail.

THURSDAY, MAY 3, 1989: Sometime on this day I'm told I am bailed out. I am taken down to the processing center, where I am then told my bail has been revoked. I am taken back to my cell.

FRIDAY, MAY 4, 1989: I am told I have an additional court date and taken down to the holding cell for transportation. I tell the deputy that I am supposed to be bailed out. He tells me to go fuck myself. I ask another deputy to help me, and he tells me the same thing. Finally one deputy checks the computer and informs me that I should have been bailed out of jail the day before. I am taken back to the processing cell and given my clothes back. I call Mom. It's five in the morning. I am hysterical. That afternoon, Dad takes me to RFK Hospital to the psych ward for admission. I am never so thankful to be in a hospital in my life.

MONDAY, MAY 7, 1989: I am picked up by Dad and taken back home. I spend a week living at home. I'm not allowed to leave the house or be alone with David. On Tuesday we all go back to court.

Ben called at five o'clock Friday morning. "I'm getting out at seven, Mom. Please come and pick me up."

Of course I recognized Ben's voice. He was my son and I had been having phone conversations with him every night at exactly 7:00 P.M. for two entire years. But this time, he sounded far away, as if he were calling from a long distance, a distance not of miles, but of spirit.

They let him out in the back alley with the clothes on his back. He was barefoot because they had lost his shoes. They had also "lost" his watch and his wallet.

He didn't cry till we got back to the house. But when he did, it didn't sound like a cry. It sounded like a wail, like the bawling of a calf who has lost its mother, or the keening of a mother who has lost her son, not once, not twice, but over and over again. It sounded like my cry. But who was it coming from—Ben or me—this agony, this torment? It was coming from both of us, in the same moment, from our different hells, the blending of a life-changing moan, the plaint of two separate sobs mingling into one horrific harmony.

We found a lawyer for Ben. Members of the Learning Disability Association I belonged to referred her. Just any criminal defense lawyer wouldn't do. We knew that for Ben to have any chance, his lawyer would have to be familiar with the territory—areas where humans are not pretty or perfect or just right in the way they learn or think or act.

Her name was Carol Telfer, and she knew what Ben was up against. Ben had held a knife to his counselor and demanded his P and I money. It didn't matter that minutes later he had laid the knife down. It didn't matter that he had cried and asked for help. The judge, she said, would not care that Ben had spun out of control because of his inability to handle the overwhelming stress he felt at the moment the drunk resident yelled in his face. It wouldn't matter that for Ben, yelling causes sensory overload and leads to a flight-or-fight response. Ben *felt* he was under attack. He wasn't really in danger, but he *believed* he was. But the judge, she said, wouldn't care about that either. The judge would think Ben was a threat to society. The judge could throw Ben in prison for a very long time.

We had to find a way to assure the judge that Ben would not be a threat to society, and to do that, she said, it would be best to have Ben placed in a long-term locked mental health facility. We had to find a place to put him before the judge did, and we had to do it fast.

List of Possible Places for Ben:

Olive Vista Center: Locked. Long term. Private pay until client is approved for SSI; $75 a day. Psychiatrist visits once every two weeks. Psychologist on premises four days a week. Group therapy four days a week. Meds. Will take high-, medium-, low-functioning patients. Violent or verbally abusive clients not accepted.

Landmark Medical Center: Locked. Long term. Ninety-four beds. Full. If bed becomes available will accept SSI. Until then private pay at

$74 per day. Gravely impaired. Psychiatrists visit one time per month. Meds monitored by nurse. Counselors. Structured program. Group therapy daily.

Community Care Centers Incorporated: Accepts Medi-Cal and SSI. One hundred and sixty-two bed facility. Locked. Group therapy. Behavioral therapy. Psychiatrist visits two times per month. Will not accept violent, combative patients.

Casa Descanso: No beds available.

Havenbrook: Locked. Will accept SSI. Psychiatrist visits two times per month. Group therapy. Individual therapy by psych intern. Private pay may apply. Nurses monitor meds. If patient becomes violent he is sent to psych ward.

In the days following, we applied to become Ben's conservators. Ben was placed in Havenbrook.

THE COURT: *206, People Versus Benjamin Levinson.*

MS. TELFER: *Your honor, there are a couple of clarifications of the conditions which have already been written on the plea form. The community service time, with the DA's agreement, can be served either at the facility where he has been placed, which is Havenbrook, or at another facility if supervised.*

THE COURT: *Very well.*

MS. TELFER: *And the "no day passes by self" means he goes to AA and OA meetings, where a staff takes him there and picks him up from there, and the DA is in agreement that that's—*

THE COURT: *Very well. . . .*

MR. MAZUR: *Now, this particular offense carries a maximum penalty of three years. When it's seen in light of the use of a knife, it carries a maximum of four years. However, based on the special situation that you were involved in, the People have agreed that you should be placed on five years of formal probation . . . Mr. Levinson, do you understand?*

DEFENDANT: *Yes.*

MR. MAZUR: *Has anyone threatened you or anyone close to you to get you to admit your guilt?*

DEFENDANT: *No.*

MR. MAZUR: *Are you pleading guilty freely and voluntarily?*

DEFENDANT: *Yes, I am.*

MR. MAZUR: *I'm going to ask you in a more formal way—Mr. Levinson, how do you plead?*

DEFENDANT: *Nolo contrary [sic], sir, no contest.*

THE COURT: *Court accepts the plea of no contest entered by the defendant.*

MS. TELFER: *This is Mr. and Mrs. LaSalle, who are the parents of Mr. Levinson.*

THE COURT: *All right.*

MR. MAZUR: *I just want to say one quick thing. Mr. Levinson, the People have entered into this plea agreement in the belief that, given the structure of the Havenbrook facility, this type of incident won't happen again, but, needless to say, it really depends entirely on you, and you have to take responsibility for your actions. And it is our hope that five years from now you'll never have to be bothered by us again.*

THE COURT: *The defendant is placed on five years' formal probation under the following terms and conditions: He is to receive credit for five days' time served. He is to perform 250 hours of community service. Is this a voluntary hospitalization?*

DEFENDANT: *No, sir.*

MS. TELFER: *Excuse me. (A conference was held between Ms. Telfer and Mr. and Mrs. LaSalle.)*

MS. TELFER: Your Honor, Mr. and Mrs. LaSalle have conservator powers to keep him there, but he is also there voluntarily.

THE COURT: All right. Mr. Levinson, do you understand and accept the terms and conditions of probation imposed by the court?

DEFENDANT: Yes.

THE COURT: That will be the order.

24

ENDLESS, SPARKLING
AMMONIA-BLEACHED CORRIDORS

*I hated that place from the moment I walked in. I thought I was being pun-
ished for being a bad person, which made me hate it even more.*

———

"DAD, ARE YOU COMING to see me this Saturday?" Ben placed the call
to John, as he always did, from the pay phone located next to Havenbrook's basement cafeteria.

"I come every Saturday. Of course I'll be there."

"That's great, because I got a pass for next Saturday so you can take
me out. Isn't that great? We could go to the Third Street Promenade!"

"You got a pass?"

"Yeah."

"But why? Don't you have to be there longer . . . before you earn a
pass, don't you have to—"

"Earn points. You have to earn enough points to get a pass. That's
why they gave it to me."

"Good for you, Ben—"

"So, anyway, could you get here early? The weekend counselor gets here at nine in the morning. So could you get here then?"

That Saturday morning, John drove thirty miles to see Ben. He had been making the same trip three times every week for the first month of what would turn out to be Ben's three-year stay at Havenbrook.

By blood and biology, John was one step removed from Ben. That was why, I told myself, his expectations of Ben were so different from mine, which in turn was also why, I told myself, he should be the one to do it. Visit Ben.

It didn't kill John to announce himself to the underpaid, bored, foreign-speaking attendant whose job it was to stand guard at Havenbrook's double-locked doors. It didn't make the hair on *his* skin prickle with outrage and humiliation as he walked through the cafeteria to the sound of open-mouthed, unmannered chewing. It didn't kill John to drive thirty miles back and forth three times a week to visit Ben, because for John it was different. Ben wasn't his son.

That Saturday, the Saturday of Ben's pass, John hit traffic, and didn't get there till half past ten. By then, Ben was ready and raring to go. He had been pacing up and down on his side of the double-locked doors for over an hour.

"Let's go, Dad," Ben said as soon as the attendant pressed the admittance bell, allowing John inside. "I have to be back by dinnertime. That's four-thirty. I'm all ready. All we have to do is get me checked out at the nurse's station."

"OK, Ben. Lead the way."

Even on Saturdays the corridors sparkled. The nurse's station was three long corridors away from the front entrance. They made it in record time, because Ben, John told me later, had never walked so fast.

"Hi, I'm Benjamin Levinson," Ben said to the weekend nurse. This was Ben's fourth Saturday at Havenbrook. By then, Ben had learned to expect a different nurse each day of the weekend. He wouldn't be familiar with her face, and she wouldn't be familiar with his.

"How do you do, Benjamin, I'm Nurse Shar. How can I help you?"

"Well, I have a day pass. This is my stepfather, John LaSalle, and he's here to take me out for the day."

"Wonderful! I bet you can't wait . . . and if you don't mind my asking, what do you have planned for today?"

"We're going to the Third Street Promenade," Ben said, all smiles.

"Oh. What a nice day for that. I just need to check the pass list and you'll be on your way." Then she picked up the clipboard marked "Pass List" from its hook on the wall and looked at it. "Just a sec, Ben, let me check one more time . . . I don't see your name here."

"Well, it's there. *It has to be.* I was told on Thursday, Pass Day, that I had a pass for this Saturday. Please check again."

"I just did, Ben. Your name is not on it."

"Look," said John, already testy from the traffic and not in the mood for another jam-up. "Ben called me on Thursday and told me he had earned a pass. That's why I'm here so early. That's why I sat in traffic for an hour on a Saturday morning."

"I'm sorry, Mr. LaSalle, but there's nothing I can do. I'm just the weekend nurse and my instructions are explicit: no one leaves without a pass."

"*But I have a pass!*" Ben yelled.

"All right, then," said the nurse. "It's probably just a mistake. Let me look up Nurse Susan's number," she said, pulling open drawers and tearing down pieces of paper pinned to the wall. "I'm sure it's here somewhere."

"But it's already eleven o'clock. Half the day is gone. Can't you just take my word and give me the pass?" Ben demanded.

"You know I can't do that . . . wait just a minute . . . I think I found it," the nurse said. "Yes, it's right here, Susan Williams. That's her. She's the one who hired me. I'll call her right now."

Nurse Shar, the weekend nurse, dialed Nurse Susan's telephone number. "I'm sorry to bother you, Susan," she said, "but I have a patient here by the name of Benjamin Levinson. He has a pass for today, but for some reason I can't seem to find his name on the—"

Then, midsentence, she stopped. The sunny expression on her face dissolved.

"Do you care to know what Nurse Susan said, Ben? Do you want me to tell you in front of your father?" Nurse Shar said, putting down the receiver.

"What? What did she say?" Ben exclaimed.

"What? What did she say?" John repeated.

"What did she say?" said Nurse Shar. "She said, 'Benjamin Levinson? Are you kidding? Benjamin Levinson? He absolutely does not have a pass.' Then she said some words I prefer not to repeat, and then she said, and here I quote, 'Don't believe a word that boy says.' She said, 'That boy is a liar and under no circumstances is he to leave these premises.' That's exactly what she said."

HAVENBROOK SMELLED LIKE canned lunchmeat. It smelled like ammonia-soaked floors. The canned lunchmeat floated in a sea of bodies, and the sea of bodies smelled of bleach, disinfectant, and ammonia. The floating bodies were mostly male and moved ever so listlessly, ever so slowly, because why would they move faster when there was no place to go? Today melted into yesterday. Yesterday melted into today. And there was so much time, such a long way to go. The only route to get where you were going was through the corridor. The endless, sparkling ammonia-clean corridor.

Up and down. Down and up. Back and forth. And you do it over and over again, because there is nothing else to do.

When you have a visitor you do it with him or her—walk up and down, down and up, back and forth. Just like you did in 2-West. Especially if you do not smoke, because smoking is an activity, too—it takes up time, it is something else to do, and you do it outside in the yard, not in the corridor.

So when I came to visit Ben, even though I didn't want to, even though I hated the place for its very nature, its nature I could not accept any more than I could accept my son's nature, I did it by way of the corridor. Ben's addiction was food, not cigarettes, so unless we wanted to be in a haze of tobacco smoke, we stayed inside.

Another place, another round of questions, because what else was there to talk about?

"What did you do today?"

"How is your asthma?"

"Are you taking your medicine?"

"Do you like your roommates?"

"Do you have any friends?"

"Are there any outings planned?"

To be quiet, to not ask questions, was to risk sitting in that empty place, that place under the words, beneath the superficial layer of questions. So I asked the same meaningless questions. I stayed for the answers, though I knew they were lies, and after that I got into my car and screamed.

For thirty miles.

If I hated that place so much, how could Ben bear it? At least I got to go home and do whatever I wanted to do, whenever I wanted to do it. I got to lock my bathroom door. My bedroom was my sanctuary; but it was more than a bed, it was a cozy chair, a closet of my own, a warm carpet for cold days, a spacious, curtainless room with a collage of family photos. I could eat when I wanted to, or not eat at all. My body would say, "You're tired. Go to sleep." It could be 9:00 P.M. or midnight or any time at all. My body would say, "You're hungry. Get something to eat." It could be 9:00 P.M. or midnight or any time at all.

I was given a room with seven other men. We had one bathroom between us. For privacy, there was a curtain around each bed. It was a hospital curtain. The only personal space I had was the area surrounding my bed. My bed became a sacrosanct place, a place of my own that I'd allow no one to violate. The same for everyone. You didn't sit on their bed. You didn't come into the space beyond their curtain unless you were invited. If you did, it was cause for a fight. When the curtain was closed you "knocked."

Beyond the curtain, there was no privacy anywhere. Bathrooms were public and shared. It didn't matter if you were taking a shower and someone had to come in and take a shit; he was going to do that and that was that. If you wanted to take a shower in the morning and you wanted hot water, you had better get up early.

They woke you up with the screech of a loudspeaker: "Good morning. Line up for meds." The loudspeaker was mounted above the door to my room and it erupted throughout the day. "Attention all patients! Groups A and B3, please meet Mary Jo in the Common Room for Money Management!" "Attention all patients! P and I money is now being distributed. Line up in the cafeteria!" "Attention all nursing staff! A medication in-service will begin at 1:00 P.M. in the staff room." "Attention all patients! Dinner will be served in ten minutes. Please go downstairs now!" "Attention, all patients! It is now time for lights-out. Please go to sleep. Good night!"

Ben, the boy who hated loud, was now the man who hated loud, the criminal who had wielded a knife for fear of loud; and now he was living in a mental facility that blared its loudness day and night. He hated that place and would run if he could. But the doors were locked. Nurses and doctors, and people training to be nurses and doctors, walked up and down the corridors with keys tied to their waists. The keys were no more quiet than the loudspeaker—they jingled and jangled—a mocking, taunting, teasing daily reminder: you're locked in, you are, you are.

"Take me home. Please, mister, please take me home," pleaded Matthew, the brilliant playwright whose "voices" began when he was twenty-one. The voices did not come from his characters, nor did they come from his rich imagination. They were unbidden, these voices; they spoke when they were not spoken to; they told him who was after him and why. The FBI and the CIA were after him. They knew where to find him, they were on their way, they would be there any minute, so "Please, mister, please take me home," he'd say each time we passed.

"No, Matthew, I can't take you home. But I can talk with you. Would you like to talk?" John would ask while I pulled at his sleeve.

I was afraid of Matthew and his voices, just as I was afraid of Carol's voices, and Jean's and Craig's and Terry's. I was afraid of all the voices trailing up and down the corridors of Havenbrook. I tried to attach each voice to a person, but the people at Havenbrook had too many voices to keep up with. And I couldn't have a conversation with them—these voices—because they didn't make sense. They said things that scared me, like their beds were bugged, their food was poisoned, they were going to hell, they were going to heaven, they were Jesus, or Mary, or God himself. All I wanted was to run upstairs to Ben's curtained cubicle, ask him my litany of questions, get in my car, and drive back home. I needed my scream. Only a scream could exorcise the voices, the smell of ammonia-bleached floors, the muttering people, the jangle of keys, and the sight of my son. Only a scream could get the picture of him out of my head—Ben lying there behind the curtain, headphones attached to his ears—enormous, mountainous, massive rolls of him lying, like a beached whale, on his bed.

For Ben it was one eye exercise in exchange for one chapter of his *Child's History of the World*. One brain test in exchange for one doughnut. For me it was one visit to Havenbrook in exchange for one thirty-mile scream, one shriek, one howling outcry in the privacy of my car.

ACTIVITIES OF DAILY LIVING
Money management: 1 point
Group therapy: 5 points
Understanding your meds: 4 points
Arts and crafts: 1 point

Social committee: 2 points

Singalong: 1 point

Grooming and hygiene: 3 points

To get your points, you have to be there, you have to participate in Activities of Daily Living, you have to show up, sit down, and raise your hand. Then you get your points. You want your points. You need them for your weekend pass. Without them, you'll have to spend Saturday and Sunday walking up and down corridors, or washing a staff person's car, or going with the other residents who were too tired, or drugged, or resistant to the bowling alley or the movies or the dollar store.

"The best days are when one of the staff takes us to the Third Street Promenade in Santa Monica and lets us go window shopping," Ben told me in answer to my question, "What do the people without passes do on weekends?"

"What about the days you go to the movies? Don't you like that?"

"I would, if I liked the movie. But we take a vote for which movie to see, and the majority wins. The majority is sleepwalking."

"So why don't you work on getting your points, Ben? Then you'd get a pass and could come home for the weekend!"

"What? And go to those stupid groups with all those sleeping people? I hate those groups. The people leading the groups are dumb as doornails. The people attending are crazier than loons. I'm not dumb *or* crazy. Why the hell should *I* go?

"Then why are *you* here, Ben?"

"*Because of you!* You put me in this godforsaken place. You and Dad got conservatorship over me and shipped me off to this nut house."

"But why, Ben? Why did we do that?"

"Because of what happened at Friendship House. But why did I have to go there in the first place? Why did I have to go to any of those horror houses? There's nothing wrong with me. I'm fine, I'm better than fine, I'm smarter than you, I'm smarter than—"

"Ben, it has nothing to do with smart, you know it doesn't. It's about living. Just living your life, just getting along with people, just holding a job, just brushing your teeth, just taking a shower, just wearing regular-size clothes, just not lying, just understanding the rules of—"

Just going round and round in the same merry-go-round dialogue. I was trying to grab the gold ring, the one that would bring Ben back from the strange and terrifying territory he inhabited, a territory I could not understand, a territory I did not want to understand. Why did *I* have to understand Ben's territory? It wasn't mine. It wasn't John's or David's. No one else I knew inhabited Ben's territory, so why should *I* have to understand him? It was *Ben* who should study *our* rules, *our* ways of social conduct, *our* mannerisms, *our* interests, *our* way of life. It shouldn't—should it?—have to be the other way around.

That's what I thought in the privacy of my heart, but in public—in staff meetings where nurses and nurses' aides, and Ben's psychology intern, and Ben's psychology intern's supervisor gathered in great monthly confabs—I was a mother tigress. *How is Ben*, they'd ask. *Is he going to group? Is he getting up on time? Is he showering, shaving, is he socializing with the other patients? He isn't? What is his problem? Is it laziness, rebellion, arrogance? What do you think it is*, they'd ask me, and I would bristle back. Ben always sat in on these monthly individualized treatment program planning meetings, and I didn't like these people talking about him as if he weren't there. I didn't like them ganging up on him as if he were on trial. I didn't like them embarrassing him, asking personal questions about him in front of an entire room full of people, in front of me, his mother.

I would sit at these meetings, my arm around Ben, and I would speak for him. "He doesn't like group because the people running it aren't smart," I'd say in front of the people running it. "He insults the nurses' aides, the ones who get paid $4.50 an hour. He asks them when they expect to be picked up by the INS, because they wake him up in the middle of the night and drag him down to the nurses' station to take his vital signs." *He doesn't like the nurses, the nurses' aides, the psychologist, the psychologist's supervisor, or this dreadful place, which smells worse than it looks,* I wanted to tell them. *He doesn't like you and neither do I,* I wanted to say. *He doesn't care if he's insulting you, because why should he? You insult him.*

His mother doesn't care either, because you don't get it. You think my son belongs here, you think he's schizophrenic or schizoaffective, or bipolar, or personality disordered, or mood disordered, or a combination of all of these. You think it's these psychiatric disorders that brought him here. You think mental problems explain why he acted so inappropriately when the drunk man yelled in his face. You think he is mentally ill the same way the rest of the people in this place are. Well, you're wrong! Do you think mental illness explains why he's always been a walking encyclopedia of knowledge? Do you think mental illness explains why he read so early and walked so late, why he doesn't make eye contact, why he lies, why he's clumsy, why he's afraid of change, why he spends all his time alone? Well, you're wrong! He's something else, something else in an entirely different category, and you of all people should know what it is.

I'll show you! I'll hunt down every book, every medical journal, every article about the brain and how it works, every periodical on human development, and I'll march right back in here next month with the entire stack in my hands. I'll have an answer then, a true, right answer to what is wrong with my son, and it will be right there on the page in black and white!

More than anything, I hated singalong. They made you sing Peter, Paul, and Mary songs, like "If I Had a Hammer," or "Puff, the Magic Dragon." They expected you to sit there like a three-year-old, like you were in preschool, and sing all those lame songs.

The staff had a meeting about me and figured out that I belonged in the low-functioning group. Their evidence was that I wouldn't follow directions,

I wouldn't go to any of the ADLs (Activities for Daily Living). I refused to socialize with the other patients.

Also, just like I used to at home, and at Concerned Living and Your Neighbors, I lied. I told one version of a story to one staff person and another version to another one. Sometimes I didn't even know the truth myself, but even if I did, I wasn't going to tell them.

The last straw was when I claimed to have a medical appointment in Westwood. The van driver was responsible for taking people to their medical appointments, dropping them off, and picking them up when they were done. So he took me to the address I gave him. But he didn't drop me off. He parked and came into the building with me. I hadn't planned for that. We stood in front of the directory looking for my doctor's suite number. "I don't see that doctor's name," the van driver said. "He's not in this building. If he even exists at all. Ben, does he even exist at all?"

After that incident I was shipped off to the psych ward at RFK Hospital. This was my third trip to that particular psych ward. By this time they knew my name.

25

PASSES

It's funny how a single person can make such a life-changing impact. For me, Doreen was that person. She saw the positive in me, while everyone else saw the negative. She believed I could turn my life around, and she made me believe it too.

———

"KATHY, WOULD YOU LIKE to help me fold the sheets?"

I asked this question because I didn't know quite what to say to Ben's girlfriend. Yes, girlfriend.

By this time, year three of Ben's stint at Havenbrook, Ben was receiving regular weekend passes.

Yes, passes. Ben could now spend whole weekends away from the facility, as long as he remained in John's and my care. It had taken two whole years, but he had finally cleaned up his act.

One day, a few weeks earlier, as Ben and I walked up and down the corridors, I saw someone who looked like Kathy, Ben's old "girlfriend" from his days in Concerned Living. But I couldn't be sure, because this girl was fat—not as fat as Ben, but still fat. "Ben, who's that?" I asked Ben. "She looks like Kathy."

"She is Kathy, Mom."

"Oh . . . what's she doing in this place?"

"They shipped her here, just like me."

"Oh . . . did she . . . uh . . . *do* something?"

"No, she didn't do anything. That's why they sent her here. She *can't* do anything. She can't even read."

"*She can't read?* But she speaks so well, she sounds—"

"Smart? Well, she isn't. But she's not stupid, either. It's just that she can't do anything. She burns stuff when she cooks. She can't take the bus, because she always gets lost. She—"

"She can't take the bus? She can't read? Two of your best things—figuring out bus routes and reading. I don't get it, Ben—why did you like her?"

"I already told you, Mom. She's a girl and she likes me. She liked me in Concerned Living and she likes me here. She's my girlfriend."

"Oh."

When I was sent to RFK, I thought it was a one-way ticket, because by that time I thought Havenbrook was sick of me and they'd never let me back. At first I didn't care, because I didn't want to go back. But when it dawned on me that there was a real chance I could end up in jail, I was overjoyed when they took me.

Back at Havenbrook, I had to start all over again as a "new" patient. Now I shared a room with three other "new" people right next to the nurses' station. I had to attend new patient orientation, and for an entire month I wasn't even allowed to go on group outings. They told me they'd be watching me closely, that I'd better follow the rules to the letter or I'd be shipped out, and this time I wouldn't be coming back. I wouldn't have made it if it weren't for Doreen.

"Ben," Doreen said on Ben's first day back from the psych ward, "You're in my group now, and I'm gonna tell it to you straight."

"What?"

"I know you hate it here. But you're doing nothing to move yourself out. If you want out you have to show people you're trustworthy. You have to stop lying and you have to follow the rules. You have to follow them to the letter."

"But I hate those ADL groups, they're so useless, so—"

"Look, Ben," Doreen interrupted. "Are you prepared to spend the rest of your life in this place?"

"No."

"Well, then, I don't care *what* you think of the groups. The rules say you go to group, and that's what you do. Period."

"But—"

"I wasn't going to tell you this, but I can see you don't get it, Ben. The consensus of the staff is that you'll have to spend the rest of your life in an institution. Do you want to prove them right?"

"No! They're wrong. They're dead wrong."

"Then prove it, Ben. *Prove them wrong!* Get with the program. Don't fight it. Don't resist. And I promise you . . . you'll get out."

There was something about Doreen that was different from the rest of the staff. She was the only one who sat me down and talked to me like that. Like she cared. Like I mattered. Like she really wanted to help me get out of that place.

So that evening, I had a talk with myself. It was obvious I was going nowhere fast. I decided then and there that I was going to follow the Haven-brook program to the letter. I would tell the truth. I would go to every ADL group, whether I wanted to or not.

The next morning I got up as soon as the loudspeaker said, "Good morn-ing." I was the first to take a shower. I shaved. I showed up for breakfast. I went to every one of my groups. I even went to singalong and sang "If I Had a Hammer."

At first the staff thought it was just another one of my manipulations. But after a while, they saw I was serious. That this was no game. I began to get perks. First I got to move to a two-person room upstairs, away from the

nurses' station. Then I began to earn passes. First, day passes. Then week-
end passes. I was allowed to take a broadcasting class at Santa Monica City
College. Once, they even let my parents take Kathy and me home with them
for the weekend.

"Kathy," I said, "would you like to help me fold the sheets?" It was
the first time I'd been alone with this girl, this girlfriend, Ben's date for
the weekend, and all I could think to talk about was laundry.

The weekend had begun on Friday afternoon, when I went to pick
them up. I stood on the outside of the double-locked doors, waiting to
be let in, and there they were—on the inside, waiting to be let out. I saw
them through the glass before they caught sight of me, each with a backpack, each with a portable stereo, peering out beyond the door. They
were looking for something, but that something wasn't me. Because
there I was, right in front of them, and yet they kept looking, as if they
were on a search that went far beyond what I could offer. I saw it in their
eyes, intent, fixed, straight ahead. It was as if whatever they were looking for was so far off in the distance, they couldn't see what was right
before their eyes. They couldn't see me seeing them, because it wasn't
me they were looking for. It was something else, something bigger than
a single person, something beyond the means of any person, because it
was—this something they were looking for—beyond any person's
means.

"Would you like to help me fold the sheets?" I asked Kathy on Sunday morning, day two of her and Ben's weekend pass. One and a half days
had passed since I had stood in front of the nurses' station at Havenbrook signing the pass list, checking them out.

"Benjamin Levinson. OK, let me see. Two whole days and one night.
That's meds for Friday and Saturday nights. That's meds for Saturday
day and Sunday day. Right?" Nurse Susan wasn't asking, she was talking
to herself, unlocking the drawer marked "Meds," counting out the foil-
wrapped packages. She was handing me a clipboard, she was pointing to

the line that said, Time, Date, Patient, Responsible Party. She was waiting for me to sign.

"Kathy Clair. OK, let me see," said Nurse Susan, going through the
entire procedure again. "That's a lot of meds, Mrs. LaSalle. Do you need
a bag?"

"Please," I said. Plastic or paper? Better or worse? Eye therapy or
movement therapy? *A Child's History of the World* or *A Child's Geography of the World*? American cheese or peas in the pod? Will you be the
daddy or the radio? Is it a lie or is it true? Is this what I'm doing—checking my son out of a locked psychiatric facility, or is this a mistake? Is this
my son, all four hundred pounds of him, or does this body struggling to
get into my car belong to another boy's mother?

Ben sat in the passenger seat next to me, and Kathy sat behind me in
the back. Still, the car felt like it was tipping to the right. Now I was asking two sets of questions—one to Ben, the other to Kathy. I could do
that. I could be social, gracious, even entertaining, and at the same time
I could worry about sleeping arrangements. Ben had already told me
where he would be sleeping: "In the guest bedroom. In the big bed. I
can't wait to sleep in a big bed again." But where, I wanted to know,
would Kathy sleep? And if she too wanted to sleep in the big bed, what
would she do when she got there?

When I first met Kathy, Ben's first and only girlfriend, my mind kept
picturing them in bed together. It was the last thing I wanted to think
about, but I couldn't help it, my mind kept landing there.

Ben's body parts, his belly, chest, neck, arms, thighs, butt, legs, and
feet had no body part shape. Put together, they made up one large
mound, with hills in various places. I had seen the hills up close. I had
visited them with their hairy curls of chest clumps, their cup-sized
breasts. I had seen their lumpy lines of stretch marks marking the landscape. I tried not to visit; I begged off, saying, "I'm too tired to tuck you
in tonight. I'll kiss you now, OK, before you get into bed?" But which
was worse: revulsion at the sight of my own son's body or revulsion at

my own incapacity to mother? So whenever Ben slept at home, I got to visit the mound and the hills and the hair and the markings. I got to sit on the bed next to them, and pat them on the forehead, and kiss them on the cheek. I got to listen to their wheeze and their whistle and then, finally, after I had counted the minutes, when it was not too soon to leave, when I could no longer hold my breath or tears or nausea, I got to leave.

I didn't ask Kathy, "How could you be attracted to Ben? How could you have sex with him? How could you touch him, or find his penis to touch?" My mouth asked regular mother-sized questions, but just like my son, who himself was not regular-sized, my thoughts were not regular-sized either.

Instead, I said, "Kathy, would you like to help me fold the sheets?"

"Sure," answered Kathy, "I'll try to fold the sheets . . . but I'm not very good at that kind of stuff."

"What kind of stuff, Kathy?"

"You know, house stuff. Kitchen stuff, laundry stuff, cleaning stuff."

"Oh."

"I never learned. My grandmother raised me and she never let me do anything."

"That's OK," I said. "It's easy. You'll get the hang of it."

But Kathy didn't get the hang of it. I held up one corner of the sheet and she held up the other. But the sheet kept dropping to the floor, and each time it dropped Kathy bent down to pick it up. But when she picked it up, she'd drag it on the floor. "I'm sorry," she said. "It's all dirty now. Now you'll have to wash it over again. And it's all my fault. It's always my fault. I told you I couldn't do it, I told you. . . ." And then she ran off. Crying.

"Don't worry, Mom," Ben said. "That's just the way she is."

At that moment I realized that Ben understood Kathy, in the same way, perhaps, as I understood him. Kathy was his girlfriend. He was looking out for her. It didn't matter whether their relationship was sexual—if they did it, or how they did it. What mattered was that Ben had found someone to care for.

Ben was on a weekend pass, in John's and my care, while Kathy, his girlfriend, was in his.

Day passes, weekend passes, passes to take the bus to school, passes to take the bus to medical appointments, passes leading out beyond the double-locked door. Passes to bigger and better things. Passes leading Ben to believe he was not only on his way out of Havenbrook but also on his way to a normal life, with places to go and people to go with. Passes not only to hope but to dreams. Grandiose dreams of who he could be and how he could be it. Dreams his precocious mind and rich imagination had been feeding all his lonely life.

26

THE HAPPIEST DAY

It was the first time a doctor made sense. What he said didn't sound foreign; it sounded familiar and it didn't make me angry.

———

"Can you bring in his files?" asked Dr. DeAntonio when I called to set up an appointment for Ben.

Ben was tired of doctors. He'd spent his entire life being examined by them, and toward what end? Toward satisfying his mother's need for an answer to the question, *What's wrong with my son?* It wasn't Ben's question, these doctors—with their scans, and scores, and schedules of medicine—were addressing. It was his mother's. And why did she need to know, anyway?

So what if he was fat?

So what if he had no friends?

So what if talked like a college professor?

So what if he had one-sided conversations?

So what if he read the same books over and over again?

So what if he preferred his own company?

Why couldn't she simply accept that that's the way he was and just leave him alone?

No, Ben didn't like doctors. All they did anyway was open their giant textbooks of psychiatric diseases. All they did was read down their list of symptoms and ask their stupid questions. *Do you hear voices? Do you stay up all night dreaming up wild schemes? Do you have thoughts of killing yourself? How many times do you check the door to see if it's locked? If you have had thoughts of killing yourself, exactly how would you do it? Is anyone after you? Exactly who is after you?* And on and on until they were satisfied.

He knew what they were doing. They were trying to squeeze him into one of the lists in their giant textbooks of psychiatric diseases. They were trying to stuff him into a category and stick a label on him.

He'd already been stuck with every label in their books, every single one of them. Has the subject heard voices? Well then, he is schizophrenic. Has he stayed up all night concocting grandiose schemes? Well then, he is manic depressive. Has he had thoughts of killing himself? Clinically depressed. Has he checked the lock on his door twenty-five times, after which he turns three times around in a circle and touches his toes? Obsessive-compulsive. Depending on which doctor examined him and which list of symptoms that doctor checked off—that's who he was, that's what he had, that's the label the doctor scribbled down in his file.

No, Ben didn't like doctors. And he definitely, absolutely *did not* want to see one more.

"Please try again, Ben. Maybe this one will be the last." Ben was twenty-three at the time and about to get discharged from Havenbrook.

I was still on the hunt to find out what was wrong with Ben because even though I had read all the books, medical journals, articles about the brain, and periodicals on human development I could find, I still hadn't tracked down what I was looking for. For that matter, what *was* I looking for?

But I did know one thing. I knew that—despite Ben's protests to the contrary—Ben needed structure. It was the structure at Havenbrook that had made all the difference in Ben's behavior. I had seen it with my own eyes. His weight was the barometer of that. In those first two years at Havenbrook, when Ben was not earning passes, he ate what they served him. No more, no less. And he lost weight. Lots of weight. One hundred pounds' worth.

But in the third year, when he was earning passes, when he was going to school, when he was using his P and I money to eat out, he gained weight. Lots of weight. One hundred pounds' worth.

"It's because I'm rushed, Mom. I have to be on time for the van driver when he comes to pick me up after class. I have to eat at school, because by the time I get back to Havenbrook the kitchen's closed. And all they have in the food mall is fast-food places."

Hamburgers and fries. Sometimes only one order of each—but sometimes, depending on how much money he had in his pocket, more. During Ben's last months at Havenbrook, he was working off his 250 community service hours at the broadcasting lab at the college. In his last month at the facility, he had landed a real job at a real radio station. He earned real money. The real part was good, but the money part was bad, because it earned him back the one hundred pounds he'd lost when he wasn't earning passes. When he was poor, Ben dined at McDonald's, and when he was rich, he gave his business to Carl's Jr. The structure of Havenbrook, before passes, when he was locked up and couldn't eat what he pleased, had saved his life. Without it, he was killing himself.

So if Ben was ever to live on his own—which he insisted he could, which I wanted him to—he was going to need help. Hands-on help. But not my hands. My hands were weary from battle fatigue. My hands were worn raw from too much tangled twine twisting between us.

The place that provided that kind of help, that kind of structure, was Regional Center, but the first time we applied the center had rejected Ben, claiming he was not a candidate for their services based on their diagnostic requirements. He wasn't retarded. He wasn't epileptic. He wasn't autistic.

Some time during his second year at Havenbrook, we appealed that decision. This time Ben was accepted for services, though he would not be able to make use of them until he "graduated" from Havenbrook. The administrative hearing officer presiding over his appeal agreed that Ben did not meet the diagnostic requirements of Regional Center, but he wrote in his decision, "In this case, given the severity of claimant's substantial handicapping condition, which originated prior to his attainment of age eighteen, and because it is likely to continue indefinitely insofar as his continued need for structured and repetitious interventions is concerned, claimant has a developmental disability."

But what *was* Ben's "severe handicapping condition"? Even the hearing officer agreed that it wasn't mental retardation, epilepsy, or autism. I couldn't stop searching for the answer to that question.

"Just one more doctor, Ben," I pleaded after someone had told me about Dr. DeAntonio. My friend had sworn, "He's an excellent diagnostician. He'll be able to help you." But what difference would finding the answer make, anyway? Ben wasn't going to change.

Sure, Ben had learned to ride a bike, climb the jungle gym, and jump on the trampoline, but so what? Was he doing any of these things now? Was he playing ball, or taking jogs in the park? No. He was still spending hours reading in his room, just as he had at three, and five, and ten, and twenty. After all these years Ben's only vegetable remained the same: peas in the pod. And when he could get his hands on it, his favorite food was still American cheese.

Now instead of reading and rereading picture books about places, like *This Is New York*, *This Is San Francisco*, and *This Is Hong Kong*, he was now reading and rereading books without pictures about places, like *Under the Sidewalks of New York* and *San Francisco: Its Bay and Its Cities*.

I understood that this was Ben, that he was not going to change, that he would always be obsessed with his special interests, that he would always talk about them, that they would always dominate his time. His interests, I understood, would forever be solitary, not social. They would ceaselessly be repetitive, involving places, not people. And finally, I even understood that it would be these special, solitary interests that would remain forever the source of his greatest pleasure.

But why? Just as Ben was obsessed with maps of city streets, I was obsessed with this question.

Finally, to get me off his back, Ben agreed to see "one more" doctor. So when I phoned to set up the appointment and Dr. DeAntonio asked that question, "Can you bring in his records?" it threw me. No other doctor had asked that.

This new doctor couldn't possibly know what he was asking. Maybe when he said "records," he was imagining a manila folder in a file cabinet, with a neatly labeled tab: "Ben: Medical Records." *Just pull open the cabinet, just find the file, just place it in your briefcase, just carry it into my office*, he must have thought. Simple, no problem. No, he couldn't possibly know what he was asking.

Ben's medical records were stored in a file cabinet of their very own. "Ben: Medical Records," it read on the outside, and when you opened it, each drawer on the inside was divided by year. I could just as easily have organized it another way. By disorder, for example. Or tests. Or places. Any method would have worked, but by year was best, because then I didn't have to look. All I had to do was keep the current year in front, open the drawer, pull it out, and stuff the paper in.

Ben's file cabinet was big and blue. I stored it behind my old bed in the garage. It wasn't reachable, but why should it be? None of the papers in Ben's file cabinet, none of the dozens of tests, letters, scans, or reports, had done a single thing to make Ben reachable.

Ben's entire life was stored in that cabinet, captured on pieces of official paper. He could have been a piece of real estate, fully inspected for termites, fully recorded for variances, fully disclosed for risk. He could have been a piece of meat, grade A, grade B. He could have been any product for buying and selling, for mincing and measuring. For manufacture.

Except he was none of these. He was a person, a human male person, and he was stuffed—all of him—from head to foot, from birth to adulthood, on hundreds of pieces of official paper. His properties stored for all of time in a blue metal fireproof cabinet in the garage behind my old bed. Warehoused, just as he was when he lived in transitional living centers, just as he was in 2-West, just as he was in jail, just as he was in Havenbrook. Out of the way, out of his mother's sight.

And here this new doctor was asking me to bring him out of hiding. Take his life in your two hands and carry it to my office. Just go into the garage. Just yank out your old bed. Just pull out the blue metal file cabinet. Just gather up the pieces of paper. Just get a bag or a barrel or a barge and drop them in. Just put them in the trunk of your car, and take them, take your son, all four hundred pounds of him, to the doctor's office.

"Well then," said Dr. DeAntonio when I explained about the papers, the hundreds of records, "just look through them. Just pick out the most pertinent."

"OK."

OK?

I waited till the last day, the day before the appointment. I'd have to cancel out my patients first; I'd have to tell them I was sick, which I was, but not in a coughing, sneezing way. In a phobic way. In an allergic-to-the-sight-of-the-blue-file-cabinet way. I'd have to take a deep breath in order to walk into the garage. I'd have to take another deep breath in order to yank out my old bed. And then I'd have to take the deepest breath of all to pull out the files.

People said I had courage, but they were wrong. I might look and sound and act like I had courage, but I didn't. Walking into that garage and yanking out the bed and pulling out the files took courage. Opening the drawers and holding Ben's years in my hands took even more courage.

But looking through the years, picturing them in my mind, remembering their sights and sounds and smells, took the most courage of all.

The appointment with Dr. DeAntonio was on a Monday. His office was located at the Neuropsychiatric Institute at UCLA, the same building that housed 2-West. Ben was waiting for me behind Havenbrook's double-locked doors, but he wasn't packed this time and he wasn't raring to go.

I had selected four years out of Ben's life, four sets of tests, teachers' evaluations, doctors' opinions, and hospital reports.

Dr. DeAntonio greeted us in the waiting area and escorted us into his tiny office. "May I see the records, please?" he inquired, barely looking in our direction. No chitchat, no questions, no friendly smile, just the passing of Ben's life from hand to hand. He didn't ask for it, but when I tried to give him some background information, he interrupted, "I'd like fifteen minutes to look through these records first. Fifteen minutes, then we can talk."

The doctor hunkered down into the pile of papers while Ben and I made small talk. We talked about his life, or rather, I asked my customary set of questions about his life. It was our usual routine; we could have done it in our sleep. Neither of us much cared what the other had to say—not Ben for my questions, nor I for his answers. Ben cared about getting out of there, leaving this building that held so many bad memories, taking the elevator down and out into the village of Westwood and eating lunch at a special restaurant. It was the bribe I'd held out if only he agreed to see this one last doctor. I cared about this one last doctor.

Finally Dr. DeAntonio turned to Ben and said these words: "Autism. Ben, you're autistic."

Whole minutes passed before either Ben or I said a word. And then, when we did speak we said the same thing in the same moment.

"Autistic?"

"Autistic?"

"Yes," replied Dr. DeAntonio. "Ben, you have autism."

"*I do?*"

"*He does?*"

"*Yes*," said the doctor. He did not smile, nor did he frown. It was just a statement of fact.

Ben was twenty-three years old when that word was spoken for the first time. So many spoken sentences had come between me and my expectations by then, so many thousands of words strung one onto the next, forming one huge heap, one painful pileup. Most of the words, though, had been repeats, all of them taken from volumes of psychiatry and mental illness. This word—*autism*—was different. It was neurological.

"But how could he have autism?" I asked when I was able to speak. "People with autism don't talk, isn't that right? Ben's *always* talked. Right from the start."

"That's a fooler," replied the doctor. "Autism is a spectrum disorder."

"What does that mean?" I asked.

"It means it takes different shapes and forms. Some people with autism have trouble with language; some don't. Autism is a pervasive developmental disorder, affecting different areas of development. It can be severe, moderate, or mild."

"But how do you know Ben is autistic? *What do those records say?*"

"They don't say anything about autism, which is just the point. None of the diagnosis in here would account for Ben's problems, which appear to be mainly social in nature, not mental. His difficulties all speak of deficits in the area of nonverbal understanding." Then the doctor turned to Ben and asked him a direct question: "Ben, did you have friends growing up?"

Ben squirmed in his chair. "Not really," he admitted. "Not the way other people do. Not—"

"Do you want friends, Ben?"

"Sometimes. But I can't really get them . . . I mean, people don't like me that much . . . I mean, it gets to be too hard . . . I'd rather be alone."

"That's because as smart as you are, Ben, and I can see you're smart, you just don't pick up the cues, the language of social interaction. So you come across as odd . . . don't you?"

"I guess. All I know is people have always looked at me funny, even before I was fat. The kids in school didn't want to play with me because I wasn't interested in what they were interested in. But it didn't matter, because I didn't want to play with them either."

"Ben, do you mind if I ask you some more questions? And your mother too?"

"Go ahead. You won't be the first—"

"I understand, Ben. But you may find my questions different from the usual ones."

"OK," said Ben.

"How do you react to change?"

"I don't like it—"

"Would you say it scares you, Ben?" I asked because I wanted to know.

"I guess it does," Ben said.

"OK, Ben. This is not to embarrass you, but would you say that you avoid social contact?"

"I just said so," Ben said.

"He's spent his entire childhood alone. But I wouldn't say he was unhappy. Were you, Ben? Were you unhappy playing alone?" I asked.

"No. Should I have been? I loved my persons and my books and my cities and listening to the radio and—"

"Which leads me to another question, Ben. What are you interested in?" queried the doctor.

"Anything about history. Anything about geography, especially cities and streets, I love streets and I love maps of streets."

"OK—" said Dr. DeAntonio.

"OK, what?" I asked.

"Well, Ben is describing a specific, narrow range of interests. Cities and streets. Have you always been interested in cities and streets?"

"Yeah. Always, since I was a little kid. Even now I read maps before I go to bed at night. They make me feel good."

"Do people nag you, Ben? Do they criticize you and tell you to change?"

"Always. All the time."

"About what kind of stuff, Ben? What do they say?"

"Well my mother tells me to make eye contact when I talk. She tells me I lecture people, and that's not how you have a conversation. She tells me to ask questions, she says I should listen more and talk less. She says don't stand so close and don't talk so loud. She tells me people aren't interested in all my facts about cities and streets. She tells me to try different foods. She says I have to get used to loud noise, because it's part of life. She tells me to read novels, not just books on information. She tells me—"

Now I was squirming. "I guess, I should leave him alone? I guess that's just the way he is and I should leave him alone?"

Dr. DeAntonio didn't respond. He wasn't there to reassure me, I could see that.

But Ben reassured me. "I think she's just trying to help," Ben said, looking over at me.

"I'm sorry, Ben," I said, teary-eyed. "It must be awful to be hounded."

"It's OK, Mom. You were only trying to help." Ben patted my leg.

Then it was over. Dr. DeAntonio handed me Ben's records and said goodbye. Still no smile, but I could tell that he meant it when he offered, "Let me know if there's anything more I can do."

It was a silent ride down the elevator. Something big had just happened in that office. A word had been spoken: *autism*. It was a frightening word, but somehow it was also a welcome word. I had never thought of my son as autistic, but when Dr. DeAntonio explained the range of autism, and when he asked those questions, and when he nodded his head and said, "OK," as if the answers added up, it all made sense. Autism.

Now what?

As we stepped out of the elevator, Ben turned to me and said, "You know what, Mom? I just found out it's not my fault. Like when I made things up? I know I lied to you, but it didn't feel like lying. I didn't know I was lying. I'm autistic. I was born that way. It's not my fault that I'm the way I am."

"Oh, Ben," was all I could say.

"Oh, Mom," was all Ben could say, because he was crying and so was I. We hugged on the street, one giant-bellied young man and his mother, who was so sad and sorry for all those lost, misunderstood years. Ben had thought it was all his fault, and so had I—how he couldn't quite get the hang of it, of life and its hundreds of unspoken rules and regulations. Life, and parents, and teachers, and people. What did they want, anyway, these people he would do anything to please, these people he so wished would like him but didn't like him, because—why? Because he was not like them. He didn't mean to be not like them. He would change if he could, but he couldn't. He just never could.

"I'm sorry, Ben," I said, and *sorry* was just a word, just a mix of letters that splattered on the sidewalk, because they were empty. They could never say what they were meant to say. I'm sorry for not knowing sooner. I'm sorry for blaming you. I'm sorry for being disappointed in you. I'm sorry for disappointing you. I'm sorry for how alone you must have felt. I'm sorry for all your pain, and mine, and Dad's, and David's. I'm just so sorry. . . .

Then I looked up at Ben's face, and although he was crying, he was smiling too.

"Don't be sorry, Mom," he told me. "This is the happiest day of my life."

27

FAMILY TIES

Being with my real dad, seeing him, hearing him talk, makes me feel comfortable. Like I'm home, where I belong.

———

WHERE WAS BEN TO GO when he got out of Havenbrook? Where was he to live?

"Yes, I *can too* live on my own, Mom. I'm ready. I'm twenty-three years old."

"But Ben, do you really think it's a good idea? Maybe in a little while . . . maybe just one more transitional living place—"

"No! I'm not going back to those awful places. I'm not crazy. Just because I'm autistic, doesn't mean I'm not smart. Even Dr. DeAntonio says I'm smart—"

"Stop it, Ben! Stop telling me you're smart. Smart is beside the point. Are you ready to organize your own affairs? Are you prepared to shop for the right foods? To live on a budget, to—"

"Of course I am. I learned that stuff here, Mom. I went to all those ADL groups. They taught me."

We could have gone round and round in circles, if it weren't for the miracle.

Steven had come back into Ben's life. After so many years of being out of touch, of losing track, of you-have-your-life-and-I-have-mine, Steven had called to tell Ben that his mother, Ben's beloved Nana, was dying, and to ask if Ben wanted to see her one last time.

Yes, he did. And so father and son saw one another again after so many years. Father and son, who had, once, long ago, shared so much. Who had sung folk songs, and recited Shakespeare, and driven to school together morning after morning, taking the detour, down, down, down into the underground parking lot with the "giant hill" and up, up, up again, into the light of day, into that place in Ben's heart reserved everlastingly for the man he would forever call "my real Dad."

"Mom, you'll never guess what!" Ben called to tell me after their first visit.

"What?"

"My dad has this apartment in Beverly Hills, and he said I could live there till the lease is up."

"He did?"

"And it's furnished and everything, so you don't have to worry about that."

"Oh."

"So do you want to see it? When do you want to see it?"

Ben's father, whom he had not set eyes on in ten years, had an apartment in Beverly Hills, and Ben could live there till the lease was up, and it was furnished, and when did I want to see it?

"I don't know." I was in shock. It was too much information to take in all at once. Steven back. Beverly Hills apartment. When could I see it?

Steven and I had lost touch, as had Steven and Ben, since Ben had returned home from boarding school. Ben was twelve years old then;

now he was twenty-three. Steven had remarried and had two children with his new wife.

There had been so many times through the years that I had wished for Steven's help, that I had wanted to call Ben's father and cry *"Steven!! Remember little Benjy? Our adorable, brilliant little boy? The boy we brought into the world, and read to, and played with, and marveled over, and loved so much? Remember him? Well, he's in trouble! He has no friends, he's cutting school, he's lying, he's in a psych ward, he's in another psych ward, he's in jail, he's in four-point restraints, he's in a locked psychiatric hospital, he has no passes, he's back in a psych ward, he has passes, he's getting fat. He's getting fatter. Oh my God, he's so fat he can hardly walk down a flight of stairs. Oh my God, Steven! Remember Ben, our little boy?"*

But, after that day in the lawyer's office, after Ben's boarding school experience, it was too late; there was too much bad blood between us. Steven had vanished out of Ben's life—and suddenly, like a bolt of lightning, striking when you least expect it, when you're least prepared—he was back.

"OK, then, Mom," Ben continued without missing a beat, "how 'bout tomorrow?"

"Tomorrow?"

"Sure, in the afternoon, right after lunch. Lunch is served at eleven-thirty, so how 'bout you pick me up at Havenbrook at twelve-thirty?"

"Well . . . I'll have to shift my patients first. I'll see if I can do it and let you know."

So at twelve-thirty there I stood, yet one more time, outside the double-locked doors of Havenbrook. Waiting. Waiting for the under-paid, bored, foreign-language-speaking attendant to put down his mag-azine, get up from behind his desk, and slouch his way over to the buzzer. He didn't know this was Ben's big day. And if he did, would he have moved any faster? Probably not. After all, it wasn't *his* big day. Maybe the attendant didn't have any big days; maybe that's why he looked so bored and moved so slowly. Maybe that's why he worked in that awful place with the Shuffling People who were always pounding on the double-locked doors. "Open up, open up!" they'd shout through the glass, but his job was to *not* open up. He was guard of the double-locked doors. He was boss of the buzzer. Maybe that was his big day.

Steven was waiting for us on the street outside his apartment. I gasped when I saw him, because, after all these years, Steven still looked the same. And he looked so much like Ben—Ben's deep-set eyes, Ben's smile. . . .

"Hi, Steven," I said, trying not to betray my discomfort. "This is so generous of you," I said, nodding toward the garden apartment behind him.

"No problem," Steven replied, smiling.

"Hi, Dad," said Ben.

"Hi, Ben," said Steven.

"The apartment is one floor up, and there's no elevator. I hope that won't pose a problem."

We both knew what he was referring to—Ben and I. Could Ben, in all his pounds of fat, walk up that flight of stairs? Could he do it without having an asthma attack, without falling down for lack of seeing where his feet were going? Could he do it once, twice, three times a day? To walk to the bus, to walk to the market, to walk to the video store?

When we walked up the flight of stairs, Ben was out of breath, but he wasn't wheezing. And I thought, that's good.

And when we toured the apartment, Steven said, "This is the kitchen. It has a microwave. It has a toaster. The pots and pans are here. The utensils are there. This is the living room. It has a TV. This is the bedroom. The sheets are there. This is the bathroom. The towels are here." Ben still was not wheezing, even though a cat and two dogs had once lived in that apartment too. Even though I could see cat hairs on the couch. And I thought, that's good.

"Isn't it great, Mom? Isn't it great?"

"It's a lovely space and very generous of you, Steven."

"Glad to do it."

"So, Dad. I'll let you know as soon as I'm discharged. OK? I can move in then?"

"Sure, Ben," said Steven.

"OK, Mom? Can I? Can I?"

"I guess so—"

And then, as we were leaving the apartment, when I was already at the bottom of the flight of stairs, I looked up to where Ben and Steven were standing, at the top of the flight of stairs. That's when I noticed Ben's shoelaces. They were untied. Ben was too fat to bend down and tie them; tying Ben's shoelaces was my job. It was my job when he was three, and it was my job when he was twenty-three.

But I couldn't do my job because I was all the way down, and Ben was all the way up.

That's when the second miracle happened. Steven was one step below Ben. He was bending down. He was tying Ben's shoelaces.

28

ASPERGER'S SYNDROME

I always take the test hoping I don't qualify. But I do. Every time. And not by a small margin, because I end up answering "yes" to every question.

———

To: *Asperger Respondents*

FROM: *Audrey McMahon, Learning Disabilities Association of America Research Committee*

We appreciate your alert response to the Learning Disabilities Association of America's Newsbriefs article of May 1991 entitled "Is Help on the Horizon?" Inasmuch as Asperger's Disorder is now included in the DSM-IV, we have that big plus of recognition going for us. We all owe a debt of gratitude to those of you who contributed voluntarily and effectively with information that enabled the Yale Child Study Center to review cases in sufficient numbers to make their data truly significant and effective. Congratulations for your part in achieving "goal one!"

THE YEAR WAS 1994, and the Yale Study Center had collected enough responses to their questionnaire, "Your Child and Asperger's Syndrome." AS had finally reached "goal one," achieving legitimate status in the bible of psychiatric disorders, the *Diagnostic and Statistical Manual of Mental Disorders*, IV-R, (DSM-IV).

For me, "goal one" had been achieved in Dr. DeAntonio's office: an answer to the question, *What's wrong with my son?* But the label *autism*, though more resounding and on target than any of Ben's former classifications, still didn't quite capture his essence.

Ben may have been autistic, but he clearly didn't fit the prototype. His language wasn't absent or delayed; it was precocious. He may have preferred information to people, but he could relate to others when he had to, and sometimes he even wanted to.

The journey of Ben had taken us down many diagnostic pathways—some false, some true, a mix of everything. Ben had not only been labeled autistic. He was also learning disabled. He had attention deficit disorder. He had an assortment of obsessive-compulsive and addictive traits. He was sometimes depressed and anxious. He had been given the labels schizoid, schizotypal, and borderline personality disorder. He had suffered from asthma and Crohn's disease since childhood.

By the time Ben was twenty-three my mailbox was filled with flyers, brochures, conference registration forms, and requests for donations from the Learning Disabilities Association of America, Children and Adults with Attention Deficit Disorder, the National Association for Mental Illness, the Association of Asthmatics of America, the California Association for Mental Illness, UCLA-NPI, Daniel Freeman Hospital, RFK Hospital, North Los Angeles County Regional Center, West Side Regional Center, Marianne Frostig Center, the Ahmanson School, the Obsessive-Compulsive Society of America, ACHIEVABLE, the Help Group, Step-Up-On-Second, and Protection and Advocacy Incorporated.

By the time Ben was twenty-three, I sat on the boards of more organizations than I could count and was considered an "expert" in neurobiological and developmental disorders. I had collaborated in producing two videos on mental illness, was a guest on a radio show on the subject of attention deficit disorder, and developed and conducted several panels and seminars for parents and professionals on neurobiological disorders.

There was this fire burning in my belly, a fire that had been there ever since I began wondering whether something was wrong with Ben. Was he better because of what he *could* do, like read and talk and tell and know, or was he worse because of what he *couldn't* do, like have friends, make conversation, and play soccer?

The fire began like most fires, with a cinder, a passing observation—*He's talking to me but not looking at me*—and grew into a flame—*He won't be the daddy, he'll only be the radio*—until it fanned out and down into my lungs—*He has no friends, he has no friends*—until I couldn't breathe, but to say his name, but to ask the question, *What is wrong, what is wrong? I must discover what is wrong.*

I used to read fiction. I used to love a good story, the way it weaved its tale with its long, take-all-the-time-you-want, liquid, languorous lines of language. I used to love to watch words stretch across the page, painting perfect pictures of inner lives weaving in and out of outer lives. But after the question *What is wrong with Ben?* there was no time for that. There was only time to concentrate on the question. There was only time to research the answer. Time was short. It was running out. Every day Ben was getting older. Every day, so was I. Every day without an answer was a day wasted.

So I went to medical libraries, I signed my name Dr. and ordered books meant for neurologists, psychologists, psychiatrists, educators, everybody and anybody who was smarter than I, who had gone to school longer than I, who read books with words I didn't understand but which I figured out, because the words had roots and I could trace the roots, even if it took me all night. It took me all night, because that was when I read them—these medical books and journals and articles—that was my bedtime reading, that was when I'd wake John up and say, "Sorry, but I couldn't wait till morning. You *have* to read this. Doesn't this sound just like Ben?"

"What! What's wrong?"

"Nothing's wrong. Look at this article, you have to read this article!"

"Now? It's two o'clock in the morning! Do I have to read it *now*? What the hell's wrong with you?"

It was the fire in my belly that was wrong with me. It was blazing, even more since Dr. DeAntonio had used that word *autism*, because the diagnosis sounded so close; it felt so right, yet it wasn't right, it still wasn't right.

Somehow in my search, I came across an article that jumped out at me, as if the words were too near, too momentous, too perfectly fitting to simply lay benignly on the printed page.

I'd found it in the middle of the night, so that's when I read it.

REVENGE OR TRAGEDY: DO NERDS SUFFER FROM A MILD
PERVASIVE DEVELOPMENTAL DISORDER?

By Nicholas Putnam, M.D.

"Nerd . . . : an unpleasant, unattractive, or insignificant person."

A more precise clinical definition of the MPDD syndrome from which nerds suffer can be offered:

In the presence of average or above average intelligence, children exhibit difficulties with reciprocal social relationships despite a definite desire for companions. These difficulties are manifest in an inability to make and keep friends, in problems understanding and responding to social cues, and in showing little empathy for the feelings of others. . . .

This definition is similar to descriptions of Asperger's Syndrome. . . . Because the disorder is "less pervasive" than autism, it is easy to misdiagnose . . . as a personality disorder. . . . Individuals with Asperger's Syndrome characteristically are socially isolated and display abnormal social interaction. . . . They may be not just shy but also abnormally garrulous or intrusive. . . . There is frequently a history of . . . an unwillingness or inability to engage in cooperative or imaginative play. . . .

The diagnosis of a nerd as suffering from MPDD . . . suggests possible interventions, and can change the way the patient and his family perceive the way he functions.

"Oh my God, John! You have to read this! You just have to!" I couldn't help myself. Like Ben with food, so was I with Ben.

But John, who was not suffering from fire in the belly, had fallen back to sleep. He could wait till tomorrow.

I had several phone conversations with this doctor, Nicholas Putnam, whom I'd never set eyes on, but whose words reverberated like no other words I'd ever read. But he, like Hans Asperger himself, was a man ahead of his time, because his prophetic paper about nerds was published four years before Asperger's Syndrome would officially appear in the DSM-IV.

And then in 1998, when the diagnosis of Asperger's Syndrome (AS) had been listed in the DSM-IV for four years, I came across a book—not just an article in a journal, not just a few questions in a manual of psychiatric disorders, but an *entire book* on the subject of Asperger's Syndrome. It was called *Asperger's Syndrome: A Guide for Parents and Professionals*, written by an Australian doctor, Tony Attwood. On page thirty-one, and set in bold type, was this title: The Australian Scale for Asperger Syndrome. Following this was a set of twenty-four direct, easy-to-answer questions to be used by parents and teachers to help identify the child with AS. Questions were to be answered by using a scale of zero (meaning rarely) to six (meaning frequently).

Does the child lack an understanding of how to play with other children?

Yes. Of course, yes, because he never played with other children. I am remembering kindergarten and the dress-up corner and the girls asking, "Ben, will you be the daddy?" No, Ben would definitely not be the

daddy, but he would be the radio. To be the daddy you have to impro-
vise—an actor without a script. Whereas to be the radio you have a
script—the weatherman's script, the sportscaster's script, the traffic
reporter's script.

*When free to play with other children, does the child avoid social con-
tact with them?*

Yes. Books were better than people, especially children. Because
books didn't tease you.

*Does the child appear unaware of social conventions or codes of con-
duct and make inappropriate actions and comments?*

Yes. Standing too close—nose to nose with people—violates a code
of conduct. Droning on and on about whatever you're interested in without regard for the other person also violates a code of conduct.

*Is the child not interested in participating in competitive sports,
games, and activities?*

Yes. No games, never games.

Is the child indifferent to peer pressure?

No. Ben seemed to care that kids didn't like him. They just never
liked him.

Does the child have an unusual tone of voice?

Yes, it's monotone.

*When talking to the child does he or she appear uninterested in your
side of the conversation?*

Yes.

Does the child use less eye contact than you would expect?

Yes.

Is the child's speech overprecise or pedantic?

Yes, like a college professor's.

Does the child read books primarily for information?

Yes.

Does the child have an exceptional long-term memory for events and facts?

I'll say! He remembers the color of his first bedroom.

Is the child confused by the pretend games of other children?

Yes. He had his own pretend games.

Is the child fascinated by a particular topic or topics?

Yes.

Does the child become unduly upset by changes in his or her routines or expectations?

Yes.

Does the child develop elaborate routines or rituals that he or she must complete?

Yes.

Does the child have poor motor coordination?

Yes.

Does the child have an odd gait when running?

Yes.

Yes, yes, yes, yes, yes!

SOURCE: Tony Attwood. *Asperger's Syndrome: A Guide for Parents and Professionals.* London: Jessica Kingsley Publications, 1998.

Here was a doctor from the other side of the world who had swooped down and spied on my son.

I wouldn't have been surprised if he had asked, *Is your son's only vegetable peas in the pod? Has he memorized every word of his two favorite books,* A Child's History of the World *and* A Child's Geography of the World? *Did he read and talk before he could walk? Did you think he was a genius and feel secretly proud? Did you think he was strange and feel secretly embarrassed? Did you watch him and think about him and worry and wonder till he was all you could care about? And when everyone—all the doctors, and therapists, and friends, and your husband, and especially Ben himself—told you to stop, that what you were doing wasn't helping, it was only hurting you and him, and the people trying to help you and him— did you still keep doing it anyway?*

Yes. You did.

There should have been two questionnaires, one for the subject and one for the subject's mother. The first identifying the diagnosis of Asperger's and the second identifying the diagnosis of Enmeshed Mother.

Here was a doctor from the other side of the world, who seemed to know Ben better than any of the dozens of doctors on this continent who had spent hundreds of hours examining him in person.

In that moment, I didn't care about anything or anybody else. I didn't care that John was playing the piano. I didn't care that he was singing into a microphone, recording a song for his demo reel. I didn't care that he had shut off the phones and was wearing headphones. I only cared about this: *Someone on the other side of the world understood my son!*

"John, John, John!" I yelled from upstairs, where I had been reading Tony Attwood's questions. But John didn't hear me. Of course he didn't hear me—he was downstairs wearing headphones.

So I ran down the stairs with the questions in my hands, as if they were gold, as if once they were flax, and my son's very life, and mine too, depended on turning them into gold, but no matter where we went, what we did, whom we asked, no one could save us. And just like that, on an ordinary Saturday afternoon, in an ordinary turn of a page, on the brink of giving up, this man appears. But he isn't Rumplestiltskin, he's Tony Attwood, and he lives all the way on the other side of the world, and he has come to our rescue.

And when I get downstairs, when I'm standing right in front of the piano, when I'm waving my arms, when I'm pointing to the headphones and mouthing, "Take them off, take them off," and when John finally sees me and takes them off, I am crying.

"What's the matter, sweetie? What happened?" John asks, walking toward me.

But I can't talk, I can only point to the gold and put the pile in front of John's eyes. John sits back down on the piano bench and takes the papers from my hands. I watch him as he reads the questions. I watch him as tears well up in his eyes. I watch him as he stands up and walks toward me. I feel him as he takes me in his arms. And then, I hear him say these words: "Oh, Barbara. It's taken such a long time."

29

NOW WHAT?

There are lots of creative and talented people with Asperger's. Without them, the world would be just ordinary. Albert Einstein's teacher once told him, "If we opened up your brain, we wouldn't find a brain. Just a lump of fat." If you ask me, Einstein had Asperger's. I'm proud to be in his company.

No, Ben did not have classic autism, the kind first brought to light by Leo Kanner, in which the diagnostic criteria captured the silent, withdrawn, aloof child. But he did have most of the characteristics described by the Viennese pediatrician Hans Asperger in a paper published in 1944 in which he studied and described four boys "who were quite unusual in their social, linguistic and cognitive (i.e., thinking) abilities." But it wasn't until 1991, when Dr. Uta Frith translated Hans Asperger's paper into English, that the syndrome became known. Earlier, in 1981, Lorna Wing published a paper in which she used the term *Asperger's Syndrome* for the first time. The children in her study demonstrated the following clinical features: "a lack of empathy, one-sided interaction, little ability to form friendships, pedantic speech, poor nonverbal communication, intense absorption in certain subjects, and clumsy and ill-coordinated movements and odd postures." But it was not until 1994, thanks in large measure to Fred Volkmar and Ami Klin and their colleagues at the Yale Child Study Center, that Asperger's Syndrome was finally included in the DSM-IV.

1994 is two and a half decades away from 1969, the year Ben was born. They say that, when it comes to their children, "mothers know best." But it is hard to trust what you know when there is no name for what you know, when nobody else knows what you're talking about, when you doubt what you know because you think, *So what if he's different? It takes all kinds—he'll grow out of it. Einstein was a genius. So what if he won't be able to talk to his wife? So what if he'll never have a wife? So what if other people think he's odd? He is odd. But who cares? Does he care, does he say he cares? Maybe you're the only one who cares, and maybe you care because maybe it's not him you care about. Maybe it's you.*

In 1992, Dr. DeAntonio said that Ben was autistic. Two years later, when the diagnosis was included in the DSM-IV, I didn't have to call for a second appointment. All I had to do was take the DSM-IV down from my office bookshelf, open it to the section on pervasive developmental disorders, the official category under which the Asperger's Syndrome diagnosis is classified, and read down the diagnostic criteria for "Asperger's Disorder, 299.80":

A. Qualitative impairment in social interaction, as manifested by at least two of the following:

  1. Marked impairment in the use of multiple nonverbal behaviors such as eye-to-eye gaze, facial expression, body postures, and gestures to regulate social interaction.

  Yes.

2. *Failure to develop peer relationships appropriate to developmental level.*

Yes.

3. *A lack of spontaneous seeking to share enjoyment, interests, or achievements with other people (e.g., by a lack of showing, bringing, or pointing out objects of interest to other people).*

Yes.

4. *Lack of social or emotional reciprocity.*

Yes.

B. *Restricted repetitive and stereotyped patterns of behavior, interests and activities, as manifested by at least one of the following:*

1. *Encompassing preoccupation with one or more stereotyped and restricted patterns of interest that is abnormal in intensity or focus.*

Yes.

2. *Apparently inflexible adherence to specific, nonfunctional routines or rituals.*

Sometimes.

3. *Stereotyped and repetitive motor mannerisms.*

Sometimes.

C. *The disturbance causes clinically significant impairment in other important areas of functioning.*

Yes.

D. *There is no clinically significant general delay in language.*

Yes.

E. There is no clinically significant delay in cognitive development or in the development of age-appropriate self-help skills, adaptive behavior (other than social interaction), and curiosity about the environment in childhood.

Yes and no. He couldn't tie his shoes until he was seven, he couldn't read the clock until he was fourteen, he couldn't button a shirt until he was seventeen, he couldn't shave until he was twenty, and he couldn't clean himself properly until he was twenty-six.

F. Criteria are not met for another specific pervasive developmental disorder or schizophrenia.

Yes.

In the year 1994, when my son was twenty-five, it was I who answered these questions about Ben, but in the year 2002, when he was thirty-three, Ben answered them himself.

I was always ashamed of who I was, so I never told the truth about anything that would embarrass me.

If you had asked me if I have trouble understanding others, I would have said no, even though the true answer was yes.

If you had asked me if I avoided social contact, I would have said no, because I wouldn't want you to think I was weird.

If you had asked me if I lacked empathy, I would have been insulted, because everyone knows good people have empathy and bad people don't.

I would have denied that I'm afraid of loud noises, that I have a narrow range of interests, and that I get upset by changes in routine.

The only questions I would have answered yes to would have been the ones about having an unusually long-term memory for events and facts; reading books for information; and being like a walking encyclopedia. That's because I liked those things about me. I thought they made me look smart.

If I thought it was good, I would have said yes, and if I thought it was bad, I would have said no.

But today, when my mom asked me if I would answer these questions, I told the truth. Participating in writing this book has forced me to remember things I tried to forget. It has helped me face the truth about who I am. Today I can admit what I like and what I don't like, what I do and don't do, what I'm afraid of and what I really care about.

I like information and I love computers. I like spending a little time with people, but not too much time. I like anything that has to do with the radio—listening to it and pretending to be Vin Scully or Dr. Demento. I love making tapes in my room, and I still read the same books over and over again, just because I like to.

I thought I could never tell the truth about any of this stuff. That if I did, it would kill me. But now I realize that that's not what would kill me. Spending the rest of my life hiding my true self—that's what would kill me.

Now we knew. There was a name for what Ben had, what he was born with, what he and we suffered with all his life. It was called Asperger's Syndrome. He'd had it before I knew what it was called, and he'd have it long after I was gone. It was a legitimate disorder, like any other, and it had earned sanctioned status in the bible of diagnostic disorders, the DSM-IV.

Now there were two happiest days: one for Ben, when he learned it wasn't his fault, and one for me, when I learned it wasn't mine. Maybe that's what I'd always been searching for—an endorsement, a good mother seal of approval, the affirmation that Ben's differences weren't my fault. But had anyone actually said it was my fault? Not in so many words, not like what happened to the mothers of autistic children born in the days of Bruno Bettelheim, when mothers were blamed outright for their kids' condition. When they were called "refrigerator mothers." Not like that.

But for so many years, I had been on a wild and frantic search. I was singleminded, and whoever got in my way had better get out of it. I'd yell and shove and step on people's toes. If a doctor saw me coming in his direction, he'd make a sharp right turn. That was my reputation. I'd earned it.

And now, suddenly my job was over. For over half my life, I had been asking the question *What's wrong with my son?* But now, as I held the answer in my hands, I felt bereft.

Had I really wanted to arrive at the end, if this was how the end was going to feel? The end, after all, is the finish, the close, the point at which the journey stops. But something didn't feel right, here at the end.

Ben was the same—with or without a label. He had the same problems. He still was friendless, he still was fat, he still felt anxious in the face of change, he still was alone. He still suffered.

And what about me? Was I any different now? Had Ben's diagnosis changed me?

Scale for Mothers of Children with Asperger's Syndrome

1. *Before your son was labeled with AS, did you honor and cherish him just the way he was?*

   No.

2. *Before your son was labeled with AS, did you accept him just the way he was?*

   No.

3. *Now that you know your son has a condition called AS, do you honor and cherish him just the way he is?*

   No.

4. *Now that you know your son has a condition called AS, do you accept him just the way he is?*

No.

I had arrived at the finish line, but I wasn't holding the prize. Ben was the prize, and I wasn't holding him.

Now what?

30

LIVING UNDER BEN'S SKIN

Even now I have only the smallest understanding of the complexities of AS, and I have barely begun to explore all the ways it affects my life and the lives of those around me.

———

I KNEW WHAT IT WAS LIKE living under my skin all these years. But how could I know what it was like living under Ben's? What it was really like. It's not that I hadn't asked. I had. I guess, before, he just wasn't ready to tell me. But thanks to the passage of time and history, and especially thanks to the opportunity to collaborate on this book, I asked him again.

Here's what he said.

IT IS ONE THING TO KNOW you are different from other people but another thing entirely to accept that fact. I knew I had Asperger's Syndrome because that's what I was told, but I never really believed it.

I've always been able to give the right answer when asked, "Do you understand what is wrong with you?" I have had enough experience in therapy and read enough books to give them what they wanted to hear. But I never believed my own answer because I couldn't really see what was different about me.

In my days at Havenbrook and in other psychiatric settings, I'd seen people who were schizophrenic begin to take medication and suddenly be free of their voices. I think I always expected the same thing to happen to me, that I'd wake up one day and be like everyone else. No longer awkward. No longer socially phobic. No longer afraid. No longer fat. Just a normal, run-of-the-mill guy, albeit brilliant and verbal.

Sadly this will never be true, because AS is a developmental disability and it cannot be cured with medication. It never goes away. Behavior modification can help with some of the behaviors, but it takes a very long time.

My best thinking will never make my problems disappear, any more than wishing I could be thin can make the extra 250 pounds I carry turn to muscle. The only thing I can do is accept my AS and try to deal with it head on. People say it's amazing that I have this much insight. But I'm glad I do, because being willing to admit and accept that I have Asperger's Syndrome has made my life easier.

When people ask, "What is it like to have Asperger's Syndrome?" I'm not sure how to reply. I'm just me. I can't tell you what it's like not to have it, so how can I tell you what it's like to have it?

I know that certain aspects of being social make me feel uncomfortable. Most of how I adapt to social situations, I've learned by rote. There are lots of things that still confuse me. Sometimes I don't know if people are joking or being serious. I take things very literally. I have had to learn to say, "Sorry, but I'm not sure if you're joking or not." I usually end up feeling pretty stupid, but at least I know what they mean.

Another thing I am working on is how to deal with people who might get upset with me because of something I've done unintentionally because I didn't know it would make them upset. For example, sometimes I am uncoordinated and end up running into someone on a crowded bus aisle or when I am in the market using a shopping cart. I always feel embarrassed when these things happen and sometimes the embarrassment turns to anger. Then I obsess on what I should have said or done differently, which makes me feel worse. I'm working on cutting myself more slack.

It has been very hard for me to understand how my actions affect other people. For other people this comes naturally, but it is something I've had to learn. I know people can't read my mind, but sometimes I act as if they can and should. I often make assumptions that turn out not to be true. This causes me a lot of problems. I don't like having to ask people for clarification or having to say things I think people should already know. Maybe this is why people with AS are considered to be lacking in empathy. It's not that I don't care; it's just that I don't see the world the way others do. This is a hard thing to admit, because I think I should see other people and understand how I affect them. As I've gotten older, I've been able to wrap my mind around this concept, but as a child it was my biggest obstacle in having friends.

To me the idea of admitting that I have trouble with social concepts like these makes me feel ashamed, because I think I shouldn't have these problems. Other people don't.

The biggest thing I have had to admit to myself is that I am not, nor will I ever be, like other people. No matter how hard I try, I will always have Asperger's Syndrome. But the miracle is that I am finally OK with that. Today I have friends. Today I share my life with others and they share their lives with me. All I have to do is be honest.

31

THE TOKEN OF THE TURMOIL

The more I was able to accept what was true for me, the easier it was to accept what was true for my mom. I used to think that validating my mother's truth would make mine less viable. Only now do I realize that I can be my own person, my mom can be hers, and neither of us is wrong.

———

THERE WAS ONE THING I could always count on: my seven o'clock conversation with Ben. It was a hook each of us grabbed and held onto, tethering us to the present moment, the present day with its "What did you do and how do you feel?" and its echoes of yesterday. Yesterday was so awful compared to today. We knew that, but we didn't dare say it, because yesterday's images were still too raw, still too painful. So now—when we did our nightly dance and I asked my standard questions, my mind wandering, my mouth moving, and Ben answering in kind—it was our way of saying, "Isn't this better? Thank you for making it better."

But something was changing. Our conversations were tilting from all about my questions about Ben to more about Ben's questions about me.

I'd ask about his day; he'd ask about mine. I'd inquire about how he was feeling; he'd ask how I was feeling. It threw me off balance, this sudden interest in my side of the street. I didn't quite know my territory in the middle of this ordinary dialogue: I talked, he listened. He talked, I listened. It was unsettling. But why? A customary conversation with my son. Conventional, normal, proscribed. Isn't that what I'd always longed for? But it felt like I'd lost something. I *had* lost something: I'd lost the role I'd played for thirty years, the role of Ben's mother. And I had nothing to replace it with.

One day, in the middle of one of these conversations, I said, "There's something different about you, Ben."

"I hope so, Mom. I certainly hope so. But tell me anyway, tell me how you experience me as different."

"I don't know, exactly . . . it's just that you seem more—"

"Interested?"

"Yeah . . . interested in—"

"I'm trying, Mom. I'm trying really hard to get out of myself and think about someone else for a change. Not just me."

I didn't reply, because hadn't I been telling him to do that, to inquire about others, to not hog the conversation, to not lecture, to listen more and talk less? Hadn't this been the very campaign I'd dedicated my life to?

"Mom," Ben said, "are you there?"

"Yeah, I'm here."

"What's wrong? Why aren't you saying anything?"

"I'm confused, I guess. I mean . . . what happened? I mean, how did you get this way? You know . . . more interested in—"

"Because of my program, Mom. I'm following the Twelve Steps, I'm reading the literature, I have a sponsor. It's the best thing I've ever done."

"I'm so glad, Ben. I'm so glad it's helping."

"Why don't you try it, Mom?"

"Me? Why should I? I don't have an eating problem. I'm not an alcoholic or an addict—"

"Not in that way, Mom. Not with a substance. But you are kind of . . . you know . . . addicted—"

"To what?"

"Me."

"How?" I wanted less of Ben, not more, so what was he talking about?

"You're addicted to changing me. Aren't you? Aren't you always trying to change me?"

Yes, but was that addiction? I was helping. I was helping my son, because hadn't he always needed my help? "But that's not the same, Ben, is it?"

"It kind of is, Mom . . . because—"

"Because what?"

"Because—can you stop? Can you stop trying to change me? I ask you to stop, I tell you and tell you. But you never do. You just keep making suggestions, you just keep giving advice when I don't ask for it. When I don't need it. *When I don't want it.*"

By then, by the "I don't want it" part, Ben wasn't talking in a monotone anymore. He was yelling. And then, after a beat, he stopped yelling. Still, when he said the next sentence, he was not talking in a monotone either, because his tone had a kind of hush in it, sort of like a voice you hear in church, a warning that I'd better get ready for what was coming next.

"As if—"

"As if what, Ben? As if what?"

And then Ben's church voice returned, and I was remembering Ben's six-month checkup and Dr. Pierce and his church voice and that pause, that very first pause when he said *anomalies* and *photos*. When he said *Boston Children's Hospital.* And I felt the same kind of fear I'd felt then.

"As if you could change me."

That's what Ben said.

I held my breath. What did he mean, as if I could?

"As if you have the power to change me. I know I'm your son, Mom, but it's not your job. You can't change me. This is the way I am."

I was silent because my heart had stopped in my chest. He was right; all these years I'd been tilting at windmills just so I didn't have to face the truth of what Ben just said. I never could change Ben. I never would.

It hit me like a ton of bricks, this truth that seemed so obvious, so transparently clear, but that, till this very moment, had been entirely hidden behind my ironclad will.

What should I do now?

Ben hadn't accepted himself any more than I'd accepted him. But at least he knew it. At least he was doing something about it. I could see it. I could feel it. He was beginning to say yes to the person he was, because he was telling the truth; he was telling *me* the truth. "It's just how it is, Mom. This is reality, and both of us—you and I—have to accept it."

BEN HAD ASPERGER'S SYNDROME, this we finally knew. It wasn't my fault. I hadn't screwed up as a mother. Or I had—but not that way. Asperger's Syndrome was neurological, part of Ben's wiring, part of his DNA. I hadn't made Ben antisocial. I hadn't made him precocious—a little grownup before his time, a walking encyclopedia of knowledge—any more than I'd made him a loner, a boy who liked things more than he liked people.

But didn't I have a syndrome too? Just because mine wasn't official, just because you couldn't locate it in the DSM-IV, didn't mean it wasn't real. And just as debilitating. It has kept and still keeps me from having what I need most: Ben. It's called Disappointed Mother Syndrome.

Type: Severe.

Prognosis: Poor.

Ben's words "You can't change me" kept reverberating in my mind. "This is the way I am" spun round and round in my brain, like the wheels of the bus. Till one day, the wheels just ground to a halt, stopped dead still in the center of the road—and I knew I had to do something drastic. I had to drag myself in another direction, whether or not I wanted to. I knew that if I was to get rid of my obsession to change Ben, I must focus somewhere else. Away from what I wanted. Away from what I insisted on having in order to be happy. I had to disentangle from Ben. Just take myself somewhere else. Anywhere else.

So I joined a volunteer group whose mandate was to visit lonely people. I envisioned myself sitting on the edge of a little old lady's bed, making her smile. Being helpful. Visiting an old lady would mean my assignment would be over sooner or later. Sooner or later she would die, and while she waited, I could hold her hand, read her a newspaper. If her memory was failing, I could listen to her same stories again and again and still smile in appreciation. I could tolerate anything if there was an end in sight. But I couldn't tolerate being powerless when there was no foreseeable end. Hadn't I already been there? Hadn't I already done that?

Then I met Jack.

Jack was all alone in the world. He needed company. I would be his company.

And so we'd meet—this man, Jack, and I—every Wednesday at two-thirty in the afternoon. By then Jack had been speaking in riddles for ten whole years. Ever since that day when he had been standing in the library stacks looking for a book on Jung, and an aneurysm burst in his brain and left him language-impaired. Jung, the dream doctor who took us deep down into another world, a world different from the world of things we could know by how it felt to touch them, see them, and smell them. Deep down and far away from the world we were used to: the world of the everyday.

So there he was, this Jack of a man-riddle, plummeting from one moment to the next, down, down, down, into a different space, a different time. There he was, no longer able to navigate a straight thought from point A to point B, lost in the middle of a dream, right in the middle of his life.

Jack was forty-three years old, small, and thin as a rail. His jet-black beard was almost as tall as he—raggedy and limp—as if once it had been proud, but now it was placid, resigned. His head was completely bald and covered with a cap that had belonged to his father. Since the aneurysm he had lost his ability to speak in a linear, logical way. This, even though he had once written poetry. Now they lived separate lives: Jack's brain, Jack's tongue. And I would be their bridge, their visitor.

And so on the day Jack told me to "addle the bulge," I knew he was trying to say something important, but I had no idea what he meant. How do you addle a bulge? Maybe he meant flatten the bulge or tighten it, but addle—how do you addle it?

I had been contemplating, meditating, musing, and measuring over Ben's bulge, all of his bulges, the ones you could see and the ones you couldn't see, for years. I was probably supposed to meet Jack just then, at exactly that moment in time, because if I had met him any earlier, I would have done with him what I'd always wanted to do with Ben.

Thrown him away. Exchanged him for a boy without a bulge. A boy who had friends. A boy who ran and raced and rocked and rolled, not a boy who sat and read. I'd have exchanged him for a boy who knew it was me he was talking to, that it mattered it was me he was talking to, not any old person for his telling and talking pleasure. I'd have exchanged him for a boy who'd never disappoint or embarrass me because he'd be how I wanted him to be, not how he was.

That's what I'd have done with this stranger, this Jack of a man-riddle, if I wasn't desperate, if I wasn't sick of myself, sick of how I felt, sick with shame for still feeling failed by the boy to whom I'd given birth. A mother who'd only accept a boy without a bulge to his name, to my name, because I was his mother, and if he had a bulge, so did I.

I had to meet Jack when I did, because if I hadn't, what would have become of me? What would have become of Ben, the boy who was missing his birthright: me, his mother? And if I couldn't love my own son, the way he was, the way God made him, I couldn't love myself.

So when I met Jack, the man who spoke in riddles, I knew he'd been sent in the nick of time.

But helping Jack in any of my old ways was out of the question. Fixing, or even fiddling, was out of the question. There was nothing I could do but to listen to Jack, to listen in a way I'd never listened before. I'd have to suspend my thoughts, my judgments, my sense of everything that made sense to me. Because Jack didn't make sense. Or he did. But only if I listened as if I were absent from the listening. Listening to Jack in that way required that I join him in his own little world.

Jack's own little world. Like Ben's own little world.

Week after week, I visited Jack in his own little world. At first, in the beginning, I visited him in the place he lived, a board and care. But then, and I don't know when, I don't know how, it changed from a board and care—just another warehouse for neglected souls with its shuffling people, and its filthy picnic tables, and its gallon-sized coffee cans stuffed with butts of hundreds of used-up cigarettes—to an entirely different place.

It was like a dream. Being with Jack was like being in a dream. You don't expect logic from a dream. You don't even want it. You want floating, and seeing and knowing on an entirely different level. You want it even if it puzzles, even if it disturbs and unsettles, because there is something lush and rich and true about it, even though you can't say what, you can't say how.

Jack said things like, "People with vociferous points of view need to have their souls underwritten." He talked about seeing "fruit loops and question marks" and traveling down a "two-veined highway." I was lost when he said these things. There was no way I could use myself, my circumstances, the life I'd lived, or read about, or longed for, to understand him. So I just stopped. I just gave up trying to understand in the way I was used to understanding, and I let the words, the poetry of the words, float over me.

I was surprised I could do this, just let go of logic and reason and dive headlong into the world of fancy and fairy tale. But being with Jack was kind of like that, like re-entering a world I'd known and loved as a child. A world that didn't rely on sense to make sense. Jack reminded me of Rumplestiltskin, the odd-looking fairy tale character who put his foot through the floor when the princess guessed his name correctly. I always liked Rumplestiltskin for his magical powers, just as I liked Rapunzel and every good witch, and every bad one too.

So when Jack said he was "ten ounces away from getting his Ph.D. when the aneurysm burst," I didn't stop him and say, "You mean, don't you, that you were close to getting your Ph.D.?" because ten ounces is as fine a measure, no better or worse, than ten minutes, or ten yards. Who am I to make Jack speak my language? I'd just have to learn to speak his.

And I did. Week after week, Wednesday after Wednesday, at exactly two-thirty in the afternoon we'd walk circles around Jack's board and care, and I'd lean into his words, just as once, long ago, Ben leaned into mine; and I'd let my mind go, I'd let it drift away, because where Jack lived, I didn't need it. My mind.

Until I met Jack, my mind was always on Ben. Figuring him out. What to do, where to do it, how to do it? It was like reading a book to see what happens. Furiously turning the page, scanning for signs of who does what to whom. How will it end? Passing over everything else, skipping over the how and where and why. Skipping over a sunny day, skipping over smiles—giving them, getting them—skipping over lazy Sunday mornings, skipping over the landscape of life, because the landscape won't get you what you're looking for. And you're looking for Ben. *Remember! You're looking only for Ben.*

But while walking with Jack, while making a series of circles on the streets surrounding his board and care, Jack would insist on stopping to notice shadows playing tricks on sidewalks, paying as much attention to the squawking of a flock of birds as he did to me. Jack didn't care about my appointment book. He didn't care that he was penciled in for a two-hour block of time: one hour to visit, the second hour reserved for the round-trip drive. He didn't care that I had a full schedule of appointments for the rest of the afternoon and evening.

Jack had other company to keep. Like Ben, Jack's company is different from mine. Mine is people. Ben's is information. Jack's is dogs and cats and shadows on sidewalks. And flies.

One day, Jack paused in the middle of our conversation to contemplate a fly. He spoke to it softly, watching it closely as it traveled up and down, as if it were testing the territory. And when not a single swat came to shoo it away, it relaxed for a long while, resting there.

At first I was impatient. Wasn't Jack in the middle of a sentence when the fly came to land? Then I was bored. I'm not interested in flies; I hadn't driven all the way down the canyon in the midst of rush hour traffic to visit one. But then, as Jack began his soothing singsong lullaby, as he stayed very still and the fly stopped its flutter, I found myself captured. I stayed very still. I stopped my flutter and my mind came to rest on the fly. On the moment. And suddenly, we were drifting—Jack, the fly, and I—caught in the web of this magical moment.

Soon I was looking forward to our Wednesday visits, and more and more I found myself adopting Jack's riddle of words, incorporating them into my own sentences in my everyday life. Things like "Why don't we sit down and become commonplace with one another" make sense to me. I like it much better than, "Why don't we sit down and be comfortable."

And when, one day, Jack says, "When you have a voice you must poem it," I realize that I have not yet poemed my voice. I realize that I have a special poem, one that is as old as Ben, because it is all about Ben, and suddenly I begin saying the poem out loud. I say it to Jack. I trust Jack to understand and accept Ben better than I do. I trust Jack not to judge me.

"I have a son who's lived in these kinds of places." And once I begin the poem, I cannot stop. I go on and on, week after week, Wednesday after Wednesday, and Jack listens and nods.

"Does he have friends?" Jack asks.

"No," I reply. "He's never had friends."

"Neither did I."

"Were you lonely?" I ask.

"I could still wrap up in that."

"So could I," I say. Wrap up in loneliness because my son is missing from my heart.

One day Jack tells me, by way of one of his riddles, that he feels like a square peg in a round hole, "like candy in a glue factory." And then I tell him how I've tried stuffing Ben into a round hole all his life, even though he, like Jack, is square, "Well, more round than square, but you know what I mean." And we both laugh.

But when we're finished laughing he beams me one of his cross-eyed stares and says, "Go on."

Go on? But where should I go and how should I get there?

By telling the truth, by telling the whole truth, by saying the worst part, the awful, shameful part. The part I've never said to anyone.

"Because, Jack," I say, "how can *I* be the right shape, if Ben isn't?"

So here I am, telling my story, my poem, to Jack, and here I am listening to his riddles and letting them be just the shape he makes them. I do not wiggle them straight when they meander, I do not tighten or tie them down into a knot or pretty them up into a perfect bow. I just enjoy them the way they are.

And then Jack says, "Hardships . . . that's the beauty of the poetry of the in. Now it's the poetry of the out."

The poetry of the out.

"Ben's in that category, too, isn't he? The out category?"

"Yes."

"And the people on the in don't know the poetry of the out?"

"That's right," says Jack. "They don't understand."

"I'm one of those people, Jack. I don't understand."

"There's beauty in it," Jack says.

Beauty.

"You mean like Ben? There's beauty in Ben, just like there's beauty in you."

Jack stops in his tracks and beams me another cross-eyed stare. His eyebrows are black and bushy and arch up, up, up, beyond this shuffling, sad, and sorry place, beyond my small-minded fear, beyond my need for

Ben to be like everyone else, to be like me, to be a person on the in, not a person on the out.

"Yes," he says softly. "There's beauty in Ben. All you need to do is find it."

"But how, Jack, how?"

"By hanging on."

"To what?"

"To the sides, the front, the framework. And the more you hang on, the more you hang on and on and on . . . the better."

"Hang on to Ben?"

"Yes. Hang on. And see the whole thing. Not in its influence, but in its wholeness."

See the whole thing.

See all of Ben. See his sides and front and framework. See his dry sense of humor, his courage in the face of all his conditions—Asperger's, asthma, Crohn's, obesity. See his love of life and learning. See his dark brown eyes that do not work together but never cease their searching. See his innocent heart trying to hide giant volumes of scholarship behind big words. See his fear trying to fake its way past all there is to do, with all its how-to rules to do it. Because fear like Ben's is not welcome. It's never been welcome.

And then Jack says, "And you'll get it, you'll find it, you'll find Ben through the token of the turmoil."

The token of the turmoil.

There has been so much turmoil—so many tokens of turmoil for Ben and me—tokens of American cheese, and peas in the pod, and persons, and lies and more lies, and places for people on the out, and more places for people on the out, and seams that burst with shit showing through, and shame and humiliation, and a mother who did what was right but could only see what was wrong.

I was supposed to be the one helping Jack—but here I was, week after week telling Jack my story—and here he was, helping me.

And then on one of our Wednesday visits, Jack says, "Remember."

"Remember what, Jack?"

"Remember *you* are the one who is changing. Don't ask Ben to change."

"But what if I can't, Jack? What if I can't?"

"You will," Jack says softly. "You will."

And that's when the breath I'd been holding for too many years escapes. It rushes out, releasing welled-up tears of dried hopes and parched dreams. It cries for the rage and blame used to cover up despair and sorrow, for the grief of a wasted day collecting into the ruin of a wasted year, for the tragedy of a work of art, abandoned and unappreciated because the frame cradling it is flawed.

It cries for the sorrow of a misunderstood heart, for the tender heart of my son, and for this uncommon man offering surrender in his outstretched hand.

I know I am finally crying my tokens of turmoil. That they are bearing witness to Ben and to me, and our long, sad journey together. I know I could never have cried my tokens if it hadn't been for Jack, with his riddles and flies, and birds and bushy eyebrows. Because, somehow, in the midst of his poetry of the out, I'd managed to find the beauty in Jack. I'd found it, because I didn't need to change a single thing about him. All I needed to do was stand very still and listen very deeply. I didn't need to make sense of what didn't make sense, because what did sense have to do with it? What did sense have to do with beauty?

It was good. It was very good.

32

FINDING BEN

Here's the big secret: I never changed. I'm still the person I was when I was little. The world just caught up to me.

———

BEN WAS WAITING FOR ME. He had been waiting for me a long time, all the while I'd been searching for him. But it was not until Jack told me what to do to find him that I knew how. Jack told me not to pay any mind to Ben's problems. He told me to look for the beauty in Ben, the beauty of the out. He told me to addle the bulge, to hang on and on and on, until I could have what I want. I wanted Ben. I wanted him back in my heart where he belonged. Where he has always belonged.

Though I recognized the deep wisdom of Jack's advice, I wondered—could I put it into action?

Jack walked me to my car, as he always did. I opened the door to my Honda Accord, sat down, and put my car into drive. Just like always. Then I started driving back up the canyon. But it felt like driving in molasses. It wasn't because of traffic. It was because my car was heading up the canyon, to my office, but my heart was pulling me back down in the opposite direction. This tug-of-war was ripping me in half, but still I kept going. Still, I went up, up, up the canyon as I always did. Back to my office. Back to my afternoon and evening with patients. I tried to keep going, but I couldn't. I couldn't keep heading away from Ben when my heart was pulling me toward him. So I stopped. I pulled over to the side of the road. And I cried.

I cried for the entire half-hour I had allotted for my drive back. I cried for having used up all those years I could have spent loving Ben. All those years I'd spent searching to find a label to attach to him. It was good to know that Ben had Asperger's Syndrome, but in the end, did it matter? In the end, I still didn't have what I had set out to find. I may have had a label, but I didn't have Ben.

I didn't have him, because I couldn't see past his outness—his monotone voice, his layers of fat, his wheezing, his lack of friends. I couldn't see past them, these traits that made him different—past them, to the person he was underneath. *I couldn't see Ben.* I couldn't find him through the lens I was looking through. And through my tears, I knew that to find him, to see him, to have him the way I needed to—as my son, not just a boy with a bag of problems, not just a man with a bag of problems for me to work on, and worry over, and fix—I'd have to take off the lenses I'd been wearing. I'd have to wipe them clean. Really, really clean. Sparkling clean. As if they were new. And then I'd have to start all over again, seeing him with this new pair of glasses. Brand-new Ben. Brand-new me.

My patients would be waiting for me, but my son, my own flesh and blood, had waited longer.

I knew what I had to do. No, I knew what I wanted to do, what I needed to do, what I'd been getting ready to do all these weeks of Wednesdays. While Jack and I were walking circles around his board and care, I was making progress. I was looking at Jack, listening to his riddle of words, yet all the while I was tilting back toward Ben.

Still crying a sea of tokens for the turmoil in my heart, I took out my cell phone and my address book. First I called my four o'clock patient and told her I would not be able to see her that day. Then I called my five o'clock patient, and my six and my seven and my eight. I spoke to secretaries, assistants, housekeepers, nannies, husbands, wives, and children. I spoke in English and I spoke in Spanish. I spoke to answering machines and I always said the same words: "Sorry, but I won't be able to make our session today."

Sorry, but I have more important things to do. Sorry, I have to find my son. He's missing, you know. He's been missing for a very long time, and for all that time I have been suffering from a broken heart. I don't look like a person suffering from a broken heart. I don't behave like one. You probably think everything is OK in my life. You probably think that I have every right to sit there in my therapist chair and listen to your broken heart, and that maybe, with just the right word, just the right memory, just the right degree of empathy, I'll be able to help heal you. But you're wrong. How can I help heal your broken heart if I can't even heal my own?

I reached all but my nine o'clock patient, though I tried his office, his home, and his cell phone. So I called my husband and asked him to leave a note on my office door saying, "Sorry, Barbara won't be able to see you today. She tried reaching you, but you weren't home."

But Ben is home. Ben has been home for thirty-three years—in all kinds of homes, in homes for people who cannot tie their shoes, or climb a jungle gym, or tell the truth, or know the truth. He has lived in homes for people on the out, people like Jack, people who have no family or friends. He has lived in homes for people who have family, but whose family failed to understand people on the out. He has lived in homes for people whose families have tried to change them back to people on the in, just because they didn't want them to be on the out. Just because they couldn't accept them that way.

And all this time, through all these years of living in each of these homes, Ben's been waiting. He's been waiting for me to find him, and see him, and take him in my arms and love him. So you see, I can't keep our appointment today, because I'm already way behind schedule. I've been running late all my life because my first appointment was with Ben, and I am thirty years late.

Today is Wednesday, Ben's laundry day. Maybe I'll catch him in between loads. Maybe I'll catch him reading his history book, waiting for the spin cycle to finish. Maybe I'll catch him in the midst of sorting his clothing into two piles—one for whites and one for darks—just as they taught him in one of his dozens of ADL groups, in one of his dozens of group homes.

Or maybe I won't catch him, because now, since leaving Havenbrook and living for a month at his "real dad's" apartment in Beverly Hills, then in two more transitional living places, then for a very long time at one more group home, now Ben is living for the first time in his very own apartment. It's a lovely, spacious apartment in an upstanding, tree-lined neighborhood. He does not have to share a bedroom or even a bathroom. The apartment, and others like it all over the city, are for people with developmental disabilities.

So maybe I won't catch him, because maybe he is downstairs visiting one of his neighbors, or maybe he is swimming laps in the pool, or maybe he's decided to switch days entirely, exchanging laundry day for library day, and he isn't even home.

Maybe he's on his way to the Long Beach Public Library, riding the Blue Line, taking out his map of the Los Angles Public Transportation System and showing a tourist how to get where he is going, where to exit, and what sights to see along the way. Or maybe he's registering for next semester's classes at Loyola Marymount University, where he will be taking classes next fall, majoring in American Studies. On his way to his goal of becoming a history professor, on his way to independence. On his way up from where he had been—for so many sad years—when he had been all the way down.

Or maybe it's too late to catch him at all, because thirty years is a long time to wait for anyone. Even your mother.

"Hi, Ben," I say into my cell phone. "Can I get you anything at Costco? Is there something I can pick up and bring?"

"*Mom? Is that you?* You mean *now*, you want to come *now*?"

"If I could. . . ."

"Sure, Mom. Come anytime."

"Could I bring you something from Costco?"

"Well, I could use some chicken breasts, and tuna, and cereal, you know the kind I'm allowed to eat, only if sugar is listed as the fifth ingredient or less, and turkey, and water, and that special bread, if they carry it, the one with no more than nine carbs per serving, but you don't have to, because tomorrow is shopping day and I'll just take the bus like always, and—"

"That's OK, Ben. It'll save you a trip. I'll be there soon."

"See you, Mom."

"See you, Ben."

But would I? Would I *see* Ben when I got there? Or would I see what I always saw—fat and a frozen expression and a messy room, and piles of dusty history books, and an unmade bed? And if I saw that, if I looked for that and saw that, would I do what I always did? Would I begin to straighten and fix and fiddle as if to say, this is wrong, this is bad, this is messy? You are wrong, you are bad, you are messy. Would I point to this and putter with that? Or would I see what I had come to find—just Ben?

Ben and I had made that trip to Costco once every month for so long. I didn't need a grocery list to shop for him, even though I had always hounded him to bring one. "I'm not taking you shopping without a grocery list," I would say, even though I knew exactly where Ben's grocery list was. It was in his head—stored along with everything else he had ever known or learned or memorized.

Chicken breasts, skinless, frozen: Two packages.
Tuna, with water, whole: Four cans.
Shredded Wheat with Bran: One big box.
Orange roughy, frozen: One bag.

Stir-fried veggies: One bag.

Salsa, mild: One big, or two small.

Salmon fillets, frozen: One bag.

Frozen peas and carrots: Two large bags.

Orange juice.

Milk, 2 percent: One gallon.

Fresh strawberries: The big pack.

Fruit cocktail, light: Four cans.

Mushrooms: One bag.

Red onions: One bag.

Evian water: As much as you can carry.

No more American cheese. Cheese of any kind was not allowed on Ben's eating plan. And Ben was dedicated to his eating plan; he lived it and breathed it. For three years it had been a way of life. Not only the food, but the love of the people supporting and guiding him, the twelve steps he practiced every day, the Higher Power he prayed to. No more fast food, no more fries or malts or hamburgers. No more McDonald's or Carl's Jr., no matter how much money he had. And he had enough.

"I have enough, Mom." Ben would tell me when I asked if he needed money.

Between the little we gave him each month and his SSI money and the columns he made with the help of his case manager—bills on one side, income on the other side—he had enough.

"I have enough, Mom. I have everything I need."

"Everything?"

"Everything. I have my own apartment and enough money to pay my bills, and a computer and a bus pass. And friends. *Mom, I have friends.*"

"Oh, Ben."

"I know, Mom. It's a miracle. So many people care about me. My friends in the program, my friends in school, my friends in the apartment house. I get rides to meetings and to the doctor. I even get to have a relationship with my real dad."

"Oh, Ben."

"I know, Mom. It's a miracle. I'm so lucky. I'm so grateful. *I have everything I need.*"

No, Ben, I thought. You don't. You don't have everything you need. You need me. You need me in a way you never had me. You need a mother who is as grateful as you are. You need a mother who has enough, who has plenty, whose life is a miracle because you are in it.

The trunk of my car is packed with cartons from Costco. And I am on my way to visit my son. Images of other visits in other places float through my mind. But were those visits, or were they missions? When had Ben changed from being my son to being my job? Was it when he had no playdates? Was it when he lied about the football team? Was it when he couldn't ride a bike or climb the jungle gym or be the daddy in the dress-up corner? It was so long ago, I cannot pinpoint the time. But as I pull into Ben's parking garage, I know one thing: I no longer remember how to be with Ben any other way.

"I'm here, sweetie," I say into the intercom.

"Be right down, Mom," Ben says.

And then he appears. I watch him walk to my car. He's wearing slippers and his long green T-shirt. It's a 2XL, when last year it had been a 3XL, and the year before a 4XL, and the year before that, a 5XL. He leans to one side as he walks because his spine has carried too much weight for too much time and his mouth has swallowed too much prednisone for too many years. But his eyes light up when they see me, not with my kind of smile—with eyes and teeth and cheeks and creases—but with Ben's kind of smile.

"Hey, Mom. What a treat! Don't you have patients today? How come you're here on a Wednesday?"

"I just missed you, Ben."

"You did? How come?"

Oh, Ben, it's too long a story. And even if I had all the time in the world, how could I put it into words? Maybe someday I'll write a book about it. Maybe someday you'll help me write it.

"Let's take the cartons upstairs," I say. "Let's put them away."

"OK, Mom. But I didn't make my bed. And my kitchen's a mess, because I wasn't expecting company."

"That's OK," I say.

But when we get into the apartment, it isn't OK. I begin to straighten up the kitchen so I can put away the groceries. I take out the old trash bag so I can put in a new trash bag. I unload the tuna and put it into the pantry. I unload the chicken and fish and frozen vegetables and put them into the freezer.

I keep my head down. I'm efficient. I have work to do. I'm helping Ben. I'm making his life easier. I've bought him groceries and now I'm putting them away. I'm being a good mother, the same mother I've always been. I'm being the best mother I know how to be.

And then I hear a voice from the other room. It's Ben. He is saying something, but his voice is low; I can hardly make out what he's saying.

But the tone of his voice sounds different. Or maybe, it's not different. Maybe I'm different. It's a Wednesday afternoon. I told my patients, "Sorry, I can't see you today," when I really meant "Sorry, I have a more important appointment to keep. Sorry, I'm going to find my son."

I have just come from visiting Jack. His words are still in my ears: "Remember," he said as we stood by my car, "your hope reaches the hope of your son, and his hope reaches me." I have come to find my son. So I put the salsa down on the kitchen table. I stand very still. And I hear what Ben is saying.

"Mom, can you come and be with me for a minute?"

I look at Ben and I see my son. He is beautiful in his green T-shirt. He is beautiful in his slippers. He is beautiful in his own smile.

And with the Costco cartons scattered all around, and the unmade bed and the half-put-away groceries and the messy kitchen, I go to Ben. I put my arms around him and he puts his arms around me. We stand there embracing for a very long time.

AFTERWORD

IT IS STILL A VERY LONG STORY, but finally I have put it to words.

Through the tears, and with Jack in the background and my son in the foreground, I now look at Ben, whom I have finally found. And I forgive myself. I love and accept Ben because I see him as he is—beautiful in his unique brilliance, courageous in his struggle to live in a world that could not appreciate him, and inspiring in his capacity to be grateful for all that he is and all that he has.

At last, I understand that I was only a mother suffering from a disappointment I had refused to come to terms with. And sometimes, from a century ago, I hear the echo of John Oliver Hobbes: "Disillusion," all come from within, "from the failure of some dear and secret hope." "But the world makes no promises," he tells us, "we only dream it does and when we wake, we cry."

If this book helps you cry, if it helps you melt the ice in your disappointed heart, if finally it helps you grieve your lost hopes and dreams, so you can say a grateful *yes* to the life you have, although it might not be the one you planned for, then I have done what I set out to do.

RECOMMENDED RESOURCES

Books and Articles on Asperger's Syndrome

Attwood, Tony. *Asperger's Syndrome: A Guide for Parents and Professionals.* London: Jessica Kingsley Publishers, 1998.

Bashe, Patricia Romanowski, and Barbara L. Kirby. *The OASIS Guide to Asperger Syndrome: Advice, Support, Insight, and Inspiration.* New York: Crown, 2001.

Gray, Carol, and Tony Attwood. "The Discovery of 'Aspie' Criteria." *The Morning News* (Jenison Public Schools), 1999. Can be found on Attwood's website (http://www.tonyatwood.com).

Klin, Ami, Fred R. Volkmar, and Sara Sparrow, eds. *Asperger Syndrome.* New York: The Guilford Press, 2000.

Ledgin, Norm. *Diagnosing Jefferson: Evidence of a Condition That Guided His Beliefs, Behavior, and Personal Associations.* Arlington, Texas: Future Horizons, 2000.

Myles, Brenda Smith, and Richard L. Simpson. *Asperger Syndrome: A Guide for Educators and Parents.* Austin, Texas: PRO-ED, 1998.

Willey, Liane Holliday. *Pretending to Be Normal: Living with Asperger's Syndrome.* London: Jessica Kingsley Publishers, 1999.

Books Dealing with Issues of
Loss and Disappointment

Kushner, Harold. *When Bad Things Happen to Good People.* New York: Avon Books, 2001.

Viorst, Judith. *Necessary Losses: The Loves, Illusions, Dependencies, and Impossible Expectations That All of Us Have to Give Up in Order to Grow.* New York: Fireside, 1998.

Mothers' Accounts

Barron, Judy, and Sean Barron. *There's a Boy in Here: Emerging from the Bonds of Autism.* Arlington, Texas: Future Horizons, 2002.

Fling, Echo R. *Eating an Artichoke: A Mother's Perspective on Asperger's Syndrome.* London: Jessica Kingsley Publishers, 2000.

Kephart, Beth. *A Slant of Sun: One Child's Courage.* New York: Quill, 1999.

Paradiz, Valerie. *Elijah's Cup: A Family's Journey into the Community and Culture of High-Functioning Austism and Asperger's Syndrome.* New York: The Free Press, 2002.

Support Groups

ASC-U.S. (Asperger Syndrome Coalition of the U.S.)
P.O. Box 351268
Jacksonville, FL 32235-1268
http://www.asperger.org/

Asperger's Disorder Homepage
http://www.aspergers.com

Prepared by R. Kaan Ozbayrak, with links to other sites.

**Asperger's Syndrome Support Network (associated with the Autism
    Victoria Family Support Service, Victoria, Australia)**
P.O Box 466
Yarra Junction 3797
Victoria, Australia
http://home.vicnet.net.au/~autism

The Autism Society of America
7910 Woodmont Avenue, Suite 300
Bethesda, MD 20814-3067
http://www.autism-society.org

Compuserve and America Online

Subscriber services and forums.

Families of Adults Afflicted with Asperger's Syndrome
http://www.faaas.org

FEAT (Families for Early Autism Treatment)
http://www.feat.org

A parent-run nonprofit group in California.

Future Horizons Publishers
http://www.futurehorizons-autism.com

The largest publisher in the world of books on autism. Find resources as
well as conferences featuring world-renowned authorities.

OASIS (Online Asperger Syndrome Information and Support)
www.aspergersyndrome.org

Ooops . . . Wrong Planet! Syndrome
http://www.isn.net/~jypsy

Provides personal and informative perspectives on Asperger's Syndrome.

Dr. Tony Attwood's Website
http://www.tonyattwood.com

A guide for parents, professionals, and people with AS and their partners.

ACKNOWLEDGMENTS

Just as finding Ben has been a journey of many years, so too has been writing this book. Five years ago, when it was still a dream, the universe supplied just the right people in just the right places at just the right times.

I called my friend Gary Le Mel at Warner Brothers Music and asked for his help. He led me to Ellen Schwartz, who introduced me to my first book proposal collaborator, Laurence Rosenthal. Laurence's keen insight, wisdom, and enormous talent shepherded me through the first incarnation of the proposal, laying the foundation for the book you now hold in your hands. Thanks to Laurence, the proposal made its way to my agent, Geri Thoma. Miraculously, Geri believed in it from the start and hung in there with me for four more years (and as many incarnations) until it came to the attention of my editor, Matthew Carnicelli. Thank you, Geri, for taking a chance on me and for championing the story you knew I needed to tell. Matthew, thank you for finding the writer in me and making her an author, and for ever so gently steering me straight when I lost my way. And thank you, Susan Moore, for being on call, even on weekends.

The friends in my life have stood by my side throughout the course of Ben's and my journeys, just as they have been by my side throughout the creation of this book.

Thank you, Phyllis Eisenberg, writer, friend, and teacher, who knew I could and said I would; Gayle Carrigan, for always being there; Renee Morris and Priscilla Lipson Darby, lifelong friends and fans.

Thank you, Vicki and Ed Friedman, first family and first readers, whose love for and unfailing faith in Ben and me have been a source of comfort and support since the beginning.

Thank you, dear friend, Sharon Shaw, for many years of loving and "seeing" me.

Thank you, Joyce Shank, for your sharp editor's eyes and ears, and for our walks and talks; Linda Crow, for reading my book proposal, hand-delivering it to Dr. DeAntonio, and cheering me on; Fran Fox, for your thoughtful read and perceptive edit; Martha Benedict, for being there at first bud and seeing me through endless computer crises; Kathryn Demas and Claire Brown, for your insights; Cathryn Michon, for listening to my whining and setting me straight.

Thank you, Joan Cathcart, fellow writer, for your collegial generosity; Andrew Pogany, for your time and astute suggestions; Maria Hjelm and Susan Leon, for helping craft my proposal; Diane Adair, for your letter-perfect transcriptions; David Burns, for sitting with me through three hundred pages of printing.

A heartfelt thanks to John Daniel, for your brilliant eye for story, craft, and editing. You created the perfect poem for Ben, and you mentored me every step of the way.

Writing a book is like being a new mother, and just as absorbing. Thank you to all my friends for your patience while I was gone, and for being there to listen to chapters, drafts, and paragraphs whenever I needed your ear. Thank you, Natalie Nankin, for seeing better with your ears; Jo Williams, for crying in all the right places; Eileen Selsky, for your razor-sharp mind and goody bags of clippings; Lynneann Zager and all the unsung heroes championing their children; Maddy Le Mel, Sharon Dunas, Arlene Rettig, for your encouragement and kindness.

Thank you, Betty Asselin and Bridget Patterson, for being my role models; and Tony Patterson, for knowing what's important.

My deepest appreciation to Dr. Mark DeAntonio for diagnosing Ben in the nick of time, and for his medical counsel; to Dr. Paul Satz, for help with Regional Center and the writing of this book; to Mel Baron and Ali Karandish, for the course on pharmacology.

I am profoundly grateful to my patients for the privilege of their trust and the lessons they have taught me.

My parents, Max and Esther Friedman, are not here to read this book, but their loving imprint is on every page. Thank you for being Ben's best friends in the whole wide world, and my greatest blessing.

Thank you, Ron Wurm. You know what for.

Thank you, Martha Escobar, for taking care of Ben, David, John, and me since the very beginning.

Thank you, beautiful David, for blessing us with your special brand of love and acceptance.

And thank you, dearest John, for being there for Ben and me each step of the way. For reading every draft with great insight. For keeping me honest. For writing me love songs and making me laugh. For being exactly who Ben needed, and for never bailing out, no matter how hard it got. You are my best friend and my greatest fortune.

And finally and most especially, I thank Ben, for being my son and the teacher I couldn't do without. I love you.

Ben's Acknowledgments

I WOULD LIKE TO THANK my family, whose love, acceptance, and support (even when I didn't want them) have made my life easier, and my own acceptance and understanding of AS more an adventure than a job.

Particularly I would like to thank my mom, who, in deciding to write this book, gave me an opportunity to express myself in ways I never thought I could. Our relationship has strengthened immensely. I respect her as a person, a writer, and most of all as my mom.

My stepfather, John, is a man I have come to count on whenever I need him. He got a lot more than he bargained for when he became my dad, and his love and honesty have been a constant over the years.

My brother, David, is an inspiration to me. Sometimes he understands me better than anyone else.

When I grow up, I want to be just like my dad. He can be tough and kind at the same time. As I've gotten to know him better, I see how similar we really are. Through getting to know him, I've come to know myself. I love him very much.

My stepmother, Suzanne, is one of the most courageous people I know. She has been supportive of me and I appreciate her love very much.

I would also like to thank my friends, who, I'm grateful to say, are too numerous to list. They are always there to support me, encourage me, and set me straight.

I would like to single out my roommate, Edwinna Hull, who is truly one of the nicest people I have ever had the fortune to meet. Also, those special friends who trudge the road of happy destiny with me, especially in Santa Monica, on Saturdays and Sundays.

Finally, I would like to thank Doreen, who gave me hope when I didn't have any. Not once, but twice. She had faith in me when I had none. I am forever in her debt.